The making of US foreign policy

MANCHESTER
UNIVERSITY PRESS

The making of
US foreign policy

Second edition

John Dumbrell
with a chapter by David M. Barrett

Manchester University Press
Manchester and New York

distributed exclusively in the USA by St. Martin's Press

First edition published by Manchester University Press 1990

This edition published 1997 by
Manchester University Press
Oxford Road, Manchester M13 9NR, UK
and Room 400, 175 Fifth Avenue, New York,
NY 10010, USA

Distributed exclusively in the USA by
St. Martin's Press Inc., 175 Fifth Avenue, New York,
NY 10010, USA

Distributed exclusively in Canada by
UBC Press, University of British Columbia, 6344 Memorial Road,
Vancouver, BC, Canada V6T 1Z2

British Library Cataloguing-in-Publication data
A catalogue record for this book is available from the British Library

Library of Congress Cataloging-in-Publication Data applied for

ISBN 0 7190 4821 4 *hardback*
    0 7190 4822 2 *paperback*

First published 1997

01 00 99 98 97   10 9 8 7 6 5 4 3 2 1

Typeset in Great Britain
by Northern Phototypesetting Co Ltd, Bolton
Printed in Great Britain
by Cromwell Press Ltd, Broughton Gifford

Contents

Acknowledgements

I wish firstly to thank David Barrett for writing Chapter 3. Various parts of this book draw on papers given to American Politics Group conferences and to Professor Anthony Badger's American History seminar. Part of Chapter 8 draws on a wider study of US-Northern Irish relations since 1969, published in *Irish Studies in International Affairs*, 1995. The second edition of *The making of US foreign policy* is a completely revised and re-written version of the 1990 edition. Both the first and second editions were commissioned by Richard Purslow. Thanks also to Nicola Viinikka of Manchester University Press; to Jenny Williams; and to colleagues in the Department of American Studies at Keele University.

John Dumbrell

Introduction to the second edition

The primary purpose of the second edition of this book is the same as that of the first: to shed light upon American foreign policy by providing an account of the structures and traditions which shape it. US foreign policy is the product of ambivalent traditions and forces. In the early Cold War period, President Harry Truman confided to his diary: 'Americans are funny birds. They are always sticking their heads into somebody's business which isn't any of theirs.'[1] Yet in 1968, Secretary of State, Dean Rusk informed British Foreign Secretary George Brown: 'Scratch any American and underneath you'll find an isolationist.'[2] The tension between, on the one hand, expansive internationalism and, on the other, a wish to disengage from the world's problems, forms an important theme in this second edition of *The Making of US Foreign Policy*. Ambivalence derives also from the fragmented environment in which decisions on US foreign policy are made. In his testimony to a House of Commons Select Committee in April 1984, Sir Nicholas Henderson (former British Ambassador to Washington) replied as follows to a question about US Administration views regarding the Falkland Islands: 'When you say the US Administration, I am sorry to be pedantic but there is the Pentagon view, the State Departmental view and the White House view.'[3] This institutional complexity and ambivalence gives this book its second major theme: the interaction between process and substance in the making of foreign policy. The third theme – the relationship between the making of foreign policy and democratic practice – arises naturally from this institutional complexity.

Whereas the first edition was written in the later years of the Cold War, this second edition is entirely a product of the post-Cold War era. The second chapter explicitly looks back on the Cold War and attempts to explain why it ended. Part of this chapter, and indeed most of the others, are in some respect concerned with the debate about what kind of American foreign policy is appropriate for the new era. As in the first edition, the first two chapters seek to summarise various theoretical perspectives. Subsequent chapters are organised around the major institutions and forces relevant to foreign policy. In the third chapter, David Barrett traces the rise of Presidential foreign policy. In so doing, he provides, in effect, a narrative of recent developments in American foreign relations. Readers who wish to familiarise themselves with this material might be well advised to address themselves first of all to this chapter. In place of the two case-studies on Cold War issues in the first edition's final chapter, this second edition offers discussion of two episodes in post-Cold War internationalism.

Notes

1   R. H. Ferrell, ed., *Off the Record: The Private Papers of Harry S. Truman* (New York, Harper and Row, 1980), p. 53.
2   Cited in A. Jay, ed., *The Oxford Dictionary of Political Quotations* (Oxford, Oxford University Press, 1996) (*New Statesman* selection).
3   Cited in Z. Steiner, 'Decision-making in American and British foreign policy', *Review of International Studies*, 134 (1987), pp. 1–18: 9.

1

The United States and international politics: ideology, theory and foreign policy

1 The ideology of American foreign policy

(a) *American ideology and the end of the Cold War* In 1987, Soviet spokesman Georgi Arbatov warned Washington that Moscow was about to do 'a terrible thing to you – we are going to deprive you of an enemy'.[1] Many commentators have seen the Cold War as functionally constructive of American identity. In his 1988 'Obituary for the Cold War', George Kennan argued that the Cold War had functioned 'to cultivate the theory of American innocence and virtue, which must have an opposite pole of evil'.[2] In this sense the Soviet Union – illiberal, atheist, dogmatic, collectivist, communist – was indeed the perfect foe.[3]

Part of America's Cold War self-image involved the association of American traditions with pragmatism and the rejection of ideology. Both before and during the Cold War, practitioners and defenders of US foreign policy tended to deny that American international relations were driven by anything so un-American as 'ideology'. Writing in 1945, for example, Thomas Bailey outlined America's goals or 'fundamental policies'. These were: isolation, non-intervention or 'non-entanglement'; the Monroe Doctrine (the protection of a sphere of influence in the Western hemisphere); freedom of the seas; the Open Door, especially in China – the 'right of American citizens to engage in industry abroad on an equal basis with other foreigners'; pacific settlement of disputes; pan-Americanism; and opportunism (minor adjustments without reference to fundamentals).[4] Goals, yes, according to Bailey, but ideology, no. For Arthur Schlesinger, jun., ideology was simply 'out of character' for pragmatic Americans.[5]

Treating 'ideology' as un-American has enabled defenders of US foreign policy to characterise opposing positions as 'ideological': over-zealous, dogmatic, undemocratic, totalitarian. Some theorists of American exceptionalism, however, tended to define 'Americanness', even 'America' itself, as an ideology. Richard Hofstadter famously declared: 'it has been our fate as a nation not to have an ideology but to be one'.[6] Reaffirming American excep-

tionalism in the wake of the Cold War, Seymour Martin Lipset echoed Hofstadter:

> The United States is organized around an ideology which includes a set of
> dogmas about the nature of a good society. Americanism ... is an 'ism' or ide-
> ology in the same way that communism or fascism or liberalism are isms ... That
> ideology can be subsumed under four words: anti-statism, individualism, pop-
> ulism, and egalitarianism.[7]

With the ending of the Cold War, apologists for and practitioners of US foreign policy tended to become more forthright about the Americanness of
one particular ideology: that of liberal democratic capitalism. Secretary of
State George Shultz declared in 1987 that 'the great ideological struggle that
has marked this century ever since the Bolshevik revolution of 1917 has
essentially been decided'.[8] Here, Shultz was clear that the Cold War was a
struggle, not between dogmatic 'ideology' and American pragmatism, but
between competing ideologies. It culminated in a victory for 'the American
creed'. (One corollary of this view, drawn out by Lipset, was that American
exceptionalism would actually weaken as other nations 'Americanised'
under post-Cold War conditions.)

(b) *Liberalism*   'Ideology', of course, bears many meanings and, no doubt,
the term can be defined so as to separate it from American liberal pragmatism. Within Marxism, 'ideology' embraces forms of thought which function
to preserve or represent class interest. For diplomatic historian Michael
Hunt, the concept of ideology comes close to that of 'culture'.[9] Generally,
however, it seems reasonable to define 'ideology' in terms of beliefs and
values which take a clear shape, a *Weltanschauung*.[10] In this sense, US foreign policy traditions do embrace – as celebrators of America's Cold War victory acknowledged – ideology. The driving ideology of US foreign policy has
been traditionally, and remains, the ideology of liberalism. (It is worth
remembering that Louis Hartz, the most celebrated modern interpreter of
American liberalism, had no doubts about its status as ideology.)[11]
   American democratic liberalism, whose main progenitor was John Locke,
may be characterised as embodying commitments to the interdependence of
democracy and capitalism; to individual liberty and the protection of private
property; to limited government, the rule of law, natural rights, the perfectibility of human institutions, and to the possibility of human progress. It
is allied to a strong sense of national mission and American exceptionalism:
the belief that American democratic history provides a model for the world.
At its heart, Lockeian liberalism embraces a commitment both to national
self-determination and to the view that the world belongs to the industrious
and the rational. Enemies of liberalism are, on the right, conservative ideologies which exude pessimism about the possibility of progress through
human agency; and, on the left, ideologies which assert that human freedom

may only be realised through a transcendence of private property and capitalism.[12]

As an ideology underpinning US foreign policy, liberalism oscillates between the poles of non-entanglement and interventionist internationalism. Historically, as in President George Washington's farewell address, non-entanglement has been held up as a consequence of American exceptionalism. According to George Washington in 1798: 'It will be worthy of a free, enlightened, and at no distant period a great nation to give to mankind the magnanimous and too novel example of a people always guided by an exalted justice and benevolence.' America's 'detached and distant situation' invited America to avoid European corruptions, to have 'as little political connection as possible' and to 'steer clear of permanent alliances with any portion of the foreign world'.[13] Non-entanglement would allow the United States to shape its frontier destiny, to remain aloof from distant quarrels, and to provide a model for the world in the process. Liberal non-entanglement doctrines drew on the Puritan, 'city on a hill' inheritance. Implicit in this tradition is the belief that US foreign policy leaders somehow lack European guile and dissimulation. John Adams (President, 1797–1801) famously denied 'any notion of cheating anybody'. Standing aloof from the wicked ways of the Old World, America could show others the way of morality. (The Swedish ambassador wrote to John Adams in 1784 that he trusted that the United States would 'have sense enough to see us in Europe cut each other's throats with a philosophical tranquillity'.)[14]

With the closing of the frontier, and especially with US assumption of global leadership after 1945, non-entanglement gave way to the liberal internationalist ideal: the protection and promotion of liberal, capitalist values on a world stage. President Woodrow Wilson appropriated the term 'liberal' to justify American entry into World War One. Liberal internationalists like President Franklin Roosevelt used the denigrating label, 'isolationist', to stigmatise the older, non-entanglement tradition. After 1945 the cause of liberal internationalism became inextricably bound up with the idea of containing a putatively expansionist, Soviet-directed communism. Containment of communism became the bedrock of US foreign policy for forty years (notwithstanding the growing disapprobation expressed towards the globalised application of the doctrine by George Kennan, the inventor of the whole notion of containment). The purpose of post-1945 US foreign policy has been summarised thus by Michael Cox: 'to create an environment in which democratic capitalism can flourish in a world in which the US still remains the dominant actor'.[15] With the end of the Cold War, a debate emerged as to whether this purpose – and its underlying liberal ideology – would be best served by a return to non-entanglement or by a new activist internationalism.

(c) *Alternatives to liberalism*   What alternatives have been presented, within the history of US foreign policy, to liberal ideology? There are at least five candidates: self-interested realism; conservatism; isolationism; Wilsonian idealism; and left liberalism. These will now, very briefly, be considered in sequence, with the underlying implication that they are most appropriately viewed as variants on and tendencies within the overarching liberal ideology. This is not to deny that there are real and important differences between these points of view – between, for example, self-interested realism and left liberalism. It is also clearly the case that both realism and conservatism have the potential to constitute ideologies antagonistic to Lockeian liberalism. The point to be emphasised, however, is that, at least in the American context, these various viewpoints have exhibited a large measure of convergence, and an unwillingness to challenge the dominant liberal ideology.

Even accounts of American foreign policy which stress its moral idealism and evangelising mission generally acknowledge the role of conscious national interest. The dialectical tension between 'ideals' and 'self-interest' lies at the heart of conventional treatments of US foreign relations. A full-blown realist interpretation would hold that US foreign policy achieves rationality and purpose only to the extent that it embodies accurate, power-oriented calculation of the national interest. Foreign policy leaders do try to maximise perceived national interest. In this respect, the behaviour of American foreign policymakers resembles that of their counterparts elsewhere in the world. However, pursuit and identification of the national interest takes place against a particular cultural, attitudinal backcloth. It is also, of course, the case that the geographical position of the United States – as realists argue – influences the content of American foreign policy. (Here, however, interpretations differ. The United States is generally regarded as having a particular security interest in the Western hemisphere. However, it was Henry Kissinger who insisted that history was made in the Northern half of the planet, and that South America was a dagger pointed at the heart of Antarctica! Realist commentators like Colin Gray have traced a long-standing US preoccupation with maintaining political divisions on the 'World-Island' of Asia and Europe.)[16]

The central point here is that power-based, national interest-oriented realism has been an influence upon, rather than a substitute for, the liberal ideology of American foreign policy. In *America's Mission* (1994), Tony Smith argues that a values-oriented, interventionist foreign policy actually coincides with realist, national security-oriented ends.[17] Even Henry Kissinger, realist and disciple of Thomas Hobbes, argues that power is most effective when it is perceived as legitimate and in tune with liberal American values.[18] Realist, geopolitical ideology in recent American foreign policy has operated as a facet of liberal internationalism, itself embodying a firm (if sometimes unstated) commitment to the national interest. Realism had an important effect on the history of the Cold War. Realist critics of the American involvement in Vietnam, for example, contributed mightily to the changing public debate over the war. But self-conscious upholders of realism, whether in the Nixon or Reagan Administrations have tended to alter the direction of US foreign policy rather than its underlying liberal and moralistic assumptions.[19] In post-Cold War conditions, President George Bush's conduct of the Gulf crisis and war (1990–91) attempted to combine relatively narrow national goals (access to oil) with moralistic commitments to democratic values. An apparently clear 'nationalist' approach was developed by some Republican Congressional leaders in the wake of the GOP 1994 mid-term election triumph. Yet even Newt Gingrich, leader of the 1994–95 'Republican revolution' on Capitol Hill, declared that the 'US must lead, period', because the alternative for the twenty-first century would be 'a dark and bloody planet'. In July 1995, Gingrich urged Americans to exert themselves 'everywhere to extend freedom'.[20]

Conservative foreign policy positions tend also to be identified with nationalism, hostility to foreign aid, commitment to high levels of defence spending and (before 1991) an intense level of anti-communism. Conservatism, especially in terms of its scepticism about the perfectibility of human institutions, does represent a genuine alternative to liberalism. From a self-consciously 'neo-conservative' position, Jeane Kirkpatrick berated liberals in the 1980s for failing to acknowledge the existence of human wickedness, taking refuge in 'pale euphemisms and blind theories of inevitable human progress'.[21] An authentic conservative tradition does exist within the history of American foreign policy: anti-imperialist, anxious about American security, sceptical about Manifest Destiny and national missions, concerned above all with the preservation of liberty at home. Defined in these terms, conservative sentiments were expressed by Daniel Webster at the time of the acquisition of California and New Mexico (1846–48). Webster feared the growth of a new, American imperialism: 'this country should exhibit to the world the example of a powerful republic, without greediness and hunger of empire'.[22] Henry Clay argued in 1852 that the best way for the United States to show 'to other nations the way to greatness and happiness' was by maintaining liberty at home as a model for imitation.[23] Samuel Flagg Bemis, diplomatic historian and celebrator of American history as expressed in foreign policy, wrote in 1936 that, after 1898, the American people decided to acquire an empire and take their place in the world: 'Actually, the United States had already taken its proper place in the world before 1898. That was in North America.'[24] Robert Taft, despite lapses into conspiracy theory and extreme partisanship, also developed a coherent conservative position during the Korean conflict (1950–53). One dimension of this concentrated on the domestic effects of war: partly inflation, but also the inevitable domestic militarisation and centralisation of power. Another related to the constitutional issues of excessive executive secrecy and unaccountability.

The Republican Senator from Ohio also stressed the dangers of America 'becoming an imperialistic nation', which failed to recognise the moral and practical 'limitations on what the United States can do'.[25] This anti-imperialist strain within American conservatism was to generate a debate in the 1970s on the putative continuity between older conservative and Vietnam generation/New Left positions. During the Korean war, Taft pointed to the possibility that interventionist liberalism might destroy the rights and lives of people whom the United States intended to defend against communism. In *A Foreign Policy for Americans*, Taft argued that forcing remote peoples to be free ran counter to American democratic ideals.[26]

Taft himself saw these democratic ideals as liberal: individual freedoms defined within the context of market liberalism and governmental non-interference. If we define liberalism in these terms, and also note that American liberalism embodies a strong commitment to the idea of America's special mission to protect liberty, we see a major problem with the articulation of American conservative thought as a genuine alternative to liberalism. Conservative positions tend to spin off in a liberal direction (as in the above quotations from Webster and Clay, with their clear evocation of the liberal non-entanglement tradition and its Puritan 'city on a hill' provenance). Pessimism about anyone's ability to serve as a model for human progress is simply absent from the mainstream of American thought. Also, as Richard Crockatt has put it, the United States lacks a tradition which unites the European organicist conservatism of an Edmund Burke and the *dirigisme* of Alexander Hamilton.[27] Taftian conservatism, although taken up in later years by conservative intellectuals like Karl Hess, in any case found it hard to survive during the Cold War. Anti-imperialist criticisms of the Vietnam War came from the left, not from the conservative wing of the political spectrum. The 'neo-conservative' foreign policy positions of writers like Norman Podhoretz and Irving Kristol in the 1970s and 1980s were redolent of moralistic liberalism.[28] Similarly, George Kennan's post-Cold War memoir, *Around the Cragged Hill*, exuded moralism. Kennan the inventor of anti-communist containment in the later 1940s, attempted in his memoir to sketch out a post-Cold War role for the United States. In true conservative vein, he started from the conservative view of man as a 'cracked vessel'; he rejected radical egalitarianism and excessive democratisation. The United States should eschew foreign adventures in favour of protection of liberty at home. Why? To serve, of course, as a 'city on a hill' and a moral example to the rest of the world.[29]

Isolationism is often regarded as an attribute of American conservatism, and ex-President Herbert Hoover's 'Gibraltar' speech of December 1950 as its post-World War Two high-water mark. In fact, both Taft and Hoover disowned the isolationist label, seeing themselves rather as critics of President Truman's overweening globalism. And 'isolationism' is a mis- and over-used term. The American foreign policy debate has always been not so much between internationalism and isolationism, but over the criteria which should govern US engagement with the world. The United States has never, strictly speaking, followed an isolationist (as distinct from a 'non-entanglement') foreign policy. Since the promulgation of the Monroe Doctrine (1823), the United States has, at the very least, been committed to regional or hemispheric hegemony. The debate of the 1930s over American involvement in a European conflict was as much a debate over neutrality as over 'isolation'. 'Corporatist' historians have challenged the whole concept of America's isolation in the 1920s and 1930s.[30] As Walter LaFeber writes: 'The United States has never been isolated or outside the world's political struggles. It was born in the middle of those struggles, and its great problem was – and has always been – how to survive those struggles while maintaining individual liberty at home'.[31]

'Isolationism' has, in fact, become little more than a term of abuse. Speaking a few weeks after the 1994 Republican victory in Congress, Anthony Lake, President Clinton's National Security Adviser (NSA) announced 'a dangerous isolationist backlash in the air'.[32] Yet, as argued in Chapter 5, the post-1994 Republican onslaught was 'nationalist' and 'unilateralist' rather than 'isolationist' A Republican bill was introduced in 1995 to reorganise the foreign policy bureaucracy, saving $6 billion over five years. Defending the bill, Senator Craig Thomas (Republican, Wyoming) held that President Clinton had 'labelled supporters of the cost-savings provisions in the bill "isolationists", overlooking the fact that we've asked every other department and agency to tighten its belt'.[33]

As is evident in Thomas's comments, the 'isolationist' label is one that few seek. Rather, it tends to be applied to three categories of foreign policy opinion: to rightist, 'America First', unilateralist and (latterly) anti-United Nations Republicans; to those who wish to give domestic reform priority over foreign adventures, usually advocating some kind of regionalist foreign policy strategy; and those simply opposed, whether from left or right, to perceived American overseas over-extension. Into the second category would come Charles Beard in his aptly titled 1934 book, *The Open Door at Home*.[34] Also, Democratic Senator Symington of Missouri, who declared during the Vietnam war that 'we should express less interest in South Asia and more in South St. Louis'.[35] In a book published in 1995, Eric Nordlinger attempted to establish a coherent, post-Cold War isolationist position, based around domestic reform priorities and regionalist diplomatic strategies.[36] Into the third category would fall Walter Lippmann during the era of the Vietnam war; compared 'to people who thought they could run the universe', wrote Lippmann, he was 'a neo-isolationist and proud of it'.[37] Among those few politicians and commentators, like Lippmann, who have been willing to risk the tag 'isolationist', few have clung to anything like a consistent isolationist position. In 1972, for example, Robert Tucker advocated 'a new isolationism', built around economic self-reliance and the nuclear shield. Within two years, he was advancing the case for US intervention in the Middle East to protect oil supplies![38]

The main tenets of the foreign policy idealism associated with President Woodrow Wilson were outlined in his 1918 'Fourteen Points' speech: open diplomacy, anti-colonialism and self-determination, free trade. Wilson's idealistic internationalism, of course, was rebuffed by 'isolationists' in the 1919 Senate vote against ratification of the Treaty of Versailles. Yet Wilsonian idealism continued to reverberate down the years. It found echoes in the 'world order' internationalism of the Jimmy Carter Administration, and in post-Cold War formulations of a global 'democratic peace' orchestrated by the United States. According to Tony Smith, the 'greatest achievements in the history of US foreign policy have come from the success of the Wilsonian vision', notably in integrating Japan and West Germany 'into a community of democratic, market states' after World War Two.[39] The Wilsonian vision resurfaced in the form of a putative 'grand bargain' with Russia in the period 1989–91: a plan, effectively rejected by President George Bush, to fund Russian integration into global free markets. The Clinton Administration's notion of 'democratic peace' also drew on Wilsonian foundations. (In July 1993, Secretary of State Warren Christopher noted: 'Democracies do not threaten their neighbors. They do not practise terrorism. They do not spawn refugees. They respond to the needs of their citizens and thereby achieve greater stability and prosperity for all[40].) The key point here, however, is that the Wilsonian inheritance stands squarely within, indeed is an intensified version of, liberal ideology. It is driven by a notion of human perfectibility guided by the example of American democracy and responsive to the needs of American capitalism. Wilson declared in 1912 that US producers had 'expanded to such a point that they will burst their jackets if they cannot find a free outlet to the markets of the world'. T. P. McCormick, summarising the work of 'corporalist' historians, equates 'Wilsonianism' with 'globalised corporatism' – 'a sort of corporate, pro-capitalist reformism'.[41] Wilson, Carter and Clinton all compromised on their commitments to democracy-promotion and human rights; they all, in effect, oscillated between 'idealist' and 'realist' versions of liberalism. Wilson intervened in six Latin American conflicts to secure regimes acceptable to Washington. American troops fought against the Red Army in the Russian Civil War (1918–20). The Carter Presidency, overtaken by events, had by 1980 reverted to an orthodox policy of containing communism. In 1994–95, the Clinton White House concurred in the extension of most-favoured-nation trading status to China, regardless of that nation's record on democracy and human rights. Under Clinton's direction, US arms sales again began to equal the record figures of the Nixon Presidential years.

Left liberalism may be defined as an attempt to take Wilsonian idealism seriously: to amputate its interventionist, militaristic and compromising tendencies. Former Vice-President Henry Wallace advocated open diplomacy with the USSR in the late 1940s. He attacked the 1946 Baruch Plan (to establish an international atomic development authority) as insufficiently generous in its promise to share atomic information. In 1947, he admonished: 'Once America stands for opposition to change, we are lost.' Unthinking counter-revolution would lead to America becoming 'the most hated nation in the world'.[42] Wallace was attacked as an appeaser and dismissed as Secretary of Commerce in 1946. He was an optimistic left liberal, believing firmly in American democratic values and the alleviation of distress through the expansion of democracy and free trade. (Wallace resigned from the Progressive Party in 1952 in support of US policy in Korea). During and after the war in Vietnam, left liberals continued to protest the influence of giant corporations and the 'military-industrial complex', in the name of democratic values. The Vietnam War caused left liberals to embrace the 'isolationist' case for the prioritisation of domestic reform. In his 1968 campaign, Robert Kennedy attacked President Johnson's claim that the war presaged 'a Great Society for all of Asia'. Kennedy urged that 'we cannot build a Great Society there if we cannot build one in our country'.[43] In 1984, the Reverend Jesse Jackson delivered a speech to the United Nations entitled: 'Foreign policy – but not foreign values'. Jackson again took up the 'city on a hill' theme: 'If we are to remain the hope of the free world, our challenge is not military escalation but a worldwide war on poverty, disease and illiteracy.'[44] Left liberals characteristically seek to interpret American values, which are presented as central to a 'republican' foreign policy, in terms of 'civic' or 'expressive' (rather than 'competitive' or 'utilitarian') individualism.[45] The liberal assumption, that foreign policy should be driven by values and that a (redefined) Americanism should provide a model for the world is rarely challenged.

2   Theory and international politics

(a) *Perspectives*   The ending of the Cold War did little to improve the reputation and attractiveness of international relations theory. Robert Conquest gave the following reaction to the 1991 abortive Moscow coup: 'If you are a student, switch from political science to history.'[46] Academic social science, geared towards the study of structures rather than of change, seemed stranded in face of the system-shattering events of the late 1980s and early 1990s. John Lewis Gaddis poked fun at the scientific pretension – 'physics envy' – of behaviourist researchers, asking: 'why did it prove easier to end the Cold War itself than to redesign the various massive data-collection projects, growing out of the events-data movement some quarter of a century ago, that were supposed to tell us how to formulate the policies that might bring an end to the Cold War?'[47]

Gaddis's barbs against the vanity of quantitative social science were well directed. Attempts, deriving from the work of J. N. Rosenau, to construct a 'normal science' of comparative foreign policy have achieved little.[48] How-ever, scepticism about overblown social scientific pretension should not lead us to abandon theory in the name of some kind of naïve, intuitive empiri-cism. 'Facts' do not speak for themselves and have little interest or value unless formed, shaped and beaten into some kind of (however tentative) theory, framework or interpretation. Since 'facts', and our perception of them, are neither free-standing nor neutral in any case, it is as well to be aware of those explicit theoretical frameworks that other researchers have found useful. The academic study of international relations frequently seems, to the layperson, overly preoccupied with methodological disputes, abstract theories and shifting paradigms. Indeed, it *should* pay more heed to the 'real world'. But theory is rarely *merely* theory; if it is, it should be aban-doned. As John Vincent wrote: 'It is difficult ... to have a truly content-free theory, or value, while our interpretation of the world of "facts" is always conditioned by our theoretical assumptions.'[49] In his 1995 Presidential address to the Society for Historians of American Foreign Relations, Melvyn Leffler presented the liberal case for a pluralism of theory: 'The search for one, all-explanatory theory is indeed a vain one (though it should be recog-nised that the assertion, that no single theory can explain everything, is itself a dogmatic and contentious one).' According to Leffler: 'if reality is too com-plex to be captured by a single theory, different theories may help the histo-rian to make sense of different parts of the phenomenon or event or process under scrutiny.'[50]

It is now my intention briefly to describe the two leading frameworks for understanding international relations which emerged from the Cold War: *neorealism* and *neoliberalism*. The relationship between these two bodies of theory and the end of the Cold War will be discussed in Chapter 2.

Neorealism is a recent expression of the classical realist tradition, with a lineage extending back to Thucydides. For a realist, the international order is inherently anarchic and conflictual, with international cooperation virtu-ally a contradiction in terms. Domestic influences over a nation's foreign policy are held to have been aggregated at the level of the nation-state, and thus have little interest to the realist analyst of world affairs. States are like billiard balls. The job of leaders is 'to judge, by experience and intuition, the requisite amount of force necessary to move one or another ball in a pre-ferred direction'.[51] Power is all, and balances of power the only way to make order out of chaos. Neorealism attempts to move on from these fundamen-tal realist tenets. This 'new' or 'structural' realism, pioneered by Kenneth Waltz, turned the focus of attention to the international system itself: 'Neo-realism develops the concept of a system's structure which at once bounds the domain that students of international politics deal with and enables them to see how the structure of the system, and variations in it, affect the inter-acting units and the outcomes they produce.'[52] The world of structural real-ism, according to Stephen Krasner, is 'a world of tectonic plates and intermittent earthquakes rather than billiard balls and frequent collisions'.[53] The nature of the international system itself – whether it is dominated by one, two or many nation-states – constrains the ability of individual states to pursue power. The Cold War's bipolarity – the global dominance by the two superpowers, the United States and the Soviet Union – constrained international politics in the direction of stability.

Contemporary neoliberalism grew from the idealist tradition associated with Woodrow Wilson, but also from the 'interdependency' school of the 1970s and from the perceived failure of realism to predict the end (certainly the peaceful end) of the Cold War. In their 1977 study, *Power and Interdependence*, Robert Keohane and Joseph Nye challenged the basic assumptions of all varieties of realism: its views on the centrality of the nation-state, force and state survival, as well as its unwillingness to countenance (in Waltz's terminology, 'reductionist') domestic issues that may affect foreign policy.[54] Keohane and Nye presented a world of complex interdependence, with states maintaining contacts at various levels and in various dimensions. According to David Lake, with 'the growth of private cross-border communications and organizations, and with the rise of economic interdependence, the "hard shell" of the state has crumbled'.[55] The rise of integrated world markets for capital is particularly important to this perspective. In the post-Cold War context, neoliberal thought regained many of the ethical concerns of the Wilsonian tradition and put great stress on the possibility of successful international organisation. Neoliberals hold that old distinctions between domestic and foreign policy agendas should be abandoned. Neoliberal values tend to assume a mutual reinforcement between political democracy and free market economics.[56]

The major rival to both neorealism and neoliberalism is Marxian 'structuralist' or 'world system' theory. In this tradition, international politics are discussed in terms of the relations between the (exploiting) core and (exploited) periphery of the global system. Even before the end of the Cold War, many 'world system' theorists saw the Soviet Union as part of this global capitalist structure, either as part of the core or as semi-periphery. 'Cold War system' theorists postulated an *alliance* between the United States and the USSR, designed to stimulate defence spending, to subjugate rivals and serve the interests of both Soviet and American elites. With 'world system' theory, the main units of analysis are neither nation-states, nor the disaggregated agents of global interdependency, but rather the dynamics of the capitalist world system itself. The Marxian structuralist approach is concerned with the spatial and structural characteristics of capitalist accumulation on a world scale. Immanuel Wallerstein's world system theory and the (originally, Latin American-oriented) 'dependency' school are probably still its best-known facets.[57] Within this tradition, the end of the Cold War involved either the globalisation of capital, predicted by Marx, or the first stage in the *dis*integration of the capitalist world system. Important attempts to challenge the neorealist–neoliberal standoff in international relations theory have also been made from the viewpoints of feminism and of post-modernism. Both feminism and postmodernism form, in Marysia Zalewski's phrase, 'part of the challenge to the hegemony of realist, positivist discourse'.[58] This challenge involves a commitment to the view that 'reality' is socially constructed and that behaviourist 'positivism' (the building of social science through the inductive method) serves particular power interests. This kind of analysis tends to proceed via the critical analysis of the 'discourse' (speeches, academic writing, arguments, rhetoric) of international politics.

(b)   *America's international power*   Since the end of World War Two, the United States has been the world's greatest – since about 1990, the world's only – superpower. America's status as a superpower depends both on military strength and on economic power. During the Cold War, international relations theorists differed about whether there could be more than one 'superpower'. For H. J. Morganthau, for example, there was a crucial different between a 'great power' and a 'superpower'. The latter was 'a great power which has no rival capable of preventing it from imposing its will upon small powers'.[59] The view expressed by Kenneth Waltz, however, was more widely accepted: rivalry between two superpowers could itself provide the basis for a double-centred, 'bipolar' global system:

> In a bipolar world, there are no peripheries. With only two powers capable of acting on a world scale, anything that happens anywhere is potentially of concern to both of them. Bipolarity extends the geographic scope of both powers' concern. It also brackets the range of factors included in the competition between them.[60]

During the Cold War, America's status as a superpower was advanced and protected most obviously by US nuclear capabilities, but also by Washington's strategy of 'preponderant power'. To quote Melvyn Leffler:

> The chief characteristic of twentieth-century American foreign policy has been the willingness and capacity of the United States to develop and exert its power beyond its nineteenth-century range to influence the economic, political and military affairs of Europe and Asia. This trend has manifested itself in the evolution of the Open Door policy, in the aid to the Allies in both world wars, in the wielding of American financial leverage, in the assumption of strategic obligations, in the development of troops overseas, in the provision of economic and military assistance, in the undertaking of covert operations, in the huge expenditures on armaments, and in the growth of the American multinational corporation.[61]

Part of the strategy of 'preponderant power' – originally developed by the Truman Administration in an *ad hoc*, rather than a conspiratorial fashion – was 'double containment': containment and disciplining of allies, through a combination of military and economic power, as well as containment of communism.[62]

Preponderant power finds its theoretical expression in the concept of 'hegemonic stability': the view that stabilisation of the international system requires there to be one dominant power, capable of imposing order on the anarchy of transnational politics and economics. ('Hegemonic stability' theory, though generally discussed in the context of international economics, also has international security dimensions.) According to the theory, stability and success within the international capitalist system are related to, even a function of, hegemonic leadership. A stable system requires a hegemon to absorb exports and to provide a currency for international transactions: 'for the world economic to be stabilised, there has to be a stabiliser, one stabiliser'.[63] Robert Keohane sees hegemony as deriving from control over raw materials, capital and markets, combined with a competitive advantage in the production of values goods.[64] Hegemonic stability theory has both realist and liberal tendencies. The realist would stress the security dimension of hegemony, and the self-interest of the hegemon (in this case, the United States in the post-1945 world order). The hegemon alone has the capacity 'to entice or compel others to accept an open trading structure'.[65] The liberal would emphasise the universal benefits, 'collective goods', aspect of hegemony; and also argue that the hegemonic function need not necessarily be performed by a single nation-state.

Hegemonic stability theory also tells us that regimes are inherently unstable, even self-destructive. This is where this theoretical debate links up with the wider debate about American decline. The strains of acting as the system's guarantor rebound upon the hegemon's domestic economy. Its capital exports, though temporarily stabilising, ultimately allow 'free-riding' small states to become competitors. The hegemon becomes economically and militarily overstretched.

Leaving aside the theory of hegemons for a moment, let us look more closely at the debate over American decline. At one level, the whole notion of decline seems absurd. Did not the United States, as George Shultz announced in 1987, win the great ideological battle of the twentieth century? With the ending of the Cold War, American military capabilities stood unrivalled. If we inquire further, however, a case can be made for relative US decline since the era of the Vietnam War. The history of the war itself illustrated the limits to American power. From the early 1970s onwards, American preponderance in key areas – competitiveness, control over capital and markets – seemed to be under threat. Increasing foreign inward investment and America's burgeoning trade and (especially) energy dependency appeared to tell the same tale. From the late 1970s onwards, annual growth rates in Europe, Japan, China and the newly industrialising Pacific rim countries, exceeded that of the United States. In 1985, the United States became a debtor nation, rapidly assuming the status of the world's largest. Servicing the national debt took up 9 per cent of federal saving in 1980; nearly 15 per cent in 1990. A 1990 Commerce Department survey of twelve 'cutting-edge' technologies found that the United States was gaining ground over its rivals in none of them.[66] During the 1992 Democratic primaries, Senator Paul Tsongas recycled a, by then, familiar joke: the Cold War is over – Japan won. US decline seemed to have been compounded by the apparent paralysis of the political process, and by chronic underinvestment in infrastructure, especially education. By the early 1990s, a large academic literature told of an American imperial overstretch, and of a fading hegemon which stubbornly resisted necessary adjustment. Some authorities also suggested that the end of the Cold War might not so much relieve America of its imperial burden, as unleash yet further 'newly arising, more vigorous rivals'.[67]

Much of the literature of decline was and is self-dramatising and overblown. The United States, like other countries, continues to experience severe difficulty in responding to dislocation in the international market economy. 'Downsizing' and the erosion of corporate profits hit at job security. Between 1970 and 1990, gaps between rich and poor in American society widened. (Between those dates, the richest 5 per cent in US society enjoyed a 35.3 per cent increase in family income; the poorest 20 per cent saw income increase by only 2.9 per cent.) Yet the middle Clinton years saw huge increases in the number of jobs at home, and the United States topped most leagues of international competitiveness. Life expectancy grew from 70.8 years in 1970 to 75.7 in 1990. By 1990, 22 per cent of the adult population had college degrees, compared to 11 per cent in 1970. According to R. J. Samuelson, Americans feel bad about doing well.[68] Even if the thesis of American decline is broadly accepted, it is evident that any such decline has been complex, problematic and patchy. The abandonment (by President Nixon in 1971) of the Bretton Woods exchange system, for example, led to a more complex exercise of American power, rather than any radical decline. Joseph Nye wrote in 1990:

> America is rich but acts poor. In real terms, GNP is more than twice what it was in 1960, but Americans today spend much less of their GNP on international leadership. The prevailing view is 'we can't afford it' despite the fact that US taxes are a smaller per cent of GNP than in other OECD nations. This suggests a problem of domestic political leadership in power conversion rather than long-term economic decline.[69]

It is certainly inappropriate to invoke any absolute decline; rather, the United States has had to adjust to interdependence and globalisation. About 17 per cent of all American trade is made up by transfers between branches of US-based transnational corporations. The complexity and diversity of the US economy, along with its renewal through immigration and new regional strategies, stands it in good stead. Moreover, America's 'soft' and cultural power, its continuing ability to embed liberal ideas in the international order, remains as strong as ever.

If the thesis of American decline needs to be treated with caution, so does the theory of 'unstable hegemonic stability'. Theorists in this area have failed clearly to delineate the links between security and economic dimensions. The theory has been criticised as ahistorical, a kind of self-fulfilling prophecy which simply serves to disguise poor planning decisions by American leaders. Also, neoliberals should always remember that the very idea of a benevolent, liberal, hegemonic world order must appear laughable in the poorer, undeveloped countries of the world. International regimes may be able to take over the work of the hegemon. Dominant powers may develop new techniques of domination; indeed, this may be seen as the main project of post-Cold War American Administrations. If we define 'hegemony' in qualitative as well as in quantitative terms, American hegemony and preponderance, though receding, may still be said to exist.[70]

3   Theory and foreign policymaking

(a) *Rationality and its limits*   Varying perspectives on the making of foreign policy emerge from the general orientations on problems of international relations outlined in the previous section. Thus, a realist or neorealist would tend to see foreign policy as structured around a more or less rational pursuit of national interest. The neoliberal would see it much more as the product of intra- and extra-state mutual adjustment and disaggregation.

Notions of rationality in decision-making have been subjected to violent attack. According to Herbert Simon, whose name is associated with the concepts of 'satisficing behavior' and 'bounded rationality', decision-makers operate in a world where choices are made on the basis of picking the least unsatisfactory option: the course of action which exhibits minimally satisfactory standards of acceptability as a basis upon which to proceed.[71] Numerous theorists have described the world of the decision-maker as oriented towards suboptimal compromise and behavioural inconsistency. The requirements of procedural rationality – clear definition of problems, identification of aims, consideration of alternatives, development of clear criteria for choice, monitoring of decisions – relate more to an ideal than to the real world. Foreign policymakers are, in practice, faced by acute difficulties, ranging from unreliable information to time and electoral pressures. As Michael Clarke has written: 'any study of a state's foreign policy over a given period quickly reveals that rather than a series of clear decisions, there is a continuing and confusing "flow of action", made up of a mixture of political decisions, non-political decisions, bureaucratic procedures, continuations of previous policy, and sheer accident.'[72]

Since the 1960s, the 'rational actor' model of decision-making has tended to become appropriated by public and rational choice theorists. Building on neoclassical free market economics and mathematical games theories, they see the goal-maximising rational actor as the logically indispensable starting point for analysis. Within this tradition, as in realism, the nation-state is often identified as a unitary 'rational actor'. (This raises the problem of making a distinction between the 'rational' interest of decision-makers, and the 'rational' interest of the nation-as-a-whole. Within rational choice theory, the notion of 'instrumental' rationality becomes relevant here: the tendency for decision-making individuals to maximise personal prefer-ences.)[73]

Rational choice and 'rational actor' approaches are not vitiated merely by the invocation of the confused, pluralistic and constrained environment in which real-world decision-makers operate. Volumes of traditional diplo-matic and international history attest that 'rational actor' interpretations can, albeit when supplemented by other approaches, provide valuable expla-nations and insights. The 'rational actor' model can act as a kind of Occam's razor, cutting back the explanatory undergrowth. Also, the fact that ratio-nality may be 'bounded' does not necessarily mean that rational frameworks for judging decision-making need be abandoned altogether. The most famous of all 'rational actor' formulations is Graham Allison's 'Model I', in his 1971 discussion of the 1962 Cuban missile crisis. Here, Allison saw ratio-nal choice as residing in the selection of 'that alternative whose conse-quences rank highest in the decision-makers' payoff function' (a rationally conceived hierarchy of goals and objectives). For Allison, rationality 'refers to consistent, value-maximising choice *within specified constraints*'.[74] E. R. May and Richard Neustadt in *Thinking in Time* (1986) attempted to specify and develop rational standards to guide decision-makers towards effective use of historical analogy. They emphasised that decision-makers should posit conditions which would cause them to abandon a particular analogy.[75] J. D. Steinbruner's 'analytic paradigm' is another attempt to develop real-world, practical rational standards: 'A given process of decision is analytic if upon examination one can find evidence that there was at least limited value inte-gration, that alternative outcomes were analyzed and evaluated, and that new information regarding central variables of the problem did produce plausibly appropriate subjective adjustments'.[76]

(b)   *Bureaucratic politics*   Most accounts of bureaucratic procedure and impact tend to emphasise irrationality. Bureaucratic organisation is seen to have a strong counter-rational dimension: institutional rivalries; inflexibility associated with standard operating procedures; decisions emanating from a process of 'pulling and hauling' between vested interests; stubborn resis-tance to all but incremental change. The bureaucratic ethos tends to be one of 'muddling through' rather than of purposeful rationality.[77]

'Bureaucratic politics' perspectives were developed largely in opposition to the 'rational actor' view, and particularly against the view that foreign policymaking may be explained entirely in terms of Presidential leadership. Theorists of 'bureaucratic politics', however, also find themselves in tension with the theories of bureaucratic rationality emanating from the work of Max Weber: the concept of rational, politically controlled bureaucracies, based on the division of labour and able to identify problems, make decisions efficiently and develop policy alternatives. It may be useful here to distinguish between the general organisational perspective on foreign policymaking – the assertion that 'organisation matters' – and the narrower 'bureaucratic politics' model. Graham Allison, although he found the distinction difficult to sustain, did originally distinguish 'organisational process' from 'bureaucratic politics'. The former characterises government as a 'conglomerate of semi-feudal, loosely allied organisations, each with a substantial life of its own'. 'Long-range planning tends to become institutionalised … and then disregarded.' Problems become fragmented and 'solved' according to short-term needs. Allison's 'bureaucratic politics' model, on the other hand, invoked 'players who make government decisions not by a single rational choice but by the pulling and hauling that is politics'.[78] Morton Halperin developed the idea further:

> most governmental actions, which look to the casual outside observer as if they resulted from specific presidential decisions, are more often an amalgam of a number of coincidental occurrences: actions brought about by presidential decisions (not always those intended), actions that are really manoeuvres to influence presidential decisions, actions resulting from decisions in unrelated areas, and actions taken at lower levels by junior participants without informing their superiors or the President.[79]

Most attempts to apply these insights have tended to conflate 'organisational process' and 'bureaucratic politics'.

Decision-makers themselves are generally in no doubt as to the power of bureaucratic fractionation. Chester Cooper, White House staffer under President Lyndon Johnson, described 1967 Vietnam War policy thus: 'There was just no interest or effort expended in orchestrating military and diplomatic moves; everyone was doing his own thing.'[80] Henry Kissinger, NSA to President Nixon, observed: 'The nightmare of the modern state is the hugeness of the bureaucracy, and the problem is how to get coherence and design in it.'[81] George Shultz, Secretary of State between 1982 and 1989, memorably described the bureaucratic wronglings within the Reagan Administration as 'worse than a university'.[82] In 1993, Vice-President Al Gore produced, as part of Bill Clinton's 'reinventing government' initiative, a plan to excise fractionated 'bureaucratic politics' from the State Department. He described a current situation 'that can easily lead to different departments in Washington receiving divergent recommendations from their officers overseas, recommendations that have been reached without any effective effort at coordination'.[83]

There can be no question that 'bureaucratic politics' insights should inform both analysis of current problems and understanding of past events. Christopher Jones, for example, has explained US technology transfers to the Iraqi government, in the decade or so prior to the Gulf War, as follows:

> The major actors within this process, the Departments of Commerce, Defense, and State, held policy positions on dual-use exports to Iraq that were based directly on their distinct bureaucratic roles. Each agency's separate organizational mission and essence caused it to have a different perception of national security and, therefore, different reasons for supporting either trade promotion or trade control.

The State and Commerce Departments won the bureaucratic contest. Defence Department doubts about the wisdom of transferring technology, with a potential military use, to Baghdad were ignored.[84] President Carter's human rights and arms control policies were subjected to consistent bureaucratic sabotage by vested interests. Christopher Shoemaker, who served on Carter's National Security Council (NSC) staff, later wrote: 'After Jimmy Carter's 1977 decision to restrict the sale of military hardware on a worldwide basis, virtually the entire security assistance community within the government set about undermining the policy until it was effectively rescinded three years later.'[85]

'Bureaucratic politics' explanations, however, cannot be all-encompassing. They cannot tell the whole story. They tend to focus on the executive branch (although there is, in principle, no reason why the approach should not be extended to Congress or to interest groups). Such explanations tend to understate the power of the President, especially in crisis decision-making. (It is possible to argue that crisis decision-making actually short-circuits bureaucratic rivalries and hence maximises a narrowly-defined 'rationality'.)[86] The characteristic research tool of 'bureaucratic politics' investigators is the interview with participants in past bureaucratic fights – a research method that, as J. Garry Clifford expresses it, 'permits participants to put excessive spin on the past'.[87] Most importantly, 'bureaucratic politics' tells us little about generalised trans-bureaucratic mindsets and assumptions. Gabriel Kolko has argued that 'bureaucratic politics' cannot alter 'the substance of basic national policies' which is rooted in 'the fundamental issues of power, interests and purposes'.[88] Bureaucratic actors are agents operating within wider structures of power. As Jenkins and Gray argued in 1983, a focus upon intra-bureaucratic bargaining reveals 'little about how relative advantages of players have emerged or how bias has developed within the system'.[89]

Nevertheless, when conceived in appropriately modest terms, 'bureaucratic politics' can achieve at least a partial level of explanation. Some of its subsets (notably 'roles' and 'implementation' theory) have also proved fruitful. The notion of people fitting into predetermined role-patterns is, in fact, a common and common-sensical one. As President Reagan approached his second term, the old actor seemed to change costume and assume the role of peacemaker. The Defence Secretary is regularly depicted as having a major difference in roles perspective compared to the Secretary of State: sensitive to military capabilities, and indeed limitations. The gap between formulation and implementation of decisions was always an important part of the 'bureaucratic politics' case. Implementation often operates as a kind of bureaucratic 'fail safe': a final assertion of the vested interests of the implementing agencies. Clarke and Smith offer three examples of the way in which implementation relates to policymaking. Firstly and most obviously, there is 'slippage': the fiasco of President Carter's 1980 Iranian hostage rescue mission, or the propensity of 'CIA assets' in the developing world to indulge in drug dealing or other activities which lose them Congressional and public support in the United States. Secondly, Clarke and Smith cite 'routine complexity', where policy implementation – exchange-rate policy is a good example – is bound, due to the complexity and unpredictability of the implementing environment, to bear only a hazy resemblance to decisions made in Washington. Thirdly, there is 'self-implementation': policies which exist at the level of rhetoric, position-taking or promises.[90]

(c) *Psychological approaches* The study of perception, cognition, memory and belief systems as they apply to the making of foreign policy is most commonly undertaken in connection with individuals, especially Presidents. A common way to proceed is for students of political psychology to isolate personality types: crusaders and pragmatists, hawks and doves, introverts and extroverts, authoritarians and anti-authoritarians. Especially influential has been the notion of a 'belief system', defined by O. R. Holsti as 'a set of lenses through which information concerning the physical and social environment is received'.[91] Individuals' belief systems are created from an amalgamation of unique experience and generational learning. The experience of fascism in the 1930s thus led one generation to conclude that it was better to risk confrontation than to appease tyrants. The 'Vietnam generation' – President Bill Clinton's generation – in its turn concluded that the United States needed clearly to identify objectives, to avoid being charged with imperialism, and to recognise limits on its power.

Measuring and categorising personality at a distance is highly problematic. Political psychologists tend to focus on speeches and writings. The 'operational coding' approach, for example, typically concentrates on the published work of leading foreign policy actors to determine how they conceptualise conflict. A similar technique is the attempt made by political psychologists to discern motivation from political speeches. David G. Winter, for example, has developed a speech content analysis technique designed to identify three distinct types of motive: achievement, affiliation and power. The achievement motive emphasises innovation, but is problematic 'in situations where effectiveness depends on motivating ... others'. Affiliation is associated with cooperation, but its adherents may react poorly to criticism. The power motive is associated with effective leadership, but may degenerate into 'profligate impulsivity'. Clinton scored highly on all three of Winter's motive scales. Attempts have also been made to classify Presidents according to 'cognitive style' (intuitive or characterised by immersion in policy detail); 'political efficacy' (people management and coalition-building); and 'conflict orientation'.[92]

The problem with many such techniques is that they tend to combine sophisticated methodology with banal conclusions. In fact, the most successful discussion of the relationship between Presidential character and performance remains that of James David Barber. He defines and describes Presidents in terms of their energy and commitment (active/passive) and in terms of the emotional satisfaction they derive from the office (positive/negative). The most successful Presidents tend to be active-positives, of whom the archetype must be Franklin D. Roosevelt. Active-positives 'want most to achieve results. Active-negatives aim to get and keep power. Passive-positives are after love. Passive-negatives emphasize their civic virtue.'[93]

Among recent Presidents, Reagan appears as passive-positive (with, in Winter's terms, a high affiliation motive). Nixon was the quintessential active-negative; Bush a less clear-cut active-positive, at least in regard to foreign policy. Each type has its dangers, with active-negatives usually being regarded as the most dangerous. But active-positives, with their passion for results, may (like Winter's power motivants) overplay their hands and fail.

'Belief systems' also impinge on the *process* of decision-making. Decision-makers seek consistency and are reluctant to accept information which upsets or challenges deeply held assumptions. To quote Robert Jervis: 'actors are more apt to err on the side of being too wedded to an established view and too quick to reject discrepant information than to make the opposite error of too quickly altering their theories. People often undergo premature cognitive closure.'[94] The result is often 'defensive avoidance' rather than rational consideration of options. Irving Janis's concept of 'groupthink' is also relevant here. Members of a 'cohesive in-group' of decision-makers may value unanimity and closing-of-ranks over rational calculation and adaptation to new information.[95]

Notes

1   C. W. Kegley and E. R. Wittkopf, *World Politics: Trend and Transformation* (5th edn, New York, St. Martin's, 1995), p. 98.

2   *New Perspectives Quarterly*, 1988 (cited in H. W. Brands, *The Devil We Knew: Americans and the Cold War* (New York, Oxford University Press, 1993), p. 205).

3   See Brands, *The Devil We Knew*; also D. Campbell, *Writing Security* (Man-

chester, Manchester University Press, 1992).

4   T. A. Bailey, *A Diplomatic History of the American People* (New York, Norton, 1954), pp. 806–7.

5   A. M. Schlesinger, jun., *The Cycles of American History* (London, Deutsch, 1987), p. 67; also, C. V. Crabb, *American Diplomacy and the Pragmatic Tradition* (Baton Rouge, Louisiana State University Press, 1998).

6   Cited in J. M. Mitchell and R. Maidment, eds, *The United States in the Twentieth Century: Culture* (London, Hodder and Stoughton, 1994), p. 14.

7   S. M. Lipset, 'American exceptionalism reaffirmed', in B. E. Shafer, ed., *Is America Different?* (Oxford, Oxford University Press, 1991), p. 16. See also S. M. Lipset, *American Exceptionalism: A Double Edged Sword* (New York, Norton, 1996).

8   *American Foreign Policy Current Documents* 1987 (Washington DC, State Department, 1988), p. 29.

9   See M. H. Hunt, *Ideology and US Foreign Policy* (New haven, Yale University Press, 1987); M. H. Hunt, 'Ideology', in M. J. Hogan and T. G. Paterson, eds, *Explaining the History of American Foreign Relations* (Cambridge, Cambridge University Press, 1991); M. J. Hogan, 'State of the art', in M. J. Hogan, ed., *America in the World* (Cambridge, Cambridge University Press, 1995), pp. 15 ff.

10   See M. Howard, 'Ideology and international relations', *Review of International Studies*, 15 (1989), pp. 1–10: 1; also, T. Eagleton, *Ideology: An Introduction* (London, Verso, 1991).

11   L. Hartz, *The Liberal Tradition in America* (New York, Harcourt, Brace and World, 1955). See also J. A. Hall, *Liberalism* (London, Paladin, 1987), pp. 166–7.

12   See P. Laslett, ed., *Two Treatises on Government*, (Cambridge, Cambridge University Press, 1960); R. Masters, 'The Lockeian tradition in American foreign policy', *Journal of International Affairs*, 21 (1967), pp. 253–77; A. K. Henrikson, 'Ordering the world', *Reviews in American History*, 12 (1984), pp. 606–11.

13   R. Maidment and M. Dawson, eds, *The United States in the Twentieth Century: Key Documents* (London: Hodder and Stoughton, 1994), pp. 248 ff.

14   See C. F. Adams, ed., *The Works of John Adams* (Boston, Little Brown, 1853), p. 178; J. B. Moore, *American Diplomacy* (New York, Harper and Brothers, 1905), p. 254. See also R. W. Tucker and D. C. Hendrickson, 'Thomas Jefferson and American foreign policy', *Foreign Affairs*, 69 (1990), pp. 135–56.

15   M. Cox, *US Foreign Policy after the Cold War: Superpower without a Mission?* (London, Pinter, 1995), p. 5.

16   C. S. Grey, 'The continued primacy of geography', *Orbis*, 40 (1996), 247–59; also, J. Lepgold and T. McKeown, 'Is American foreign policy exceptional?', *Political Science Quarterly*, 110 (1995), 369–85.

17   T. Smith, *America's Mission: The United States and the Worldwide Struggle for Democracy in the Twentieth Century* (Princeton, Princeton University Press, 1994).

18   See H. Kissinger, *Diplomacy* (New York, Simon and Schuster, 1994).

19   See R. Dallek, *The Style of American Foreign Policy* (New York, Knopf, 1983), p. 258; W. D. Anderson and S. J. Kernek, 'How "realistic" is Reagan's diplo-

      macy?', *Political Science Quarterly*, 100 (1985), pp. 389–409.
20   *Time*, 7 April 1995, p. 22; A. J. Bacevich, 'The impact of the new populism',
      Orbis, 40 (1996), pp. 31–43: 37.
21   J. J. Kirkpatrick, *Legitimacy and Force*, vol. I (New Brunswick, Transaction,
      1988), p. 26.
22   E. Shewmaker, 'Daniel Webster and American conservatism', in N. A. Graeb-
      ner, ed., *Traditionals and Values: American Diplomacy, 1790–1945* (Lanham,
      University Press of America, 1985), p. 134.
23   See N. A. Graebner, ed., *Ideas and Diplomacy* (New York, Oxford University
      Press, 1964), p. 287.
24   S. F. Bemis, *A Diplomatic History of the United States* (New York, Holt, Rine-
      hart and Winston, 1936), pp. 803–4.
25   *Congressional Record*, 1951, A4762.
26   R. A. Taft, *A Foreign Policy for Americans* (New York, Doubleday, 1951); also,
      O. R. Holsti, 'The study of international politics makes strange bedfellows',
      American Political Science Review, 68 (1974), pp. 217–42.
27   See R. Crockatt, 'A new Burke', *Times Higher Education Supplement*, 25 Aug.
      1989.
28   See J. Ehrman, *The Rise of Neoconservatism: Intellectuals and Foreign Affairs,
      1945–1994* (New Haven, Yale University Press, 1995).
29   G. Kennan, *Around the Cragged Hill* (New York, Norton, 1993).
30   See T. J. McCormick, 'Drift or mastery?: A corporatist synthesis for American
      diplomatic history', *Reviews in American History*, 10 (1982), pp. 318–30.
31   W. LaFeber, *The American Age* (New York, Norton, 1989), p. 34.
32   A. Lake, 'The need for engagement', *State Department Dispatch*, 5 Dec. 1994,
      p. 804.
33   *Congressional Record*, 1995, S11890 (8 Aug.).
34   (New York, Macmillan, 1934).
35   Cited in J. Rourke, *Congress and the Presidency in Foreign Policy Making* (Boul-
      der, Westview, 1983), p. 148.
36   E. A. Nordlinger, *Isolationism Reconfigured: American Foreign Policy for a New
      Century* (Princeton, Princeton University Press, 1995).
37   See R. Steel, *Walter Lippmann and the American Century* (London, Bodley
      Head, 1980), p. 586.
38   R. W. Tucker, *A New Isolationism: Threat or Promise?* (Washington DC,
      Potomac Associates, 1972); Nordlinger, *Isolationism Reconfigured*, p. 16.
39   T. Smith, 'A Wilsonian World', *World Policy Journal*, 12 (1995), pp. 62–6: 65.
40   Cited in *ibid*.
41   LaFeber, *The American Age*, p. 254; McCormick, 'Drift or mastery?', pp. 324,
      326.
42   See C. W. Kegley and E. R. Wittkopf, *American Foreign Policy: Pattern and
      Process* (3rd edn, New York, St. Martin's, 1987), p. 71; G. White and J. Maze,
      Henry A Wallace: His Search for a New World Order (Chapel Hill, University
      of North Carolina Press, 1995).
43   J. Witcover, *85 Days: The Last Campaign of Robert Kennedy* (New York,
      William Morrow, 1988), p. 49.
44   R. D. Hatch and F. E. Watkins, eds, *Reverend Jesse Jackson: Straight from the
      Heart* (Philadelphia, Fortress Press, 1987), p. 225.

45 See Hunt, *Ideology and US Foreign Policy*, pp. 159, 193–4; R. N. Bellah, et al., *Habits of the Heart: Individualism and Commitment in American Life* (Berkeley, University of California Press, 1985); M. J. Sandel, *Democracy's Discontent: America in Search of a Public Philosophy* (Cambridge, Harvard University Press, 1996).

46 See J. L. Gaddis, 'International Relations Theory and the end of the Cold War', in S. M. Lynn-Jones and S. E. Miller, eds, *The Cold War and After* (Cambridge, Mass., MIT Press, 1993), p. 382.

47 J. L. Gaddis, 'History, Science and the Study of International Relations', in N. Woods, ed., *Explaining International Relations since 1945* (Oxford, Oxford University Press, 1996), p. 44. A riposte is provided in J. L. Ray and B. Russett, 'The future as arbiter of theoretical controversies', *British Journal of Political Science*, 26 (1996), pp. 441–70.

48 See S. Smith, 'Theories of foreign policy: an historical overview', *Review of International Studies*, 12 (1986), pp. 13–29; M. Light, 'Foreign policy analysis', in A. J. R. Groom and M. Light, eds, *Contemporary International Relations: A Guide to Theory* (London, Pinter, 1994), p. 100.

49 J. Vincent, 'The place of theory in the practice of human rights', in C. Hill and P. Beschoff, eds, *Two Worlds of International Relations* (London, Routledge, 1994), p. 29.

50 M. P. Leffler, 'New approaches, old interpretations, and prospective reconfigurations', *Diplomatic History*, 19, 1995, pp. 173–96, 179.

51 R. L. Rothstein, 'On the costs of realism', *Political Science Quarterly*, 87 (1972), pp. 346–62: 351.

52 K. N. Waltz, 'Realist thought and neorealist theory', in C. W. Kegley, ed., *Controversies in International Relations Theory: Realism and the Neoliberal Challenge* (New York, St. Martin's, 1995), p. 74.

53 S. Krasner, 'Regimes and the limits of realism', in S. Krasner, ed., *International Regimes* (Ithaca, Cornell University Press, 1983), p. 367.

54 R. O. Keohane and J. S. Nye, *Power and Interdependence* (Boston, Little, Brown, 1977).

55 D. A. Lake, 'Realism', in J. Krieger, ed., *The Oxford Companion to Politics of the World* (New York, Oxford University Press, 1993), p. 772.

56 See M. W. Zacher and R. A. Matthew, 'Liberal International Theory: Common Threads, Divergent Strands', in Kegley, ed., *Controversies in International Relations Theory*.

57 See I. Wallerstein, *The Capitalist World Economy* (London, Cambridge University Press, 1979); R. Little, 'International Relations and the Triumph of Capitalism', in K. Booth and S. Smith, eds, *International Relations Theory Today* (Cambridge, Polity Press, 1995), pp. 74 ff.; S. Amin, *Accumulation on a World Scale* (New York, Monthly Review Press, 1974).

58 M. Zalewski, 'Feminist theory and international relations', in M. Bowker and R. Brown, eds, *From Cold War to Collapse* (Cambridge, Cambridge University Press, 1993), p. 137. See also J. Vasquez, 'The post-positivist debate', in Booth and Smith, eds, *International Relations Theory Today*; R. J. Walker, *Inside/Outside: International Relations as Political Theory* (Cambridge, Cambridge University Press, 1993).

59 H. J. Morgenthau, 'From great powers to superpowers', in B. Porter, ed., *The*

Aberystwyth Papers (London, Oxford University Press, 1972), pp. 129–30.

60   K. N. Waltz, *Theory of International Politics* (New York, Addison-Wesley, 1979), p. 171.

61   M. P. Leffler, 'National Security', in Hogan and Paterson, eds, *Explaining the History of American Foreign Relations*, pp. 206–7; also, M. P. Leffler, *A Preponderance of Power: National Security, the Truman Administration and the Cold War* (Stanford, Stanford University Press, 1992).

62   See C. Layne and B. Schwarz, 'American hegemony – without an enemy', *Foreign Policy*, 92 (1993), pp. 5–21.

63   C. Kindleberger, *The World in Depression* (Berkeley, University of California Press, 1973), p. 305.

64   See R. O. Keohane, *After Hegemony: Cooperation and Discord in the World Political Economy* (Princeton, Princeton University Press, 1984).

65   S. D. Krasner, 'State power and the structure of international trade', *World Politics*, 28 (1976), pp. 317–47: 321.

66   See J. Petras and M. Morley, *Empire or Republic? American Global Power and Domestic Decay* (New York, Routledge, 1995), pp. 25–62; M. A. Bernstein and D. E. Adler, eds, *Understanding American Economic Decline* (Cambridge, Cambridge University Press, 1994); C. F. Bergsten, 'Japan and the United States in the New World Order', in T. Rutner, ed., *The United States in the World Political Economy* (New York, McGraw-Hill, 1994).

67   M. Blachman and D. Puchala, 'When empires meet', in C. Kegley, ed., *The Long Postwar Peace* (New York, Harper Collins, 1991), p. 184; P. Kennedy, *The Rise and Fall of the Great Powers* (New York, Random House, 1987); D. Calleo, *Beyond American Hegemony* (Brighton, Wheatsheaf, 1987).

68   See R. J. Samuelson, *The Good Life and its Discontents: The American Dream in the Age of Enlightenment 1945–1995* (New York, Times Books, 1996).

69   J. S. Nye, *Bound to Lead: The Changing Nature of American Power* (New York, Basic Books, 1991), pp. 259–60. Also, J. Gowa, *Closing the Gold Window* (Ithaca, Cornell University Press, 1983); H. R. Nau, *The Myth of American Decline* (Oxford, Oxford University Press, 1990); J. G. Ruggie, 'International regimes, transactions and change – embedded liberalism in the postwar economic order', *International Organization*, 36 (1982), pp. 379–415.

70   See Susan Strange, 'The future of the American empire', *Journal of International Affairs*, 42 (1988), pp. 1–17; J. Gowa, 'Rational hegemons, excludable goods, and small groups: an epitaph for hegemonic stability theory?', *World Politics*, 41 (1989), pp. 307–24; A. Wyatt-Walter, 'The United States and Western Europe: the theory of hegemonic stability', in Woods, ed., *Explaining International Relations*.

71   H. A. Simon, *Administrative Behavior* (New York, Macmillan, 1957).

72   M. Clarke, 'The foreign policy system: a framework for analysis', in M. Clarke and B. White, eds, *Understanding Foreign Policy: The Foreign Policy Systems Approach* (Aldershot, Elgar, 1989), p. 38.

73   See F. C. Zagare, 'Rationality and deterrence', *World Politics*, 42 (1990), pp. 238–60.

74   G. T. Allison, *Essence of Decision* (Boston, Little, Brown, 1971), pp. 29–30; my emphasis.

75   E. R. May and R. E. Neustadt, *Thinking in Time* (New York, Free Press, 1986).

76 J. D. Steinbruner, *The Cybernetic Theory of Decision* (Princeton, Princeton University Press, 1974), p. 45.

77 See C. E. Lindblom, 'The science of muddling through', *Public Administration Review*, 19 (1959,) pp. 79–88.

78 Allison, *Essence of Decision*, pp. 67, 92, 144; G. T. Allison and M. H. Halperin, 'Bureaucratic politics: a paradigm and some policy implications', *World Politics*, 24 (1972), pp. 40–79.

79 M. H. Halperin, *Bureaucratic Politics and Foreign Policy* (Washington DC, Brookings, 1971), p. 293.

80 C. L. Cooper, *The Lost Crusade: America in Vietnam* (New York, Dodd, Mead, 1970), pp. 373–4.

81 Halperin, *Bureaucratic Politics*, p. 15.

82 G. P. Shultz, *Turmoil and Triumph: My Years as Secretary of State* (New York, Scribner's, 1993), p. 275.

83 Office of the Vice-President, Accompanying Report of the National Performance Review, 'From Red Tape to Results', *Department of State and US Information Agency* (Washington DC, US Government Printing Office, 1993), p. 6.

84 C. M. Jones, 'American prewar technology sales to Iraq: a bureaucratic politics explanation', in E. R. Wittkopf, ed., *The Domestic Sources of American Foreign Policy* (New York, St. Martin's, 1994), p. 293. See also B. W. Jentleson, *With Friends like These: Reagan, Bush and Saddam, 1982–1990* (New York, Norton, 1994).

85 C. C. Shoemaker, *The NSC Staff: Counseling the Council* (Boulder, Westview, 1991), p. 30. See also J. Spear, *Carter and Arms Sales* (Basingstoke, Macmillan, 1995); J. Dumbrell, *The Carter Presidency: A Re-evaluation* (Manchester, Manchester University Press, 2nd edn, 1995), ch. 7; D. C. Kozak and J. M.. Keagle, eds, *Bureaucratic Politics and National Security* (Boulder, Lynne Reinner, 1988).

86 See J. R. Oneal, 'The rationality of decision making during international crises', *Polity*, 20 (1988), pp. 598–627.

87 J. G. Clifford, 'Bureaucratic politics', in Hogan and Paterson, eds, *Explaining the History of American Foreign Relations*, p. 145.

88 G. Kolko, *Confronting the Third World: United States Foreign Policy, 1945–1980* (New York, Pantheon Books, 1988), p. xii.

89 B. Jenkins and A. Gray, 'Bureaucratic politics and power', *Political Studies*, 31 (1983), pp. 177–93, p. 188; S. Lukes, *Power: A Radical View* (Basingstoke, Macmillan, 1974).

90 M. Clarke and S. Smith, 'Perspectives on the foreign policy system: implementation approaches', in Clarke and White, *Understanding Foreign Policy*, pp. 165 ff.

91 O. R. Holsti, 'The belief system and national images', *Journal of Conflict Resolution*, 6 (1962), pp. 244–52: 245.

92 D. G. Winter, 'Presidential psychology and governing styles: a comparative psychological analysis of the 1992 Presidential candidates', in S. A. Renshon, ed., *The Clinton Presidency: Campaigning, Governing and the Psychology of Leadership* (Boulder, Westview, 1995), pp. 115 ff. See also D. M. Snow and E. Brown, *Puzzle Palaces and Foggy Bottom* (New York, St. Martin's, 1994), p. 69; S. Smith and R. Little, eds, *Belief Systems and International Relations* (Oxford, Blackwell, 1989); S. G. Walker, 'The interface between beliefs and behavior',

Journal of Conflict Resolution, 21 (1977), pp. 129–68; G. H. Shepard, 'Personality effects on American foreign policy', *International Studies Quarterly*, 32 (1988), pp. 91–123.

93   J. D. Barber, *Presidential Character: Predicting Performance in the White House* (Englewood Cliffs, Prentice-Hall, 1985), p. 10.

94   R. Jervis, *Perception and Misperception in International Politics* (Princeton, Princeton University Press, 1976), p. 187. See also R. B. McCalla, *Uncertain Perceptions: US Cold War Crisis Decision Making* (Ann Arbor, University of Michigan Press, 1992).

95   I. L. Janis, *Groupthink: Psychological Studies of Policy Decisions and Fiascoes* (Boston, Houghton Mifflin, 1982).

2

US foreign policy: past into future

1 Interpreting American foreign policy

(a) *National mission* Invocation of the concept of 'national character' immediately invites charges of romanticism and reification. Christopher Hill, British historian of the seventeenth century, declared in his 1989 Conway lecture: 'To resort to national character as an explanation means that you have no explanation: national character changes with history.'[1]

The centrality of ideas of national mission and exceptionalism, however, to the dominant liberal foreign policy ideology was noted in the previous chapter. The notion of 'Americanism' or 'American national character' includes an optimism about human behaviour and perfectibility, a pragmatic belief in the solubility of the world's problems. It appears also to embody a notion of deliverance from evil: the idea that justice and liberty may be achieved if only the correct dragon is slain. American faith in technology can also reasonably be cited as a facet of the national character. Such attitudes have had an effect on US foreign policy, as has the American public ethos of commitment to capitalism and democracy. These cultural forces are not reducible to economic interest. (Indeed, as Stephen Krasner argues, very powerful nations share with very weak ones the luxury of being able to pursue 'ideological', non-economic goals)[2].) Notions of national mission (to spread democracy) combine with liberal ideology to produce the character-istic argument – articulated originally by Thomas Jefferson – that, for US foreign policy, 'interests' and 'morality' are identical.[3]

The historical trajectory of 'national mission', from the 'city on a hill' Puritan legacy through the frontier to the late nineteenth-century incursions into the Philippines and the Caribbean, is clear. For Frederick Jackson Turner, the frontier was 'a gate of escape from the bondage of the past'.[4] America's democratic mission was both to transcend and recreate the past. The experience of state-building in the western territories, along with the subjugation of Native Americans, fed into and shaped America's emergence as a world power. The 'cultural' or 'national character' inheritance is complex; it combines elements of cultural racism with a commitment to anti-colonialism. Important 'national mission' and 'cultural' interpretations have been made of, for example, the 1941–45 war against Japan and of the Vietnam War.[5]

For many American policymakers, the Cold War seemed to represent the precise coincidence of 'interests' and 'morality': capitalism and the spreading of liberty. Problems arise, of course, when the two appear no longer to be mutually supportive. At one level, there is the perennial problem of selectivity. On what grounds may a foreign policy predicated on the identity of 'interests' and 'morality' stand back from the whole-hearted promotion of liberty? From this dilemma arises an ultimately unsustainable commitment to universality and globalism. At another level, there is the problem of the identity between 'interests' and 'morality' itself. During the Vietnam War, a host of critics – from George Kennan to Senator William Fulbright – argued that national interests (including domestic peace) were being sacrificed to 'morality'. In the post-Cold War context, this debate re-emerged as a disagreement between globalist democracy-promoters and proponents of a selective engagement geared to national interest. The end of the Cold War also stimulated a debate about the degree to which shifting patterns of immigration, uncertainties deriving from the Vietnam War and Watergate eras, and the social and cultural divisions of the 1980s, had undermined any cohesive 'national character'.[6]

(b) *Realism and balances of power*   The American realist tradition, as exemplified by Reinhold Niebuhr, takes issue with Thomas Jefferson's view about the identity of 'interests' and 'morality'.[7] Nations must protect their integrity and their interests, and will do whatever is necessary so to do. This view was made explicit in one of the Cold War's great founding documents: NSC document 68 of 1950 (NSC-68, largely composed by Paul Nitze). According to NSC-68:

> Our free society, confronted by a threat to its basic values, naturally will take such action, including the use of military force, as may be required to protect those values. The integrity of our system will not be jeopardized by any measures, covert or overt, violent or non-violent, which serve the purposes of frustrating the Kremlin design.[8]

Yet, as noted in the previous chapter, American realism always has the tendency to be overtaken and absorbed by moralistic, messianic liberal internationalism. This is indeed apparent in the text of NSC-68 which combines a tough-minded realism with a denunciation of 'evil men' in Moscow. George Kennan, the author of the 1946 'long telegram' and 1947 'X' article in *Foreign Affairs*, considered Stalin to be deranged, but nevertheless traced the roots of Soviet aggression to Russia's expansionist, geopolitically driven traditions. Again, however, Kennan's realism, with its implicit acceptance of 'spheres of influence', became the servant of a universalistic, moralistic theory of anti-communist containment.

Geopolitical imperatives for the United States are generally held to include the containment of Soviet (after 1991, of Russian) expansionism, the maintenance of access to raw materials (notably oil in the Persian Gulf region), and the safeguarding of US naval superiority in the Atlantic, Pacific and Indian oceans. As Stephen Pelz puts it, realist commentators 'portray U.S. decision makers as responding to threats to the vital assets of the United States or as taking advantage of the opportunities that the international system gives U.S. leaders to increase the security of the nation by expanding its military strength or by making alliances'. Only 'when such international incentives and disincentives fail to explain policymakers' actions' need the realist consider other causes.[9] Realists also draw attention to the 'security dilemma': in 'seeking power and security for themselves, states can easily threaten the power and security aspirations of other states'.[10]

The 'security dilemma' constantly threatens to undermine balances of power. These are defined, in realist thought, as more or less stable systems which distribute benefits and manage threats. In its history, the United States is seen to have participated in various multipolar and bipolar balance of power systems, prior to the creation of the Cold War system in the late 1940s. According to William Odom: 'International systems do not spring up spontaneously. Leaders of the major powers create them.' In 1995, Odom, a former deputy to Zbigniew Brzezinski on President Jimmy Carter's NSC staff, urged President Clinton to create a new 'concert of great powers'. (Odom's 'great power' list included the G-7 industrial partners – Germany, France, Britain, Italy, Canada, Japan – 'plus Russia').[11]

As argued in the previous chapter, in the discussion of ideology, American liberalism tends to penetrate and supersede realism. The realist analysis of the pre-1914 period, for example, has problems with America's failure to help preserve the power balance against Germany. Realism, and its 'security studies' stepchild, has also suffered from an overly restrictive view of 'security'. Reviewing the field in 1995, David Baldwin concluded that contemporary security studies were 'poorly equipped to deal with the post-cold war world, having emerged from the cold war with a narrow military conception of national security and a tendency to assert its primacy over other public policy goals'.[12] Several authorities argue that security studies need to take more account of social, economic and environmental 'threats'.[13] Michael Hunt points to further lines of criticism of realism:

> The very identification with the state, with current policymaking, and with the underlying assumptions of the foreign policy elite that gives realism its strength also limits its intellectual range and analytic scope, in effect trapping realists ... in a framework of inquiry that has a pronounced national as well as gender and class bias.[14]

(c) *Imperialism*   Historians who focus on 'national mission' see the motor force of American foreign policy as the desire (however well or ill-conceived) to spread political and economic liberty. Geopolitical realists interpret it in terms of protecting interests and filling power vacuums. A third school urges the explanatory claims of imperialism and the wish (or need) to secure overseas outlets for 'surplus' American production. In the context of most major foreign policy debates, this perspective is labelled 'revisionist'. (It should be noted, however, that 'revisionism' refers simply to the challenging of received orthodoxy and has no essential left or Marxian inclination. In the case of the Vietnam War, for example, 'revisionism' refers simply to the work of writers like Guenter Lewy,[15] who oppose the view that the war was immoral and unjustifiable.) 'Revisionist' versus orthodox debates have been waged over, for example, interpretations of the Spanish–American war (1898), of US entry into the two world wars, and of the origins of the Cold War.

The inspiration for much revisionist writing, and for leftist interpretations of US foreign policy generally, lies in the work of William Appleman Williams (1921–90). For Williams, the 'essence of American foreign relations' was the 'evolution of one fragile settlement' planted on the 'perimeter of a vast and unexplored continent into a global Empire'.[16] The search for markets abroad, especially after the closing of the frontier, through Open Door policies, was the engine of expansion. Williams combined a commitment to the primacy of economics, a radical American populism, and an account of expansion derived from the frontier thesis of F. J. Turner. Such eclecticism left Williams open to charges of ambiguity and theoretical naïveté. (In an essay published in 1995, Bruce Cumings listed the various positions ascribed to Williams by his critics: 'a pro-Communist, a revisionist, a reductionist, an American exceptionalist, the author of the new orthodoxy in diplomatic history, or, by implication, a dishonest historian who ignored the millions who died at the hands of world-historical monsters'[17].) Yet, to be fair to Williams's critics, it is not entirely clear whether he saw the history of US foreign relations as driven unavoidably, deterministically, by the search for markets; or, whether he was actually calling on America's leaders to change course.[18] Was American idealistic liberalism itself an empty expressions of economic interest? Or had it simply become perverted by greedy capitalists, and was thus capable of being redeemed from them? Williams was no crude conspiracy theorist. Yet he did not resolve the problem of reconciling a commitment to the primacy of economics with a belief in the independent force of ideas: the problem formulated by Marxian structuralists in terms of 'relative autonomy'. One way out of Williams's dilemma, of course, is to write more orthodox Marxist history, with an unambiguous commitment to revolutionism over reformism. The work of Gabriel Kolko indicates that such an approach need not lead to an arid reductionism. Another alternative is the unabashed radical populism of

Noam Chomsky.[19] What Williams and his New Left followers did was to reinvigorate diplomatic history, turning it once again (as Charles Tansill and Charles Beard had for an earlier generation) away from a paralysing concentration upon 'high politics'.

Williams's influence is felt in the work of Thomas J. McCormick, who locates his study of the US 'hegemonic project' against the backdrop of Wallerstein's 'world system' theory.[20] 'Corporatist' diplomatic historians also look to Williams. Within the corporatist perspective, government and business elites are seen as combining, non-conspiratorially, to set a predictable, ordered pattern of foreign relations that is conducive to profit. Such collaboration is rooted in liberal notions of a 'middle way' between unfettered business and socialistic solutions. President Herbert Hoover's idea of the 'associative state' and President Eisenhower's attraction towards the 'corporate commonwealth' are examples of this 'middle way'. (The corporatist school has been criticised for failing adequately to define the central concept of 'corporatism', and also for being more successful in treating periods of foreign policy consensus than in accounting for consensual breakdown.)[21]

For W. A. Williams, the Open Door was imperialism. This view echoes the older historical debate over the putative imperialism of free trade. The term, 'imperialism', of course, is a slippery one. K. N. Waltz has correctly ridiculed its use to describe virtually any relationship between unequal partners.[22] Certainly, in the legal-formal sense, the United States is an imperial power only to a very limited degree. Since the Philippines became independent in 1946, the United States may be said to have maintained a quasi-imperial relationship (in the legal-formal sense) with Puerto Rico, Guam, the Panama Canal Zone, American Samoa, the Virgin Islands and parts of the Territory of the Pacific Islands. The United States was born from colonial rebellion. Anti-imperialists within the American political tradition have condemned 'economic' as well as 'political' imperialism. (Senator Robert La Follette, for example, urged Woodrow Wilson in 1917 against allowing 'financial imperialism' to propel the United States into World War One[23].) Yet the United States also has an imperialist tradition – an 'empire which is so desperately anxious not to be an empire'.[24] Walt Whitman celebrated and predicted 'The New Empire' in 1860: 'I chart the new empire, grander than any before'. In 1899, Henry Blake Fuller, anti-imperialist and supporter of William Jennings Bryan, replied:

> G. is for Guns
> That McKinley has sent,
> To teach Filipinos
> What Jesus Christ meant.[25]

It is overly fastidious to restrict use of the world 'imperialism' to its legal-formal sense. American determination to prevent unwanted (leftist) political change in Latin America, for example, at least approaches the status of impe-

rialism. To extend the term beyond the legal-formal dimension is not frivolous. It raises fearsomely tricky questions about the relationship between
power, influence and control. Yet it does try to take seriously the conventional definition of 'imperialism' as a condition where key decisions are
made by 'persons, processes and institutions foreign to the colony'.[26] 'Hegemony' and 'preponderant power' are more satisfactory concepts than imperialism. From the perspective of the developing world, especially Latin
America, however, the terms may not seem very distinct. Imperialism, like
hegemony and preponderant power, is seen, for example, to have a cultural
dimension. Gill and Law point out that Latin American radicals have
depicted Mickey Mouse as an instrument of US imperialism: a symbol of the
individualistic North American way, as well as a trademark of the powerful,
transnational Disney corporation.[27]

2 Explaining the end of the Cold War

(a) *Background*   The ending of the Cold War called into question virtually
all pre-existing assumptions about international relations and about US foreign policy. Literature on these subjects, published between the late 1940s
and early 1990s, tended to suffer from extreme partisanship and from ahis-
toricity. Put simply, it was difficult to imagine that the Cold War would *ever*
end; even more difficult to see how the end could come peacefully. How
could there be a post-Cold War American foreign policy, except perhaps a
policy for combating nuclear winter?

Most people were surprised by the events of 1985–91. Some individuals,
for example, Senator Daniel Patrick Moynihan,[28] have claimed that they did
predict the imminent collapse of the Soviet empire amid nationalistic tensions. Cases can be made that the end of the Cold War was foreseen by some
liberal capitalist hawks; by those analysts who did emphasise Soviet weakness; by George Kennan himself, or by Paul Nitze in NSC-68; by various
writers on interdependency, industrialisation, modernisation and 'long
cycles' of great power influence; even by Ronald Reagan himself.[29] Academe,
however, especially academic social science, stood accused of having missed
the predictive boat.

Most accounts of the Cold War's end concur that central importance
should be accorded to Mikhail Gorbachev's 'new thinking': the decision of
Soviet leaders in the late 1980s to abandon traditional, confrontational
modes of thought and behaviour. Raymond Garthoff contends: 'the American role in ending the Cold War was necessary but not primary'.[30] All assertions about the Cold War, however, are controversial. Let us begin at the
beginning. What was the Cold War? When did it end? (Has it ended?) Most
commentators accept that the Cold War was a mixture of geopolitical and
ideological struggle, primarily between the United States and the Soviet
Union. (Part of the case against social science theory has been that it tended

to neglect the ideological contest.) Walter LaFeber and Fred Halliday have each attempted further to classify and catalogue competing visions of what exactly constituted the Cold War. LaFeber has distinguished four dimensions: a continuation of 'the ongoing struggle, dating back at least to World War I ... between the United States and the European countries to determine the kind of Europe that should evolve, and to decide how great a role America will have in that determination'; secondly, 'the ongoing struggle between the world's commercial centres and the outlying countries' – the 'periphery' – 'that provide markets and raw materials'; thirdly, a war 'fought within the United States' to turn 'an individualistic, open, commercial and domestic-oriented society into a consensual, secret, militaristic, international force'; and, lastly, 'the long conflict between the United States and the Soviet Union' which, at least in nascent form, predated the Bolshevik Revolution of 1917.[31] Halliday has also isolated four approaches to understanding Cold War dynamics: great power geopolitical conflict; 'subjectivist' theories (advanced by writers like Irving Janis and Robert Jervis, though also on occasion even by Henry Kissinger[32]) of perception and misperception; 'internalist' theories, whereby dominant groups in the USA and USSR were seen as using the Cold War to control their own and client populations; and 'inter-systemic conflict' (ideological, military and economic antagonism between 'two distinct systems').[33]

It emerges from the LaFeber–Halliday typologies that not all viewpoints would accept that the Cold War, except possibly in name, had ended by 1991. The geopolitical conflict, for example, especially if it is seen to pre-date 1946 (much less 1917), is seen by some realist commentators as continuing. Similarly, those understandings of the Cold War which never accorded centrality to the US–Soviet rivalry would hardly accept that Cold War dynamics have ended. Into this category we may place LaFeber's core–periphery dimension, characteristic of world systems theory. Noam Chomsky maintains that the phase of core control of the periphery called 'the Cold War' ended with the fall of the Berlin Wall; then the US invaded Panama to show that nothing had changed.[34] Some 'internalist' theories would also presumably argue that the Cold War had not so much ended as moved on. Writers who see the Cold War primarily as functionally constructive of American identity might argue that the United States is simply looking for a more credible enemy.

Despite all this, let us presume that the Cold War, defined primarily as a geopolitical-ideological contest between superpowers, *has* ended. *When* did it end? Garthoff holds that it had ceased by 1990, *before* the Soviet collapse. Halliday contends that the end came with the 'rapid, almost effortless surrender' by the Soviet leadership, a body 'that had hitherto shown remarkable tenacity and ingenuity in rivalling the West'.[35] The end may thus be judged as the point where ideological and competitive 'surrender' became not only manifest, but virtually incapable of being reversed (either by means of a conservative seizure of power in Moscow, or a change of direction). Cases can be made for exalting various arms deals, the opening of the Berlin Wall, the East European revolutions of 1989 (with the prior dropping by Moscow of its Brezhnev Doctrine) or 1990 German reunification as 'the end'.[36] Thomas Risse-Knappen identifies it 'as the point in time when the "Soviet threat", which dominated Western foreign and defense policy outlooks throughout the post-1945 era, ceased to exist'. Risse-Knappen concludes that the Cold War ended 'in the eyes of the American public' between late 1988 and 1990.[37] Some US policy leaders, however, took the Soviet threat seriously at least up until the 1991 coup, and to some extent until the Soviet break-up. Let us concur with George Bush, who declared in Paris in November 1990: 'The Cold War is over'.[38] (In Cold War history, of course, nothing is simple. Periodisation of the war, the oscillation between confrontation and cooperation, is still controversial. Some commentators argue that the war ended when it became a 'controlled contest', driven by 'nuclear learning' on both sides; or, possibly when the Soviet leadership – long before 1985 – lost its faith in Marxism-Leninism[39].)

(b) *'Reagan victory'?*   As noted above, Gorbachevian 'new thinking' holds centre ground in most accounts of the Cold War's end. However, among those writers who do focus on the United States, primary attention tends to be devoted to the Reagan Administration (1981–89) and its impact on the Soviet reform and disintegration process. The 'pure' 'Reagan victory' thesis is advanced by Margaret Thatcher: '[Reagan's] policies of military and economic competition with the Soviet Union forced the Soviet leaders, in particular Mr Gorbachev, to abandon their ambitions of hegemony and to embark on the process of reform which in the end brought the entire communist system crashing down.'[40] In January 1988, Vice-President Bush declared that Gorbachev's policies were the result of 'our strength' and 'our resolve'.[41] In characteristically mock-heroic mode, Reagan himself announced in 1989: 'People tell me that I won the Cold War.'[42]

The pure 'Reagan victory' thesis attributes American victory to the early Reagan defence spending and economic squeeze. The thesis has been extended in a number of directions. Stephen Sestanovich, for example, has argued that not only Reagan, but also Margaret Thatcher and President Bush were responsible: 'What they did ... was hand [Gorbachev] a gun and suggest that he do the honorable thing.'[43] Several historical accounts of the period extend considerable credit to Bush's management of potentially dangerous crises in the Cold War's final days.[44] Some 'Reagan victory' commentators place special emphasis on Reagan's Strategic Defence Initiative (SDI, or 'Star Wars') – the laser defence system proclaimed in 1983; others accord pride of place to the Pershing II deployments in Western Europe. Writers such as Peter Rodman stress the Reagan Administration's anti-Sovietism in the developing world – the Reagan Doctrine – as much as defence and economic squeeze.[45] Many pro-Reagan commentators are prepared to acknowledge Gorbachev's central role, but still see Reagan as inciting the new Moscow policies. Attempts have also been made to credit the 'four-part strategy', developed by Reagan and Secretary of State George Shultz, with Cold War victory. (The 'four-part strategy' aimed to engage the USSR on separate fronts: on arms control, human rights, trade, and regional issues. It represented the final break with the 'linkage' thinking of the early and mid-1970s, whereby Soviet behaviour was to be influenced across a wide range of issue areas with the primary aim of securing arms control agreements.)[46] Extensions of 'Reagan victory' include the argument, advanced by Nathan Glazer, that it was as much Reagan II, the more flexible post-1984 President, as the tough Reagan I, who won the day.[47] Many authorities also hold that post-1946 containment triumphed, with Reagan giving history the final push. At its most expansive, 'Reagan victory' shades into the view that the world in the late 1980s was merely witnessing the ineluctable ascendancy of liberal capitalism.

The provenance of 'Reagan victory' thinking is interesting. At one level it constituted an attempt to recapture the legacy of Reaganism for the cause of conservative anti-Sovietism. At the time, many conservatives were distressed by President Reagan's second term flexibility towards Moscow. Whatever their provenance, 'Reagan victory' arguments deserve to be taken seriously. Reagan's personal unpopularity in liberal and leftist circles, especially in Western Europe, made it difficult for many commentators to extend any credit to his Administration: to recognise Reagan's personal anti-nuclearism, his desire to be a second term peacemaker, or to acknowledge Secretary Shultz's skills as a pragmatic counterweight to White House and Pentagon ideologues. Important qualifications do, however, have to be made to 'Reagan victory'. The Reagan Administration's operations were often ramshackle. The anti-Soviet 'squeeze' strategy (promoted by Richard Perle at the Defence Department) was never applied consistently; technology transfers and grain sales were actually resumed (after the Carter Administration bans) in the early 1980s. Confusion in Washington and the attitude of America's European allies ensured that the economic aspects of détente were never entirely dismantled. The Reagan Doctrine and anti-Sovietism in the developing world was also applied more than a little erratically. Washington's 1980s anti-Sovietism proved overblown and deeply compromised in Central America. It achieved little in the Middle East, although it was certainly more effective in Afghanistan. In the Philippines, the Reagan Administration eventually cast itself loose from the discredited Marcos regime. In Africa, State Department specialist Chester Crocker attempted, often in opposition to the White House, to construct a pragmatic foreign policy for the South. In the Horn of Africa, the Administration essentially followed a policy of unabashed pragmatism. In a sense, the Cold War was won in the developing world; but as part of the reduced appeal of the Sovietised development model, rather than as a result of the Reagan Doctrine. Soviet withdrawal from the Third World was not unrelated to American competition. But it flowed also from 'new thinking', which had its own dynamic, above and beyond any straightforward reaction to Reaganism.[48]

It should also be appreciated that Reagan's second term flexibility had causes that went deeper than his desire to be remembered as a peacemaker. From late 1986 onwards (with mid-term electoral reversals and the eruption of the Iran–Contra scandal), the Reagan–Gorbachev dialogue was conducted against the background of US Presidential weakness and vulnerability. Reagan II was a response to various failures and pressures in the first term. The Administration had encountered great difficulty in convincing both American and allied opinion of the potency of the 'Soviet threat'. The US nuclear freeze and Western European peace movements both complicated the first term messages being received in Moscow, and sent warnings to the Administration. David Cortright has made the claim that the freeze movement forced the Reagan Administration 'to negotiate with the Soviet Union', with peace movements generally 'shaping the zero-option proposal, stalemating the MX missile, rejecting civil defence planning, ending anti-satellite weapons testing, imposing limitations on SDI funding and testing, and preventing military intervention in Central America'. Such claims do not accurately convey the complexities of Presidential–Congressional relations in this period. (Even Cortright admits that the peace movements were unable 'to alter the core structures of the war system'[49].) However, as Mary Kaldor has argued, the role of the Western freeze and peace movements, as well as of the East European dissidents, cannot be written out of the history of the Cold War's end.[50] It is also widely acknowledged that various transactional, interdependency and disarmament movements – like Joseph Rotblat's 'Pugwash' – influenced Soviet 'new thinking'. It can be argued that it was détente itself which communicated notions of interdependence eastwards: that it was precisely the degree to which détente was not dismantled which emboldened the Kremlin to consider disarming. Reaganism may then be seen as an obstacle to reform, particularly to the extent that Reagan's first term bellicosity strengthened the hand of Moscow hardliners. Georgi Arbatov, director of the Soviet Institute for USA and Canadian Studies, argued in 1991 that 'Reagan made it practically impossible to start reform after Brezhnev's death ... and made it more difficult for Gorbachev to cut military expenditures'.[51]

'Reagan victory' interpretations of the end of the Cold War are, at least in their 'pure' form, insensitive to the *Soviet* dynamics. At one level, there is Senator D. P. Moynihan's point: 'Surely, the Cold War might have come to an end on its own without the US having to become a debtor state in the process.'[52] Soviet reform was rooted in structural problems of the command economy, in generational changes and intra-Communist Party cleavages. Examination of the diplomatic history of the period also leads to the conclusion that Moscow, after 1985, was making all the running. The important breakthroughs for Reagan's 'negotiation from strength' policy came only after Gorbachev's 1985 accession to power.

What of SDI and the 'squeeze' on Soviet defence spending more generally? Soviet commentator Igor Klyamkin maintains that a combination of SDI and the Pershing missiles in Western Europe convinced Moscow that 'a systemic restructuring of society' was needed in order to solve 'our defence problems'.[53] The Soviet leaders took SDI seriously. Gorbachev raised the possibility of SDI technology being used for offensive purposes. Former Ambassador Anatoly Dobrynin records that the USSR did genuinely fear a US nuclear attack, although Soviet leaders had become 'less paranoid' by 1984. The new laser defence system seemed like comic-strip fantasy to many in the West. But it threatened to make obsolete an entire generation of Soviet nuclear weapons, and, in effect, to give the United States a destructive first-strike capability. Both Soviet and American concern with SDI proved the undoing of arms agreements and the Reykjavik summit of 1986. Indeed, there is also no question that Moscow's 'new thinkers' were alarmed by spiralling arms costs. By the mid-1980s, almost one quarter of Soviet Gross National Product was being taken up in defence spending. Yet Moscow's defence spending levels remained fairly constant throughout Reagan's Presidency. Fred Chernoff concludes:

> The burden was indeed crushing for the Soviet economy, and no doubt had an enormous impact on the leadership's decision to reverse 45 years of postwar foreign policy. But the conclusion that the data forces upon us is that the burden was in place well before the military buildup of the 1980s began and did not accelerate appreciably thereafter.[54]

In fact, during the entire Cold War, it proved exceedingly difficult to demonstrate any direct correlation between US and Soviet defence spending shifts. On both sides, pressures to increase spending appear to have operated almost independently of the objective 'threat'.[55] As for SDI, it seems extraordinarily unlikely that Moscow was unaware of the high degree of uncertainty attending the operation of 'Star Wars'. In his memoirs, Gorbachev recalls Reagan's 'bizarre' advocacy of SDI 'science fiction'.[56] Reykjavik notwithstanding, the Soviets *never* received any American commitment on SDI abandonment, postponement or downgrading.

(c) *The liberal idea, capitalist triumph, and the limits of realism*   One obvious rejoinder to the 'Reagan victory' thesis is, of course, the assertion that deeper processes were at work. Gaddis invokes 'tectonic' forces, underpinning the interactions of diplomatic history. (According to Gaddis, these forces included the rise of the liberal idea; the divorce, in an advanced nuclear age, between economic and military power; the 'collapse of authoritarianism'; and 'the inability of command economies to cope with the growing demands of post-industrial societies'[57].) Discussion of 'deeper processes' does not imply that the events of 1985–91 were 'inevitable'. Individuals and contingencies do matter. The end of the Cold War foregrounded elite, rather than mass behaviour. (Eric Hobsbawm points out that 'none of the regimes in Eastern Europe were *over-thrown*'.) No individual mattered more than Gorbachev, who did not merely 'uncork change'.[58]

Most accounts of the Cold War's end emphasise the triumph of liberal capitalism. These run the gamut from celebratory invocations of the 'liberal idea' to leftist narratives of the globalisation of capital. In the former category, Francis Fukuyama's 'end of history' thesis has received the most attention. According to Fukuyama, who formulated his ideas as a member of the State Department's Policy Planning staff, realism had simply failed to anticipate the historic (and peaceful) triumph of liberalism. The end of the Cold War indicated that, for mankind, 'all the really big questions had been settled'. Only liberal democratic capitalism is able to fulfil the two key human needs: the desire for individual recognition (the Platonic concept of *thymos*) and the requirement of material comfort. Fukuyama, in his celebration of liberal democracy, tended to ignore not only nationalist and religious fundamentalist upsurges, but also the experience of *authoritarian* capitalism in the Far East. He also gave enormous weight to the power of ideas.[59] Some of this 'march of democracy' literature also ignores the evolution of Chinese communism and overstates the 'absolute' failure of its Soviet counterpart. To quote Fred Halliday: 'what is perhaps most striking is that this attempt to escape the conventional path of capitalist development was for a time remarkably successful, not least in the ideological and military challenge it posed to the West'.[60] Soviet economic stagnation became especially damaging since it occurred in an era of global economic growth. Western consumerism was a vital ingredient in, and focuser of, the ideas battle, as was the development of global interdependence. Halliday's concept of international 'homogeneity' – 'It was the T-shirt and the supermarket, not the gunboat or the cheaper manufactures that destroyed the legitimacy and stability of the Soviet system'[61] – is useful. US public diplomacy played a part here. In 1995, Connecticut Senator Joseph Lieberman, attempting to deflect Republican budget-cutters, argued that American broadcasting services to Eastern Europe – Voice of America and the US Information Agency – 'ultimately cracked the Berlin Wall'.[62] More important, however, was the role and survival of détente, in communicating ideas and expectations eastwards. Former Central Intelligence Agency (CIA) head Robert Gates has, surprisingly, given President Jimmy Carter credit for defending and spreading the liberal idea in his human rights policy.[63] Global interdependence and the communications revolution, in so far as they affected Eastern Europe and the USSR, accelerated the proliferation of political and economic liberal ideas.

As noted in the previous chapter, some advocates of leftist 'world system' theory interpret the Soviet collapse as illustrating the globalisation of capital, predicted by Karl Marx. In this view, the end of the Cold War witnessed the rise of a global 'market civilisation' – 'a social and cultural transformation in which links between work, effort, savings and life chances (and death) more generally are reified through ideological representations commensurate with growth in the power of capital'.[64] Global 'market civilisation' is seen to have its own contradictions and seeds of decay. For Immanuel Wallerstein, Soviet collapse was actually a 'geo-political catastrophe' for the United States. The USSR, having for so long served the integrative function of 'safe enemy', threatened disintegration by quitting the 'Cold War system'.[65]

Though most frequently associated with the left, theories of the 'Cold War system' also have a more conservative provenance. Rightist views of the Cold War system stress, even celebrate, its stability. Theories accounting for Cold War stability include those pertaining to the logic of nuclear deterrence and various positions touched on in the previous chapter: theories of hegemonic stability, bipolarity, and regime formation, cooperation and collaboration. To the extent that arguments concerning post-1970 American decline are accepted, it can be agreed that the Cold War system fell through a process of mutual superpower disintegration and loss of global control. (On the American side, the defeat in Vietnam seems to have been the key event in this process.) However, the Cold War system ended not primarily through joint USA–USSR weakening, but through Soviet capitulation and implosion.

The Cold War's end – especially the Soviet retreat from power – posed special problems for realist theory. Kenneth Waltz's theory of structural realism did not really encompass any explanation for change in the system, much less the Soviet Union's voluntary retreat from empire.[66] Robert Gilpin's notion of defensive retrenchment can be used to explain Soviet retreat,[67] although it is hard to argue that Eastern Europe was anything other than a primary sphere of influence (and hence, in conventional realist terms, inviolable). In terms of adapting to the end of the Cold War, realists have either embraced a 'Reagan victory' analysis, or – in Lebow's words – 'have sought to save their core insights by treating the end of the Cold War as a special case and reformulating their propositions to take it into account'.[68] Realist defender William Wohlforth offers the following refinements: 'decision-makers' assessments of power are what matters'; 'declining challengers are more likely than declining hegemons to try to retrench and reform rather than opt for preventive war'; 'sudden decline or civil strife in the losing side of a struggle is less destabilizing globally than such decline or strife on the winning side'. In so far as the end of the Cold War may be traced to Soviet domestic factors ('reductionism', in Waltzian terminology) structural realism is discredited. (Wohlforth maintains that structural realism is actually a straw man, and that his own analysis is based on classical realism, neorealism and 'a pragmatic empirical focus on the decision-makers' capability assess-

ments'.)[69] Matthew Evangelista has also attempted to defend classical realism by means of focusing on elite perception rather than 'objective' power
structures.[70]

Many commentators have attacked realism's failure to allow for a peaceful transformation of superpower relations. Most explanations of peaceful
system change assign a key role to nuclear weapons. In this way, deterrence
and 'nuclear learning' – increasingly sophisticated skill in crisis avoidance
and management – can be used not only to theorise Gaddis's 'long peace',
but also its peaceful transformation. Against this John Mueller has argued
that war actually became unthinkable before the advent of nuclear weapons,
and that only the aberration of a Hitler could account for the post-1918 use
of war as a means to achieve world domination.[71] Less controversially,
'nuclear peace' theorists have been attacked as understating the dangers of
'accidental' nuclear war, nuclear proliferation, or the temptation that leaders may resort to 'the threat that leaves something to chance'.[72] The ending
of the Cold War was not occasioned primarily by nuclear issues, although
the declining importance – against a background of 'nuclear learning' – of
military might was an important factor in the Soviet crisis.

Persuasive explanations for the end of the Cold War lie in an understanding of the interaction between Gaddis's 'tectonic' forces and elite behaviour
and perceptions. The Cold War embraced inter-systemic geopolitical and
ideological rivalry within the wider framework of a 'Cold War system'. Both
the rivalry and the system crashed through Soviet capitulation and the consequences of the 'new thinking'. At the root lay Soviet economic stagnation.
Lenin wrote that 'the competition between capitalism and socialism will be
resolved in favour of the system that attains a higher level of economic productivity'.[73] But even economic productivity is not everything. The 1989
revolutions were 'catching-up-revolutions'[74] in political as well as economic
terms. The sharpest drop in Soviet economic output relative to that of the
United States occurred in the early 1970s, not the 1980s.[75] By the 1980s, the
communist *idea* had become discredited: in Eastern Europe, in developing
nations, among many Soviet citizens, even to party bosses. (Gorbachev, of
course, wished to save rather than to destroy Soviet communism. Yet 'new
thinking' essentially abandoned traditional categories of ideological competition with the West.) America's reaction was cautious and unimaginative.
Reagan's unwillingness merely to repeat Eisenhower's cool reaction to
Moscow post-Stalin overtures was important. Bush's strategic conservatism
had statesmanlike as well as excessively cautious elements. To an extraordinary degree, however, American leaders were able to allow events to take
their course. Writing in 1951, George Kennan actually considered the possibility of the Soviet leadership acquiescing in its own Cold War defeat.
'Stranger things may have happened', wrote Kennan, 'though not much
stranger.'[76]

3   American foreign policy after the Cold War

(a) *New agendas?*   During the early Bush years, if not before, it became evident that anti-communist containment, the capstone of US foreign policy since the late 1940s, could no longer provide much of a guide to the nation's decision-makers. There ensued a major debate on future foreign policy options. Heated and partisan, the debate tended to assume that, although the United States had won the Cold War, it was now faced by a new array of problems; conspicuous among them was international fragmentation – ethnic, economic and geopolitical – and disorder. By way of making sense of this debate, some key positions may be isolated: firstly, President George Bush's own response to calls for a new lead – the New World Order; secondly, advocacy of unilateral US policing of global disorder; thirdly, various populist and neo-isolationist positions; fourthly, 'new agenda liberalism', incorporating both Wilsonian democracy promotion and interdependency concerns; and, lastly, what Tim Hames has called 'retrenched international-ism' – a position close to the Clinton doctrine of selective engagement.[77]

George Bush's notion of the New World Order was announced to Congress during the 1990 Persian Gulf crisis. Here was an 'order struggling to be born ... a world where the rule of law supplants the rule of the jungle, a world in which nations recognize the shared responsibility for freedom and justice, a world where the strong respect the weak'.[78] In his descriptions of the New World Order, George Bush attempted to adapt the *pax Americana* to a world of multipolar interest, but to a world also where American power still held sway. The United States would provide leadership, as in the Gulf War, but would not act alone in order to achieve 'peaceful settlement of dis-putes, solidarity against aggression, reduced and controlled arsenals and just treatment of all peoples'.[79] The New World Order was an attempt to harness Wilsonian promotion of democracy and markets to American security inter-ests. It was also an attempt to institutionalise the termination of 'Vietnam syndrome' inhibitions on the use of American military force. According to Joseph Nye, the New World Order involved an uneasy marriage between realism and Wilsonian idealism: 'The problem for the Bush Administration was that it thought and acted like Nixon, but borrowed the rhetoric of Wilson and Carter.'[80] Burgeoning international *dis*order – notably in the former Yugoslavia – combined with the unhappy experiences of the US mil-itary in Somalia to undercut the New World Order.

One alternative to the multilateralist New World Order was simple, uni-lateralist, 'globocop' world policing by the United States. Retention of America's ability and will to act unilaterally, rather than through the United Nations or *ad hoc* international coalitions, became a leading goal for Repub-lican critics of the Clinton Administration. The extreme, 'unipolar', or 'solo superpower' position,[81] however, remained a minority viewpoint in the post-Cold War debate. The classic expression of this position was provided in the

February 1992 Defence Planning Guidance for the Fiscal Year 1994–99, a leaked interagency study development by the Defence and State Departments, along with NSC staff. Even this ('no rivals') document declared that the United States should not 'become the world's "policeman", by assuming responsibility for righting every wrong'. The United States should, however, retain the military capacity to 'prevent any hostile power from dominating a region whose resources would, under consolidated control, be sufficient to generate global power'. The United States would provide 'adult supervision' for a disorderly world.[82] Framed entirely in realist terms, and clearly distinguishable from Bush's own New World Order, the 1992 Defence Planning Guidance represented the most extreme denial of post-Cold War expectations for a 'peace-dividend' and international retrenchment.

Bush's New World Order was a concept designed to halt the rise of post-Cold War isolationism. One populist version of isolationism found its expression in the 1992 and 1996 Presidential primary campaigns of Republican candidate Pat Buchanan. Shortly before his success in the 1996 New Hampshire primary, Buchanan gave his views on President Clinton's despatching of US troops to Bosnia as part of the Dayton Agreement peace-keeping force: 'Bosnia is a back-water civil war in a country that didn't exist five years ago, where no vital American interest is engaged. Get the American army out of there and let the Europeans patrol their own borders.' He went on to criticise Clinton's 1995 plan to rescue the Mexican peso: 'We cannot afford to balance the budgets of foreign countries when we cannot balance our own.'[83] Buchananite America Firstism, many tenets of which were shared by Congressional Republican opponents of the Clinton Administration, posited a range of demons: the United Nations; 'foreign policy as social work'; unrestricted immigration; foreign aid; unfair foreign penetration of American markets; and (to use a phrase of Republican Senator Jesse Helms) 'deadbeat diplomats'.[84]

More considered versions of 'America First' were also on offer, however, in the early and mid-1990s. Several writers and commentators sought to wean post-Cold War America away from any 'imperial temptation' and from the excessive, par-interventionist moralism which had led the US astray in the Vietnam War era. Alvin Rubinstein inveighed against 'the new moralists', arguing that foreign policy, 'like domestic policy, must be affordable, supportable, and demonstrably in the best interests of the country at large'.[85] Michael Mandelbaum criticised the Clinton Administration for not abiding by its own analysis of the deficiencies of 'the foreign policy of Mother Teresa'.[86] In his study *Isolationism Reconfigured* (1995), Eric Nordlinger attempted to move beyond narrowly realist and introverted versions of America First. Lower defence budgets would facilitate domestic restructuring. A reconfigured isolationism could operate on three tiers: a 'minimally effortful national strategy in the security sphere; moderately activist policies to advance our liberal ideals among and within states; and a fully activist economic diplomacy on behalf of free trade, possibly modified by fairly managed trade relations with Europe and Japan'. A dismantling of the national security state, with positive implications for the cause of domestic democracy, might yet be a fruit of the American Cold War victory.[87]

Post-Cold War advocates of democracy-promotion abroad tended to cast their arguments, not in terms of a global crusade, but rather as – in Larry Diamond's words – 'one of the cheapest, most cost-effective ways of advancing the national interest'. In this connection, promoting democracy was equated – as in the tradition of Woodrow Wilson – with the expansion of market economics; and with international peace. 'A more democratic world would be a safer, saner, and more prosperous world for the United States.'[88] Such assertions stimulated a major academic debate in the late 1980s and early 1990s as to whether, in fact, liberal democracies ever have gone to war with each other.[89] Alongside self-interested democracy-promotion, post-Cold War liberal internationalists also urged the United States to take the lead in shaping planetary environmental policy, and to revive President Carter's human rights policy. Jessica Tuchman Mathews, formerly of Carter's NSC staff, urged the United States to take the lead in coordinating global responses to the challenge of interdependence, and argued for a new definition of 'security': 'Security measured against the strength of an opponent will steadily give way to the measure of global security, defined principally by environmental threats and the conditions of economic interdependence.'[90] Writing in 1990, former Ambassador Richard Gardner asserted that there was 'now a broad bipartisan consensus that human rights should be part of the US foreign policy agenda'; How 'a nation treats its own citizens is no longer its own business alone'.[91] Viewing the Bosnian conflict in 1992, Leslie H. Gelb wrote: 'Morality requires doing everything possible to stop slaughter everywhere.'[92]

President Clinton's first term foreign policy contained elements of many of these various foreign policy positions: ambiguous commitments to multilateralism; America First prioritisations of domestic agendas; democracy-promotion (NSA Anthony Lake's doctrine of 'enlargement') and stated advocacy of human rights. The Republican Congressional victories of 1994 stimulated the Administration to a new foreign policy activism. However, the preferred foreign policy of the Clinton Administration may be characterised as a kind of retrenched and economistic Wilsonianism: a combination of 'selective engagement', modest democracy-promotion and prioritisation of foreign economic policy. By 1994, a hierarchy of interests seemed to have emerged. Activist involvement appeared most likely in relation to regional security problems, especially those with a significant domestic overspill (including immigration and drugs-trafficking issues); to nuclear proliferation and international terrorism; to agendas (like the Northern Irish peace process) with significant domestic mobilisation; and to areas of particular historical concern, notably the Middle East and post-Soviet Russia.

Activism over Bosnia in 1995 undercut the selective engagement stance of 1993–94 to considerable degree. In 1995, Defence Secretary William Perry advanced a new hierarchy – of vital, important and humanitarian interests. 'Vital' interests would present the United States with the option of unilateral military action. 'Important' ones would be better handled multilaterally. 'Humanitarian' interventions might occur, but only with minimal risks and clear objectives. The Administration remained committed thus to 'retrenched internationalism' and some military cutbacks, albeit still driven to some extent by Wilsonian ideals. The White House's 1996 National Security Strategy document emphasised that 'our involvement must be carefully tailored to serve our interests and priorities'. Yet part of this strategy was democratic 'enlargement':

> The core of our strategy is to help democracy and free markets expand and survive … This is not a democratic crusade; it is a pragmatic commitment to see freedom take hold where that will help us most … our efforts must be demand-driven – they must focus on nations whose people are pushing for reform or have already secured it.[93]

In the immediate post-Cold War period, there was general agreement that the United States had to re-set its foreign policy compass. Most commentators and decision-makers agreed that the new order would be one of geoeconomic interdependence; but also that fragmentation would pose threats to international, and US, security. The world seemed simultaneously to be coalescing (through swift communications and the apparent triumph of liberalism), and splitting asunder (via local conflicts, the collapse of empires and the rise of 'rogue' or 'backlash' states like Iraq and North Korea). Nevertheless, by the mid-1990s, some of the assumptions of the immediate post-Cold War period seemed less certain. With (significantly restructured) communism still strong in Eastern Europe, the certainty of liberal triumph weakened. Some academics began to question the globalising trajectory of capitalism, arguing for state-centred analyses of accumulation.[94] Russia in the mid-1990s seemed less a country in which power had been transferred from the old party elite, more one in which large sections of the *nomenklatura* had simply donned new labels. American commentators began to talk about renewing old doctrines, rather than inventing new ones. In 1996, for example, three writers in *Foreign Affairs* even attempted to resurrect the old, anti-communist 'falling domino' theory. The United States, according to Chase, Hill and Kennedy, needed to identify key 'pivotal states' as the new dominoes which should not be allowed to succumb to 'chaos and instability'.[95] G. J. Ikenberry argued that in 'world historical terms, the end of the Cold War is an overrated event'. The United States was not engaged in any 'third try' at world order (as after the two world wars) but – according to Ikenberry – was still leading the thriving liberal order which had been created in the late 1940s.[96]

What was clear in the post-Cold War foreign policy debate was the continued vitality of American liberalism. The debate revolved, as Nordlinger contended, around 'four dualisms': realism–idealism; internationalism–isolationism; 'a sense of extraordinary power and the anxieties of weakness'; and 'expectations of consistent success and its achievement at no more than modest costs'.[97] Informing and driving all four dualisms was the impulse to export democracy, to do good, to – at the very least – provide a model for the world. Even while recommending an isolationist path, William Pfaff acknowledged in 1989:

> Americans remain 'globalists' in their fashion, prisoners of the progressive tradition, even as they chant the glories of American nationalism. We are not philosophical realists, willing to leave Russians, Nicaraguans, Cubans – or Afghans or Poles – alone if they would leave the United States alone. We are not philosophical pessimists, prepared to argue that international life is mean, and foreign policy a way to make the best of bad choices.[98]

Both Bush's New World Order and Clinton's first term retrenched internationalism – although they certainly recognised limits to American power and interests – represented affirmations of this liberal, philosophical optimism.

(b) *Democratic processes?* The Cold War encouraged Presidential aggrandisement, unaccountability and unrestricted nuclear crisis management. The national security state did not go unchallenged during the years of the Cold War. Indeed, the defeat in Vietnam provoked a wide-ranging effort to restrain, prise open and democratise the whole national security process. However, the logic of bipolar confrontationalism and nuclear diplomacy always tended to point away from goals of democracy and accountability.

The ending of the Cold War seemed to offer new opportunities for democratic foreign policy. Shorn of its Cold War mission – involving it, in Loch Johnson's phrase, in an impulse 'to both guard and destroy democracy'[99] – perhaps even the Central Intelligence Agency might at last be subject to positive democratic control. Many commentators looked to an enhanced, post-Cold War Congressional role. According to James Lindsay, for example, the 'demise of the Soviet Union … lowered the perception of external threat and with it the political costs to members of Congress who choose to challenge the president'.[100] To the extent that post-Cold War priorities would be in economic, rather than traditional security areas, strong Congressional involvement seemed inevitable. Norman Ornstein commented in an essay published in 1994:

> [G]eoeconomics increasingly drives geopolitics, compared to a Cold War agenda where geopolitics drove geoeconomics. For Congress, this means that the fuzzy line between domestic and foreign policies and politics grows even fuzzier; the number of members of Congress who assert their role in foreign policy increases, as does the number of interested groups.[101]

Post-Cold War foreign policies of interdependence seemed to indicate fragmented and diffuse policy-making processes. Presidential ability to identify
the 'national interest' would become even more problematic. New actors –
notably, interest groups and state governments – might enter and complicate
the process, at least diluting centralised leadership, if not actually promoting
democracy.[102]

Yet, not all indicators signalled an end to the national security state and an
amelioration of the imperial, foreign policy Presidency. After all, if the post-
Cold War world really was one of enhanced fragmentation and insecurity,
might this not actually augment Presidential authority?[103] The 1992 Defence
Planning Guidance hardly boded well for the cause of decentralised democratisation. Neither did President Bush's handling of the Gulf War. The working out of democratic purposes and procedures in the post-Cold War context
will provide an important theme of subsequent chapters.

Notes

1 *Guardian*, 29 May 1989.
2 See S. D. Krasner, *Defending the National Interest* (Princeton, Princeton University Press, 1978), pp. 340, 345.
3 See A. Wolfers and L. W. Martin, eds, *The Anglo-American Tradition in Foreign
   Affairs* (New Haven, Yale University Press, 1956), p. 156. See also S. P. Hunt-
   ington, *American Politics: The Promise of Disharmony* (Cambridge, Harvard
   University Press, 1982).
4 F. J. Turner, *The Significance of the Frontier in American History* (Ann Arbor,
   American Historical Association, 1966 [1893]), p. 211.
5 See C. Thorne, *Allies of a Kind: The United States, Britain and the War against
   Japan, 1941–1945* (London, Hamilton, 1978); L. Baritz, *Backfire* (New York,
   Morrow, 1985); W. L. Williams, 'United States Indian policy and the debate
   over Philippine annexation', *Journal of American History*, 66 (1980), pp.
   810–31; C. Thorne, *American Political Culture and the Asian Frontier,
   1943–73* (London, British Academy, 1986); C. Thorne, 'American political culture and the end of the Cold War', *Journal of American Studies*, 24 (1992),
   pp. 303–30. See also R. J. Payne, *The Clash with Distant Cultures* (Albany, State
   University of New York Press, 1995).
6 See J. Citrin, E. B. Haas, C. Muste and B. Reingold, 'Is American nationalism
   changing? Implications for foreign policy', *International Studies Quarterly*, 38
   (1994), pp. 1–31.
7 R. Niebuhr, *Nations and Empires* (London, Faber and Faber, 1959); also,
   G. Weigel, 'Exorcising Wilson's ghost', in B. Roberts *US Foreign Policy after the
   Cold War* (London, MIT Press, 1992).
8 R. Maidment and M. Dawson, eds, *The United States in the Twentieth Century:
   Key Documents* (London, Hodder and Stoughton, 1994), pp. 279 ff.
9 S. Pelz, 'Balance of power', in M. J. Hogan and T. G. Paterson, eds, *Explaining
   the History of American Foreign Relations* (Cambridge, Cambridge University
   Press, 1991), p. 112.

10 B. Buzan, *People, States and Fear* (2nd edn, London, Harvester Wheatsheaf, 1991), p. 295.

11 W. E. Odom, 'How to create a true world order', *Orbis*, 39 (1995), pp. 155–72: 156, 171; also, W. Y. Smith, 'US national security after the Cold War', in E. R. Wittkopf, ed., *The Future of American Foreign Policy* (2nd edn, New York, St Martin's, 1994).

12 D. A. Baldwin, 'Security studies and the end of the Cold War', *World Politics*, 48 (1995), pp. 117–41: 133.

13 See, e.g., E. A. Kolodziej, 'Renaissance in security studies?', *International Studies Quarterly*, 36 (1992), pp. 421–38.

14 M. H. Hunt, 'The long crisis in diplomatic history', in M. J. Hogan, ed., *America in the World* (Cambridge, Cambridge University Press, 1995), p. 99.

15 G. Lewy, *America in Vietnam* (New York, Oxford University Press, 1978).

16 W. A. Williams, *From Colony to Empire* (New York, Wiley, 1972), p. 476. See also W. A. Williams, *The Tragedy of American Diplomacy* (New York, Dell, 1972) and *Empire as a Way of Life* (New York, Oxford University Press, 1980).

17 B. Cumings, 'Revising postrevisionism, or, the poverty of theory in diplomatic history', in Hogan, ed., *America in the World*, p. 43.

18 See L. C. Gardner, ed., *Redefining the Past: Essays in Diplomatic History in Honor of William Appleman Williams* (Corvallis, University of Oregon, 1986); J. A. Thompson, 'William Appleman Williams and the "American Empire"', *Journal of American Studies*, 7 (1973), pp. 91–104; P. Buhle and E. Rice-Maximim, *William Appleman Williams: The Tragedy of Empire* (London, Routledge, 1996).

19 See, e.g., G. Kolko, *Vietnam: Anatomy of a War* (London, Unwin Hyman, 1987); N. Chomsky, *World Orders: Old and New* (New York, Columbia University Press, 1994).

20 T. J. McCormick, *America's Half Century: United States Foreign Policy in the Cold War and After* (2nd edn, Baltimore, Johns Hopkins University Press, 1995), p. 3.

21 See, e.g., M. J. Hogan, 'The search for a synthesis: economic diplomacy in the Cold War', *Reviews in American History*, 15 (1987), pp. 493–8.

22 *Theory of International Relations* (New York, Addison-Wesley, 1979), p. 33.

23 Cited in E. N. Nordlinger, *Isolationism Reconfigured* (Princeton, Princeton University Press, 1995), p. 188.

24 Niebuhr, *Nations and Empires*, p. 28.

25 Cited in W. LaFeber, *The American Age* (New York, Norton, 1989), pp. 130, 211.

26 R. W. Stirling, *Macropolitics* (New York, 1974), p. 204.

27 S. Gill and D. Law, *The Global Political Economy* (London, Harvester, 1988), p. 155.

28 D. P. Moynihan, *Pandaemonium* (Oxford, Oxford University Press, 1993), pp. 41–4.

29 See D. Deudney and G. I. Ikenberry, 'Soviet reform and the end of the Cold War', *Review of International Studies*, 17 (1991), pp. 225–50; J. L. Gaddis, *The United States and the End of the Cold War* (New York, Oxford University Press, 1992), pp. 30, 222; T. Hopf, 'Getting the end of the Cold War wrong', *International Security*, 18 (1993), pp. 202–8; M. Cox, 'Radical theory and the new

Cold War', in M. Bowker and R. Brown, eds, *From Cold War to Collapse* (Cambridge, Cambridge University Press, 1993), p. 47; C. Kegley, 'How did the Cold War die?', *Mershon International Studies Review*, 38 (1994), pp. 11–41; J. L. Ray and B. Russett, 'The future as arbiter of theoretical controversy', *British Journal of Political Science*, 26 (1996), pp. 441–70.

30 R. L. Garthoff, *The Great Transition* (Washington DC, Brookings, 1994), p. 755.

31 W. LaFeber, 'An end to *which* Cold War?', in M. J. Hogan, ed., *The End of the Cold War* (Cambridge, Cambridge University Press, 1992).

32 I. L. Janis, *Groupthink* (Boston, Houghton Mifflin, 1982); R. Jervis, *Perception and Misperception in International Politics* (Princeton, Princeton University Press, 1976); H. Kissinger, *White House Years* (Boston, Little, Brown, 1979), p. 411.

33 F. Halliday, *Rethinking International Relations* (Basingstoke, Macmillan, 1994), pp. 171–7.

34 Chomsky, *World Orders: Old and New*, p. 44.

35 See R. L. Garthoff, 'Some reflections on the history of the Cold War', *SHAFR Newsletter*, Sept. 1995, p. 12; F. Halliday, 'The end of the Cold War and international relations', in K. Booth and S. Smith, eds, *International Relations Theory Today* (Oxford, Polity Press, 1995), p. 47.

36 See J. Wright, 'The end of the Cold War: the Brezhnev doctrine', in R. Summy and M. E. Salla, eds, *Why the Cold War Ended* (Westport, Greenwood, 1995).

37 T. Risse-Knappen, 'Masses and leaders', in D. A. Deese, ed., *The New Politics of American Foreign Policy* (New York, St Martin's, 1994), pp. 244–5.

38 Cited in D. Reynolds, 'Beyond bipolarity in space and time', in Hogan, ed., *The End of the Cold War*, p. 245.

39 See A. Lynch, *The Cold War is Over – Again* (Boulder, Westview, 1992); M. Cox, 'Rethinking the end of the Cold War', *Review of International Studies*, 20 (1994), pp. 187–200.

40 M. Thatcher, *The Downing Street Years* (London, Harper Collins, 1993), p. 813.

41 Cited in S. Blumenthal, *Pledging Allegiance* (New York, Harper Collins, 1990), p. 86.

42 Cited in A. Carter, 'Did Reagan "win" the Cold War?', in Summy and Salla, eds, *Why The Cold War Ended*, p. 19. See also P. Schweizer, *Victory: The Reagan Administration's Secret Strategy that Hastened the Collapse of the Soviet Union* (New York, Atlantic Monthly Press, 1993); J. Winik, *On the Brink* (New York, Simon and Schuster, 1996).

43 S. Sestanovich, 'Did the West undo the East?', *The National Interest*, 31 (1993), pp. 26–33.

44 See particularly P. Zelikow and C. Rice, *Germany Unified and Europe Transformed* (Cambridge, Harvard University Press, 1995).

45 P. W. Rodman, *More Precious than Peace* (New York, Scribner's, 1994).

46 See G. P. Shultz, *Turmoil and Triumph* (New York, Scribner's, 1993) pp. 488–9; T. W. Simons, *The End of the Cold War?* (New York, St Martin's, 1990).

47 N. Glazer, 'How important was Reagan?', *The National Interest*, 28 (1992), pp. 102–8.

48 These various points are developed further in J. Dumbrell, *American Foreign*

Policy: Carter to Clinton (Basingstoke, Macmillan, 1996), chs. 4–6.

49 D. Cortright, 'The peace movement role in ending the Cold War', in Summy and Salla, eds, *Why The Cold War Ended*, p. 88.

50 See M. Kaldor, 'Taking the democratic way', *The Nation*, 22 April 1991.

51 Quoted in C. W. Kegley and E. R. Wittkopf, *World Politics* (New York, St. Martin's, 1995), p. 103.

52 Moynihan, *Pandaemonium*, p. 50.

53 Cited in J. B. Dunlop, *The Rise of Russia and the Fall of the Soviet Empire* (Princeton, Princeton University Press, 1993), p. 5.

54 F. Chernoff, 'Ending the Cold War', *International Affairs*, 67 (1991), pp. 111–26. Also, M. Gorbachev, *Memoirs* (London, Doubleday, 1996), p. 455; A. Dobrynin, *In Confidence* (New York, Random House, 1995), p. 523.

55 See, e.g., S. Marullo, *Ending the Cold War at Home* (New York, Harper and Row, 1993), p. 90. Also, R. Lebow and J. Stein, *We All Lost the Cold War* (Princeton, Princeton University Press, 1993).

56 Gorbachev, *Memoirs*, p. 406.

57 Gaddis, *The United States and the End of the Cold War*, p. 166.

58 E. Hobsbawm, *Age of Extremes* (London, Abacus, 1994), p. 487.

59 F. Fukuyama, *The End of History and the Last Man* (London, Hamish Hamilton, 1992), p. xii.

60 Halliday, 'The end of the Cold War and international relations', p. 43.

61 *Rethinking International Relations*, p. 97.

62 *Congressional Record*, 1965, S1154–5 (11 May).

63 R. M. Gates, *From the Shadows* (New York, Simon and Schuster, 1996), p. 177.

64 S. Gill, 'Globalisation, market civilization, and disciplinary neoliberalism', *Millennium*, 24 (1995), pp. 399–424: 406, 410.

65 See I. Wallerstein, 'The world-system after the Cold War', *Journal of Peace Research*, 30 (1993), pp. 1–6. Also, I. Wallerstein, *After Liberalism* (New York, New Press, 1995).

66 See R. N. Lebow, 'The long peace, the end of the Cold War and the failure of realism', in R. N. Lebow and T. Risse-Knappen, eds, *International Relations Theory and the End of the Cold War* (New York, Columbia University Press, 1995).

67 R. Gilpin, *War and Change in World Politics* (Cambridge, Cambridge University Press, 1981).

68 Lebow, 'The long peace', p. 25.

69 W. C. Wohlforth, 'Realism and the end of the Cold War', *International Security*, 19 (1994–5), pp. 91–129. Wolhforth has also edited an important volume of first-hand recollections and commentary: *Witnesses to the End of the Cold War* (Baltimore, Johns Hopkins University Press, 1996).

70 M. Evangelista, 'Internal and external constraints on grand strategy: the Soviet case', in R. Rosencrance and A. A. Stein, eds, *The Domestic Bases of Grand Strategy* (Ithaca, Cornell University Press, 1993), p. 93.

71 J. Mueller, *Retreat from Doomsday: The Obsolescence of Major War* (New York, Basic Books, 1989).

72 T. Schelling, *The Strategy of Conflict* (Cambridge, Mass., Harvard University Press, 1960), p. 187.

73 Cited in S. Bialer, 'Gorbachev's program of change', *Political Science Quarterly*,

103 (1988), pp. 406–59: 410.

74 J. Habermas, 'What does socialism mean today?', in R. Blackburn, ed., *After the Fall: The Failure of Communism* (London, Verso, 1991).

75 See Evangelista, 'Internal and external constraints', p. 157.

76 G. F. Kennan, 'America and the Russian future', *Foreign Affairs*, 29 (1951), pp. 351–70: 368.

77 See T. Hames, 'Foreign policy and the American elections of 1992', *International Relations*, 11 (1993), pp. 315–30. Also, R. N. Haass, 'Paradigms lost', *Foreign Affairs*, 74 (1995), pp. 43–58.

78 *Public Papers of the Presidents of the United States: George Bush: 1990: Book II* (Washington DC, US Government Printing Office, 1991), p. 1219.

79 Cited in J. S. Nye, 'What New World Order?', in Wittkopf, ed., *The Future of American Foreign Policy*, p. 50.

80 Ibid., p. 51.

81 See Hames, 'Foreign policy and the American elections of 1992'; C. Krauthammer, 'The unipolar moment', in G. T. Allison and G. F. Treverton, eds, *Rethinking American Security: Beyond Cold War to New World Order* (New York, Norton, 1992).

82 P. E. Tyler, 'US strategy plan calls for insuring no rivals develop', *New York Times*, 8 March 1992. See also M. T. Klare, 'US military policy in the post-Cold War era', in R. Miliband and L. Panitch, eds, *The Socialist Register 1992* (London, Merlin, 1992).

83 US Information Service, 'Elections 96: Foreign Policy Views of Republican Candidates' (London, US Embassy, 1996).

84 See *Congressional Quarterly Weekly Report*, 21 October 1995, p. 3214; A. C. Bacevich, 'The impact of the new populism', *Orbis*, 40 (1996), pp. 31–43.

85 A. Z. Rubinstein, 'The new moralists on a road to hell', *Orbis*, 40 (1996), pp. 277–95: 293; R. W. Tucker and D. C. Hendrickson, *The Imperial Temptation* (New York, Council on Foreign Relations, 1992).

86 M. Mandelbaum, 'Foreign policy as social work', *Foreign Affairs*, 75 (1996), pp. 16–32: 20. See also S. Hoffman, 'In defense of Mother Teresa', *Foreign Affairs*, 75 (1996), pp. 172–5.

87 Nordlinger, *Isolationism Reconfigured*, p. 4.

88 L. Diamond, 'Promoting democracy', in Wittkopf, ed., *The Future of American Foreign Policy*, pp. 104, 106.

89 See, e.g., B. M. Russett, *Grasping the Democratic Peace: Principles for a Post-Cold War World* (Princeton, Princeton University Press, 1993); H. S. Farber and J. Gowa, 'Polities and peace', *International Security*, 20 (1995), pp. 123–46.

90 J. T. Mathews, 'Preserving the global environment', in Wittkopf, ed., *The Future of American Foreign Policy*, p. 110.

91 R. N. Gardner, 'The comeback of liberal internationalism', in B. Roberts, ed., *US Foreign Policy After the Cold War* (Cambridge, Mass., MIT Press, 1992), p. 357.

92 *New York Times*, 26 June 1992.

93 *A National Security Strategy of Engagement and Enlargement* (Washington DC, US Government Printing Office, 1996), pp. 18, 32. See also J. S. Nye, 'Conflicts after the Cold War', *The Washington Quarterly*, Winter 1996, pp. 5–24; R. Haass, 'Foreign policy by posse', *National Interest*, 41 (1995), pp. 58–65.

94 See, e.g., D. D. Marshall, 'Understanding late twentieth century capitalism: reassessing the globalization thesis', *Government and Opposition*, 31 (1996), pp. 193–215.

95 R. S. Chase, E. B. Hill and P. Kennedy, 'Pivotal states and US strategy', Foreign Affairs, 75 (1996), pp. 33–51.

96 G. J. Ikenberry, 'The myth of post-Cold War chaos', *Foreign Affairs*, 75 (1996), pp. 79–91. See also J. G. Ruggie, 'Third try at world order? America and multilateralism after the Cold War', *Political Science Quarterly*, 109 (1994), pp. 553–70. Note also Ikenberry's analysis of 'structural', 'institutional' and 'situational' leadership, in G. J. Ikenberry, 'The future of international leadership', *Political Science Quarterly*, 111 (1996), pp. 385–402.

97 Nordlinger, *Isolationism Reconfigured*, pp. 263–4.

98 W. Pfaff, *Barbarian Sentiments: How the American Century Ends* (New York, Hill and Wang, 1989), p. 188.

99 L. K. Johnson, 'New directions for US strategic intelligence', in J. E. Winkates, J. R. Walsh and J. M. Scolnick, eds, *US Foreign Policy in Transition* (Chicago, Nelson-Hall, 1994), p. 95.

100 J. M. Lindsay, *Congress and the Politics of US Foreign Policy* (Baltimore, Johns Hopkins University Press, 1994), p. 32.

101 N. J. Ornstein, 'Congress in the post-Cold War world', in D. Yankelovich and I. M. Destler, eds, *Beyond the Beltway* (New York, Norton, 1994), p. 114.

102 See D. A. Deese, 'The hazards of interdependence', in D. A. Deese, ed., *The New Politics of American Foreign Policy* (New York, St. Martin's, 1994).

103 See P. E. Peterson, 'The international system and foreign policy' in P. E. Peterson, ed., *The President, the Congress, and the Making of Foreign Policy* (Norman, University of Oklahoma Press, 1994).

3   *David M. Barrett*

Presidential foreign policy

1   Introduction: Presidents choose between war and peace

In July 1965, the government of the United States faced a choice of monumental proportions: either send hundreds of thousands of soldiers to South Vietnam and try to save the faltering non-communist government of that country, or call it quits to America's military presence in Southeast Asia. For over a decade, the US government had subscribed to the proposition that the 'loss' of South Vietnam to communism would signify another triumph for the Soviet Union and Red China (as Americans then called the People's Republic of China) in their efforts to move the entire world towards communism. As exaggerated as that American fear may seem in retrospect, most Republicans and Democrats in the United States shared that fear.[1] Thus the American government had committed tens of thousands of military advisers and billions of dollars for over a decade to doing what was necessary to 'save' South Vietnam.

In September 1994, while the stakes were perhaps not so critical as in 1965, leaders of the US government were losing patience with the dictators of the government of Haiti, who refused to accede to United Nations resolutions and US pressure to give up power so that the democratically elected President Jean-Bertrand Aristide could be restored to office. Waves of Haitians took to the seas in ramshackle boats, headed for US shores, causing severe immigration problems for the American government. Shows of force by the US Navy had not worked any better than diplomacy. Even as those latter efforts continued, the US military was directed to be ready in the event of a decision to intervene in the poverty-stricken nation in the Caribbean Sea.

The decision of whether or not to transform America's military presence in Vietnam and, twenty-nine years later, intervene in Haiti rested almost entirely with one person, the President of the United States. How had it come to this, that one person – admittedly a powerful one, but still just one person in American government – could decide whether or not American boys would possibly die (and kill) in small countries little known to the US public? The question demands attention because there is no doubt that the founders of the American republic (those who wrote and ratified its Constitution) had emphatically not wanted decisions of war and peace to be made by a single individual, not even the President.[2] Furthermore, the remarkable end of the Cold War, with its great impact on international and domestic politics, might have been expected to alter the powers of the Presidency in the 1990s.

The President in July 1965 was Lyndon B. Johnson; in October 1994, Bill Clinton. The decision, in both cases, was for massive military intervention. The results of Johnson's decision for the United States over the following seven and a half years were disastrous – over fifty thousand soldiers killed and ultimate defeat in Vietnam. For Clinton, results were far better, with the dictators agreeing to give up power, just minutes before the US forces were to invade. But Johnson was not the first, and Clinton perhaps will not be the last President to send troops to conflicted faraway corners of the world. How, indeed, had it come to this?

2 The founders, Presidents, and foreign policy

The men who wrote the Constitution of the United States in Philadelphia in 1787 were determined that neither a President nor the Congress (and certainly not a military leader) would be empowered to engage America in a war and lead that effort. They separated foreign policy powers, in general, and war powers, in particular. The President would be 'commander-in-chief' of the military, ensuring that generals and admirals would answer to an elected civilian leader. But Congress would hold the powers to declare war and to raise and support an army and navy. There would be no Presidential wars, if the founders had their way.

Alexander Hamilton, one of the advocates of the new Constitution in 1787, provides the most persuasive testimony for this, because he favoured a 'strong' Presidency. He compared the President's war powers to those of the British monarch:

> It would amount to nothing more than the supreme command and direction of the military and naval forces, as first general and admiral of the Confederacy; while that of the British king extends to the declaring of war and to the raising and regulating of fleets and armies – all which, by the Constitution under consideration, would appertain to the legislature.[3]

Similarly, James Madison, perhaps more responsible than any other figure for the creation of the Constitution, wrote after its adoption of 'the necessity of a rigid adherence to the simple ... fundamental doctrine of the constitution, that the power to declare war, including the power of judging the causes of war, is fully and exclusively vested in the legislature'.[4]

More broadly, in terms of foreign policy, the President would appoint and receive ambassadors and would, with the 'advice and consent' of the Senate, make treaties with other countries. There would be no American foreign policy embodied by the President: instead, both Congress and the President would guide America's relations with the world. There were some disagreements at the Constitutional convention over foreign policy powers. Many feared Congress might be too slow to respond to a sudden attack by a foreign power on the United States. Thus a proposal to empower Congress to make war was changed to the power to declare war. But, except for such emergency 'protection of the community against foreign attacks', war powers were divided, with Congress, not the President, given the authority to decide for or against such bloody and costly entanglements.[5]

For most of the nineteenth century and the early twentieth century, it worked out that way. Presidents played a key role in foreign policy, to be sure, but were mostly deferential to the will of Congress. In 1801, for instance, Tripoli declared war on the United States and attacked its naval vessels in the Bay of Tripoli. President Thomas Jefferson (1801–09) explained to Congress how the Americans under his command responded: 'Unauthorised by the constitution, without the sanction of Congress, to go beyond the line of defence, the vessel, being disabled from committing further hostilities, was liberated with its crew.'[6] It was constitutionally impermissible for a President and those under his command to go further, without Congressional authorisation, thought Jefferson. Mostly, the nineteenth century was a long era of what political science professor (later President) Woodrow Wilson characterised in 1888 as 'Congressional government' – 'the predominant and controlling force, the centre and source of all motive and of all regulative power is Congress'.[7]

3   Theodore Roosevelt, Woodrow Wilson, Franklin Roosevelt and the growth of Presidential power

Towards the end of the nineteenth century, America began to experience changes which slowly transformed the Presidency. A growing capitalist economy accelerated a shift from a mostly agrarian society to a much more industrialised one, with millions of immigrants pouring into the country for jobs and new lives. With industrialisation came more international trade and relative prosperity, but also complex societal problems – urban slums, overburdened public education systems, and public health dilemmas, to name but a few. With such problems came the beginnings of what political scientists call the 'welfare state', and what many ordinary Americans simply refer to as 'big government'.

Along with this came the belief that the United States had an important role to play in international affairs. Rejecting the advice of President George Washington in his famous Farewell Address to 'avoid entangling alliances' with other countries,[8] Presidents Theodore Roosevelt (1901–09) and Woodrow Wilson (1913–21) personified the new thinking about America's role in the world and the Presidency's role in managing American government and foreign policy. Simple deference to Congress was out. Wilson thought the President uniquely endowed to represent the democratic values of the American people in world affairs. He thus threw himself into an exhaustive (albeit failed) mission to persuade the necessary two-thirds of the Senate to approve American entry into the League of Nations. Theodore Roosevelt was similarly internationalist and aggressive in asserting Presidential power. He later explained: 'I declined to adopt the view that what was imperatively necessary for the nation could not be done by the President unless he could find some specific authorization to do it.'[9] Therefore, in an era when the United States became involved in the Spanish–American War and World War One, a new view of Presidential power ascended.

Nonetheless, the approach of World War Two made it clear that Presidents could go only so far in involving the United States in a military conflict. Strong isolationism arose in America in the aftermath of World War One, in the belief that the United States had wasted the lives of thousands of young men in a war that achieved nothing for America. President Warren G. Harding (1921–23) typified this view with his popular pledge to return the country to 'normalcy', a state of affairs distinguished by peace, prosperity, weak government, and little involvement with European affairs. Controversial as this view was as Europe entered another great conflict in the late 1930s, Congress reflected such isolationist sentiment.

Passing a Neutrality Act in 1936 with President Franklin Roosevelt's (1933–45) reluctant agreement, Congress frustrated the President's efforts to align the United States closely with Britain and its allies in the fight against Germany's Hitler. Franklin Roosevelt had been conspicuously successful in the 1930s in adding to the Presidency's domestic powers, as he fought a deep economic depression. But on questions such as war, his powers were partially restrained. Thus his confidential aide, Harry Hopkins, faced the difficult problem on a mission to Britain of 'explaining our constitutional provision that only Congress can declare war. Churchill understood this – perhaps he had learned it at his [American] mother's knee – but there were others of eminent rank in the British government who could not seem to get it through their heads.'[10]

Only an attack by Japan on the United States' Pacific Ocean naval base at Pearl Harbor in Hawaii in December 1941 induced Congress to get behind the President and declare war on Japan and Germany. During the war, Roosevelt was very much the leader of America's foreign policy. Left open to question, though, was the future of the Presidency's powers in foreign affairs after the war's end. If events followed the patterns set after the Civil War and World War One, Congress would then reassert itself.

4   Harry Truman and the modern American foreign policy Presidency

Despite Constitutional provisions dividing foreign policy powers, and the founders' intent that only Congress should take America to war, events and decisions after World War Two transformed the Presidency's role to one of long-term dominance in foreign affairs. The events grew out of the Cold War with the Soviet Union and other communist countries. Faced with what he and most American leaders perceived as Soviet adventurism, President Harry S Truman (1945–53) responded in a number of important ways. Truman's approach is best illustrated by his response to communist North Korea's invasion of non-communist South Korea in the summer of 1950. Seeing the incursion as part of larger communist designs for world domination, Truman told his Secretary of State Dean Acheson: 'We've got to stop the sons of bitches, no matter what.' Flying to Washington after receiving news of the invasion, Truman reflected how 'Communism was acting in Korea just as Hitler, Mussolini, and the Japanese had acted ten, fifteen, twenty years earlier'. Without waiting for authorisation from Congress or the United Nations, Truman ordered troops along with air and naval support to defend South Korea. As he hoped, Congress and the UN followed his lead, the latter with a Security Council resolution (passed in the absence of the Soviet Union) calling on UN members to oppose the North Korean invasion. Significantly, Truman declined to ask for a Congressional resolution authorising or approving his war decision, even after the fact. Acheson later explained:

> At the moment, troops of the US were engaged in a desperate struggle in and around Pusan [South Korea]. Hundreds, thousands of them were being killed … if, at this time, action was pending before Congress, by which hearings might be held, and long inquiries were being entered into as to whether or not this was the right thing to do, or whether the President had the authority to do it, or whether he needed congressional authority for matters of that sort – we would be doing about the worst thing we could possibly do for the support of our troops and their morale.[11]

Truman's and Acheson's actions represented a new era in the history of Presidential foreign policy power.

Some members of Congress objected. Senator Robert Taft said Truman had 'simply usurped authority, in violation of the laws and the constitution', while Senator Arthur Watkins complained that 'the United States is at war by order of the President'. In response, the Truman Administration claimed that 'the President, as Commander in Chief of the Armed Forces of the United States, has full control over their use thereof'. It was a sweeping assertion and defence of Presidential dominance in foreign affairs. One leading commentator writes that previous American history 'offers no example of a President who plunged the nation into war in order to repel an attack on some foreign nation'.[12]

Truman fully subscribed to the previously described views of Theodore Roosevelt on Presidential power and to a controversial Supreme Court decision written by Justice George Sutherland. The Justice set forth the modern theory of 'inherent' Presidential power over foreign affairs in the 1936 *Curtiss-Wright* decision, writing of a 'plenary and exclusive power of the presidency as sole organ of the federal government in international relations'.[13] Though the Court decision was based on a questionable reading of the Constitution, Presidents since the Truman era have often cited Sutherland's opinion. Significantly, Congress retained its constitutionally mandated power of the purse – the power to fund or not fund any governmental activity – during this period. But as an institution, it deferred to President Truman's Korean policy and supported it with budgetary outlays, despite the misgivings of some of its members. A new era in Presidential power had begun, the modern era of presidential 'prerogatives', in which authority is unilaterally asserted in foreign affairs, justified by constitutional construction and interpretation.[14]

The Truman era was significant for another reason in the history of the Presidency and foreign policy – the creation by Congress, with the National Security Act of 1947, of bureaucracies in the White House and elsewhere in Washington, DC, to assist the President in coordinating foreign/defence policies, by gathering and integrating information and by providing expertise and coherent advice. No longer would Presidents have to rely mostly on officials in the State Department, located across town from the White House, for such assistance; the creation of the NSC staff, working in or next door to the White House, was a significant enhancement of the executive branch's ability to lead in foreign affairs, as were the creation in 1947 of the CIA and the Department of Defence.[15]

Truman's assertions of Presidential power in foreign policy (and the acquiescence of Congress, many constitutional scholars and the Supreme Court itself) did not occur in a political vacuum. They happened in an era when, despite America's creation of the atomic bomb and its rise to a position of supreme political, military and economic power, there was widespread fear and distrust of the nuclear-armed (as of 1949) Soviet Union. Sharing Truman's view of America's role in world affairs, most other political actors in Washington and the nation saw the Presidency in a necessary, significant new role. Its occupant was not just leader of the United States, but also leader of the 'free world'.[16] Thus, when Truman and subsequent Presidents would pursue controversial policies with other nations, even critics of that particular policy would (however reluctantly) usually subscribe to the reigning view of the President as the leader in foreign affairs.

5   Vietnam, the Persian Gulf and Haiti: tests of the limits of Presidential dominance in foreign affairs

The broad pattern of foreign policy decision-making since 1945 has been one of the Presidency as prime mover. And yet there has been some change across time in the foreign policy powers of the Presidency. One way to observe this is to examine the power of the Presidency in three different conflicts from the Cold War and post-Cold War eras.

(a) *Vietnam*   A dramatic example of the modern President's leadership on international matters is the case of America's relations with Vietnam. For over two decades, from the early 1950s until the mid-1970s, presidents from both the Democratic and Republican Parties moved the United States deeper and deeper into a seemingly unshakeable commitment of American resources in Southeast Asia.

Despite a traditional American ideal of anti-colonialism, the Truman Administration allied itself with France in that country's fight against Ho Chi Minh's movement to eject the French and establish a unified, communistic Vietnam, free of foreign domination. Dealing with such problems as the 'fall' of China to communism (with the victory of Mao Tse Tung's revolution), the war in Korea and the Cold War, Truman started sending aid to the French in 1950. He did so with the support of Congress. After France gave up and withdrew from Vietnam in 1954, the country was divided by a peace conference into communist North Vietnam and non-communist South Vietnam. The United States, under President Dwight Eisenhower (1953–61) allied itself with the South. By sending hundreds of advisers and billions of dollars, the United States committed itself to a flawed regime in South Vietnam, with problems of corruption and human rights abuses. In line with President Truman's general policy of anti-communist containment, President Eisenhower enunciated the so-called 'domino theory'. This was the idea that the fall of Vietnam would represent the beginning of a 'crumbling process' that would spread to the rest of Asia and beyond. By 1958, the Eisenhower Administration was sending South Vietnam more military aid than it was to any other nation. Eisenhower may have kept America at peace, but he also kept America in Vietnam.[17]

Democrat John F. Kennedy (1961–63) followed the Republican Eisenhower into the White House. In his famous Inaugural Address, Kennedy promised the United States would 'pay any price, bear any burden ... support any friend, oppose any foe to assure the survival and success of liberty'.[18] Friends were usually thought to be those governments which were anti-communist, whether or not they were democratic. Meanwhile, the USSR enunciated a policy of supporting Third World guerrilla movements' wars of 'national liberation' against despotic or colonial-style governments allied with the United States. Not surprisingly, Kennedy's Administration held an objective of preventing communist domination of South Vietnam. But this became harder and harder to achieve, as Vietcong guerrillas and North Vietnamese soldiers continued to defeat the South Vietnamese army. By the end of 1962, there were 11,000 American advisers (military personnel) in Vietnam.

At the same time, various sectors of the South Vietnamese society became disenchanted with the autocratic President Ngo Dinh Diem. Just weeks before his own death, President Kennedy approved of a plan permitting South Vietnamese military leaders to stage a coup to overthrow Diem. Kennedy and his advisers hoped that a non-violent coup might be possible, and would lead to a more stable and popular government of South Vietnam. Instead, President Diem was assassinated by the coup's leaders (who had worked closely with the CIA and other American government officials in planning the coup). Thus, an American President, again with virtually no consultation with Congress, had drawn the United States deeper into the Vietnam quagmire. When JFK was murdered three weeks after Diem's death, there were 16,000 US advisers in Vietnam.

President Lyndon Johnson (1963–69) pledged to support the late President's policies 'from Berlin to South Vietnam'. Johnson's attitude to the conflict was deeply affected by analogies taken from the (relatively) successful limited war in Korea, as well as by memories of the 1930s.[20] In August 1964, after North Vietnamese torpedo boats attacked US ships in the Gulf of Tonkin, on one or possibly two occasions, Johnson consulted his advisers and ordered a retaliatory air raid against North Vietnam.[21] He also obtained from the Democratic majority in Congress a mandate to take whatever actions he believed necessary 'to repel any armed attack against the forces of the United States and to prevent further aggression'.[22] The Resolution passed unanimously in the House of Representatives and with only two opposing votes in the Senate. It was another dramatic expansion of the President's war powers. In the first half of 1965, the South Vietnamese military lost more and more battles with the Vietcong and North Vietnamese. While Johnson gave serious attention to those who urged American withdrawal, most of his advisers favoured a major military commitment.[23] On 28 July, Johnson (without a Congressional declaration of war, but with the Tonkin Resolution on the books) announced on live television: 'I have asked the commanding general, General Westmoreland, what more he needs to meet this mounting aggression. He has told me. We will meet his needs.'[24]

Johnson hoped that sending troops would force the communists to agree to a peace treaty that would save South Vietnam, but the Vietcong and North Vietnamese met the Americanisation of the war with stubborn resistance. American soldiers began dying by the thousands, with no victory in sight. Increasingly, some members of Congress and the general public started questioning Johnson's constitutional right to have entered the war. Still, Congress supported the President's policies throughout the Johnson

Administration with appropriations of money for the war. Feeling trapped, unable either to win or pull out, Johnson did not seek re-election in 1968. Not only anti-war demonstrators on college campuses, but a majority of all Americans had lost their faith in him as a war leader.[25]

By 1973, when the United States withdrew, Vietnam had divided American society and weakened Presidential primacy in the area of war powers. Over the veto of (Republican) President Nixon, Congress (still held by Democrats) passed the War Powers Resolution in 1973, in an explicit effort to fulfil the intent of the framers of the Constitution of the United States that 'the collective judgement of both the Congress and the President would apply to the introduction of United States armed forces into hostilities ... and to the continued use of such forces'.[26] In the years since the War Powers Resolution was passed, what one scholar calls the Constitution's 'invitation to struggle' over foreign policy has continued between Presidents and Congress.[27] None of the Presidents who have taken office since 1973 has given their full support or agreement to the War Powers Resolution.

In retrospect, few would deny that Vietnam policymaking across decades was almost always dominated by Presidential preferences and actions. The failures of Vietnam, in combination with other failed policies, led some analysts to question whether the United States has an imperial Presidency. Nonetheless, the Presidency continued to dominate foreign policymaking for most of the 1970s and 1980s, leading some to wonder whether Vietnam really had lessened the Presidency's powers. What did change, though, in the late 1980s and early 1990s, was world politics, with the end of the Cold War.

(b) *The Gulf War*   The war between a US-led alliance of nations, acting under United Nations resolutions, and Iraq came in January 1991, by which time the Cold War was virtually over. The Berlin Wall had been down for over a year and the Soviet Union would cease to exist by the end of 1991. Therefore, it is hard to view the Persian Gulf War as purely a Cold War or post-Cold War event, though mostly it would seem to fit in the latter category. After all, the leaders of the two sides – President George Bush (1989–93) and Soviet leader Mikhail Gorbachev – found multiple areas of agreement in the final two years of the Cold War. Here, without attempting a general history of the war in the Persian Gulf, I wish to ask how powerful the Presidency seemed to be in leading the United States to war with Iraq, and to view possible contrasts with Vietnam-era Presidencies.

Late in the summer of 1990, when Iraq invaded Kuwait, the US Congress (with Democrats in the majority), the public and the news media looked to the Bush Administration for a response. Although it took some weeks for a clear policy to emerge, it was the Presidency, not the Congress, which dominated policy. It was (Republican) President Bush who decided, with Congressional acquiescence, that thousands of US military personnel would be sent on an emergency basis to Saudi Arabia, which loomed as a possible target of further aggression by Iraq's dictator, Saddam Hussein. More importantly, Bush decided in late October 1990 (without informing Congress or the public for some days) that the United States would move from that early 'defensive' posture in the Persian Gulf to an 'offensive' posture which would permit them and their allies to eject Iraqi troops from Kuwait. This meant that close to half a million US military personnel would be sent to the area in preparation for possible war. None of this had been authorised by Congress, which had passed a resolution that autumn which merely expressed support for the early defensive measures. As for consultations prior to Bush's decisions, they were sporadic and without depth.[28]

Had anything really changed since Vietnam? In some respects, the answer must be no. The decision to send hundreds of thousands of troops around the world to defend an ally had largely been made by a President, with little Congressional involvement. Indeed, as late as January 1991, President Bush said of a proposed Congressional resolution to permit him to authorise US forces to go to war: 'I don't think I need it.'[29] On this and other occasions, Bush stated that he had all the power he needed, by way of the Constitution's 'commander-in-chief' clause and a set of United Nations resolutions authorising actions against Iraq.

In some respects, though, times *had* changed since Vietnam. Witness the comments of a Republican member of the House of Representatives, Susan Molinari (New York):

> The American people voted for George Bush. They did not vote for King George. There is only one constitutional body, one constitutional vehicle, to send this Nation to war. It is the Congress ... I say that if George Bush attacks Iraq without explicit declaration of war from Congress, it should be an impeachable offense.[30]

President Bush ultimately decided that his Administration should seek Congressional authorisation, which was given on 12 January 1991. And in response to charges of domineering behaviour, the Administration claimed that Bush's consultations with many members of Congress in the late summer and autumn of 1990 had been extensive, prior to the actual vote in 1991. The brevity of the war tremendously enhanced George Bush's standing with the public and the Congress, but only for a while. If the debate and unambiguous resolution authorising war were examples of the 'new' era of the Presidency's lessened foreign policy dominance, so was the reaction of the public in the latter part of 1991, into 1992. In previous decades there had been a truism in American politics which held that Presidents who managed 'their' wars successfully won re-election to another term. But that bit of conventional wisdom fell into the dustbin of history, as did Soviet communism. A year after the Persian Gulf War was over, few Americans discussed it. With a persistent economic recession much more on their minds,

Bush's popularity faded. Whether or not the war was 'his', it did not matter much to the public, once it was over.

(c) *Haiti*   The United States' intervention in Haiti in September 1994, authorised by the United Nations, came at a point when the Cold War was unambiguously over. The republics which made up the former Soviet Union all had more or less friendly relations with the United States. Therefore, the concern which hung over US policymakers for decades in dealing with other nations of the Western hemisphere – the possibility of growing Soviet influence, as with Cuba and Nicaragua – no longer existed.

The Haitian situation flared up during the Bush years, in 1991, when President Aristide was ousted by a military coup and fled to the United States. Despite a series of sanctions and warnings over the following years, the dictatorship headed by General Raoul Cedras continued to hold power, while systematically repressing virtually all political opposition. Late in the Bush Presidency and through most of the first two years of the Clinton Presidency, thousands of Haitians took to the seas, attempting to make it to US shores, in hopes of being accepted as political refugees. This created dilemmas which the Clinton Administration and many others found unacceptable.

As for Presidential–Congressional relations prior to the eventual US intervention in Haiti in 1994, what is striking is how little the Presidency's powers seemed to have waned, despite the end of Cold War conditions which had long been thought to provide a basis for those powers. Like the cases of Vietnam and the Persian Gulf, substantive consultations by President Clinton with Congressional leaders prior to his major decisions were few, at least from the vantage point of most members of Congress. On 14 September 1994, for example, Senator William Cohen (Republican of Maine), widely known for his non-partisanship, told the Senate that there had not been 'genuine consultations' with any leaders of the House and Senate, nor any 'conveyance of ... the original intent or plans or options they might have in mind'.[31] As for explicit Congressional authorisation of a US invasion of Haiti, President Clinton took a stand which sounded familiar but ironic, in light of his youthful opposition to the Vietnam policies of Presidents Johnson and Nixon: 'Like my predecessors of both parties, I have not agreed that I was constitutionally mandated to get' the permission of Congress to use military force abroad.[32] Clinton did not rely exclusively on force: he also sent a diplomatic delegation including former President Carter, retired General Colin Powell, and Senator Sam Nunn (Democrat of Georgia) to urge Cedras to step down. Literally, as the US 82nd Airborne Division was on its way to invade Haiti, Cedras agreed. On 15 October 1994, President Aristide returned to Haiti and resumed holding office. Despite the successful (and peaceful) intervention, the US Congress was grudging in its reaction. Neither house of Congress had voted for an invasion, nor for that matter had public opinion favoured such a course. Said House Foreign Affairs Committee Chairman Lee Hamilton (Democrat of Indiana): 'We have not approved of the policy, we have not disapproved of the policy. We simply default.' Later, Congress passed a resolution indicating that Clinton should have sought its authorisation, prior to the intervention.[33]

What lessons are to be derived from the Vietnam, Persian Gulf, and Haitian cases in the Cold War and post-Cold War eras, in relation to the power of the President? It would appear that the Presidency's war powers are still enormous, despite the lack of a Cold War almost to guarantee that the public and Congress will rally around the President. This does not mean that such White House powers will not slowly decline in the coming years. Many analysts believe this will happen. One can speculate that the next time there is a unilateral Presidential decision to intervene abroad militarily, and if that intervention turns out to be a major disaster, only then will Congress choose finally and decisively to limit such Presidential policymaking in the future. But there is no consensus among scholars and policymakers that this will happen; nor is there one, more generally, over how much, if at all, the Presidency will decline in other foreign policy powers.[34]

6 Decision-making styles and choices of recent Presidents

Each President must make important choices about how to structure the foreign policy advisory system which serves him. One key choice is whether or not to centre most foreign policy decision-making in the White House and thus become a 'hands-on' manager of day-to-day problems in foreign affairs. The alternative is to place much of this responsibility on the Secretary of State, leaving the President free to deal with a limited number of foreign policy problems.

A remarkable example of a White House centred foreign policy system comes from the Nixon Administration. After his election in 1968, Richard Nixon met with Harvard Professor Henry Kissinger to discuss the latter's possible appointment as NSA. In his memoirs, Kissinger writes that Nixon spoke of a 'massive organisation problem ... He had very little confidence in the State Department. Its personnel had no loyalty to him ... he was determined to run foreign policy from the White House.'[35] So he did, with Kissinger's help, and with Secretary of State William Rogers's frequent ignorance. On issues ranging from opening relations with China to negotiating a peace treaty with North Vietnam, President Nixon purposely kept his own Secretary of State in the dark, while Kissinger travelled the world on secret diplomatic missions. Decisions and important deliberations occurred at the White House, not the State Department. Kissinger recalls, for example, that Nixon excluded Rogers from the President's 'first meeting with Soviet Ambassador Anatoly Dobrynin ... The practice, established before my own position was settled, continued. Throughout his term, when a State visitor was received in the Oval Office by Nixon for a lengthy discussion, I was the only other American present.'[36]

Most recent Presidents have chosen to centre much of the foreign policy action in the Oval Office and in the nearby office of the NSA, though none has taken the practice to the extremes that Nixon did. Like him, they have felt frustrated or suspicious about the willingness and capability of the huge State Department bureaucracy to carry out their orders or those of the Secretary of State. John Kennedy respected his Secretary, Dean Rusk, but as President, Kennedy wanted to be (in effect) his own Secretary of State. So, with the assistance of his NSA, McGeorge Bundy, and the advice of persons scattered throughout his Administration, Kennedy kept a close eye on foreign relations.

In the Administrations of Presidents Carter and Reagan, the NSAs conflicted with the Secretaries of State. This does not mean that Secretaries Cyrus Vance (in the Carter Administration) and George Shultz (in the Reagan Administration) had little influence on foreign policy. But, the writings and testimony of Vance and Shultz recount the continual struggles they faced in trying to be their respective Presidents' top foreign policy official.[37]

President George Bush was determined to control the making of US foreign policy, as this was the issue area for which he felt strongly qualified. He appears to have given serious thought to constructing a team of foreign affairs advisers who had high intelligence and strong wills, but also egos of manageable proportions and loyalty to the President. This permitted Bush to rely heavily on both his NSA Brent Scowcroft, and his Secretary of State James Baker. No two persons in those jobs can avoid conflict, and there were plenty of rivalries between officials in the State Department and on the staff of the NSC. Still, compared to most other Administrations, Scowcroft and Baker worked together extremely well in helping Bush direct foreign policy.

In many respects, President Clinton's style in the White House is different from that of Bush. Most obviously, Clinton came into the White House without the sort of passion Bush had for foreign affairs. In the early years of his Presidency, Clinton often seemed inattentive to discussions of international problems; sometimes he cancelled planned meetings to make time for other events relating to domestic issues and politics. As time went on, though, Clinton appeared to become comfortable and even enthusiastic about confronting such issues. And he learned that no modern President can turn foreign policy over to his Secretary of State or his NSA. To an extent, Clinton did that by default early in his Presidency. The result was a lack of strategic direction which was widely perceived in and out of Washington. French President Jacques Chirac, for example, returned from the United States in June 1995, where he had met with an American President who seemed confused and vacillating. Chirac announced derisively that the position of leader of the free world was 'vacant'.[38]

Another choice the President must make is how they wish advice on foreign policy is to be presented to them. Will many advisers on foreign policy have direct access to the President, or will most information and advice be routed through one or a few key advisers? John Kennedy, Lyndon Johnson and Bill Clinton were highly informal in their interactions with advisers. Kennedy was known to call up lower level bureaucrats in the State Department or elsewhere in the government, bypassing normal channels to seek advice. Though Johnson met regularly with a small group of top advisers, known as the Tuesday Lunch Cabinet, on Vietnam War matters, he also talked with a diverse assortment of long-time political friends and advisers who lacked official standing.[39] Similarly, Clinton heard daily from his first Secretary of State Warren Christopher, in person or in writing; however, note the significance of the fact that, among those attending free-wheeling, weekly, policy and politics meetings, held at night-time in the President's living quarters of the White House, was the Deputy NSA Samuel Berger. Domestic politics and foreign policy were thoroughly intertwined in Clinton's first term.[40] While such evidence from a current Administration is always fragmentary, Clinton (like Kennedy and Johnson) appears to have had the approach to advisers referred to as a 'hub in the wheel' style, with a number of different advisers having direct access to the person at the centre of government, the President. Often, these advisers have no idea who else the President is consulting.

Presidents Truman, Eisenhower and Nixon preferred more formal systems of receiving advice. These men employed so-called 'pyramid' advisory structures, which place the President at the top of the decision-making system and allow a very few persons to transmit the advice of others to the Chief Executive. Presidents Truman and Eisenhower placed their Secretaries of State just below them at the top of their advisory systems. Therefore much of the advice these Presidents received was routed to them by their Secretaries. Eisenhower also relied heavily on formal meetings of the NSC to present him with alternatives in addressing problems on the international scene. Richard Nixon relied heavily on Henry Kissinger as the prime collector and conveyor of foreign policy alternatives. Still, the extent to which Presidents have confined their advisory interactions to the 'hub in the wheel' or 'pyramid' models should not be exaggerated. Recent research suggests that Presidents Eisenhower and Johnson, for example, sought more diverse types of advice than had been previously thought.[41] No political scientist or historian can ever know with certainty all of the people to whom a President spoke and which conversations were most crucial.

Ultimately, an adviser is anyone chosen by a President to counsel him (or her, in the future) on a problem. Sometimes this is one with little or no official standing. A good example comes from the brief Presidency of Gerald Ford (1974–77), who took office after Richard Nixon resigned. When Cambodian forces seized an American ship and its men off the shores of Cambodia in 1975, Ford met with top advisers to consider an American response.

Beyond recovering the American hostages, advisers such as then Secretary of State Henry Kissinger leaned toward a 'strong response' – heavy air strikes – as a form of punishment against the Cambodian government. In a room full of foreign policy heavyweights – the Secretaries of State and Defence, various military leaders, the Vice-President, and the Director of the CIA – the atmosphere was tense. Kissinger emotionally warned Ford that if the United States failed to respond to the challenge, it would be a serious blow to American prestige around the world. Suddenly, as Ford recounts in his memoirs:

> from the back of the room, a new voice spoke up. It was [White House official photographer David] Kennerly, who had been taking pictures of us for the past hour or so ... 'Has anyone considered', he asked 'that this might be the act of a local Cambodian commander who has just taken it into his own hands to halt any ship that comes by? ... you can blow the whole place away and it's not gonna make any difference.'

Ford recalls that there was a moment of silence in the Cabinet room before discussion resumed. When decision time came, Ford decided that 'what Kennerly had said made a lot of sense. Massive air strikes would constitute overkill.'[42] Instead, the President directed that a rescue attempt proceed as planned, accompanied by only limited air strikes against a few military targets. This was neither the first nor the last time that a crucial 'adviser' to a President would be a friend, a family member or some other person not listed on an Administration's official personnel chart.

Some political scientists have extolled the benefits of a 'multiple advocacy system' serving the President.[43] Such an advisory systems brings the President diverse points of view on foreign policy issues, with key members of his Administration (or others from outside the Administration) debating their differences in front of the President. While one can hardly argue against the ideal of a President confronting wide-ranging, in-depth presentations of competing policy alternatives, there are certain prices to be paid for employing such systems. Presidents as diverse as the outgoing Bill Clinton, the formalistic Dwight Eisenhower and the almost reclusive Richard Nixon have sometimes often found large meetings unwieldy, because irrelevant advice and discussions take up valuable time.[44] A stronger Presidential concern is over leaks. It is a fact of modern American political history that all Presidents – Democrats and Republicans, liberals and conservatives – have been driven to extreme frustration by leaks to the press about debates and differences among top figures in the Administration. Even more upsetting to Presidents have been leaks about imminent Presidential decisions – sometimes disgruntled Administration personnel leak a tentative Presidential decision to the press, in hopes that a negative reaction from Congress or other quarters might force the President to change his mind and not announce the decision. No matter that Presidents themselves often leak information to the press –

they see this as a Presidential prerogative, they are infuriated when others do it. President Ronald Reagan's response to leaks was to sign a directive requiring all top office-holders to take polygraph examinations (so-called 'lie detector' tests). But Reagan's second Secretary of State George Shultz refused to submit to such examinations. While sympathetic to Reagan's frustration over leaks, Shultz went public with his criticism of the tests. He told reporters: 'The minute in this government I am told that I'm not trusted is the day I leave.'[45] Shultz offered his resignation to Reagan over the matter, but the President refused to accept it, withdrawing the lie-detector policy instead.

Rejecting such spectacular solutions as the Reagan polygraph plan, previous Presidents have often restricted the most important decisions of crucial foreign policy issues to relatively small groups of trusted advisers. While Presidents have been accused of tilting too strongly against multiple advocacy approaches to decision-making, they understand the costs associated with meetings of large groups of people to discuss key issues. Yet the alternative, that of a President seeing only a small number of advisers, has obvious problems – he may be cut off from important opinions in the American political environment. He may not understand, for example, how strong a protest may come from Congress in response to a particular action, unless there are advisers to warn him.

More importantly, if a President relies on the counsel of only a few advisers, he may choose an unwise course of action. Certainly, John Kennedy came to believe that a wider pattern of advisory interactions might have turned him against the 1961 Bay of Pigs fiasco. And Ronald Reagan might have avoided the Iran–Contra scandal had he directed his NSC to present him with more acceptable solutions to the problem of American hostages being held in Lebanon than selling arms to Iran in hopes of freeing the hostages.

7 Presidential leadership on foreign policy issues: recent Presidents, from Nixon to Clinton

(a) *Nixon* Despite the disgrace brought about by his concealment of evidence in the Watergate scandal and his unprecedented resignation from the Presidency, Richard Nixon (1969–74) led an Administration of unusual importance in foreign affairs. The great crowning achievement of the Nixon era was opening relations with the People's Republic of China, which had been estranged from the United States for over two decades. Since the communists headed by Mao Tse Tung, took power in 1949, the United States had clung to the fiction that the government of the little island nation of Taiwan was the real government of China. This was justified on the basis that the one-time leader of all of China, Chiang Kai Shek, had taken his government-in-exile to Taiwan after being overthrown in the Revolution. For years afterward, conservative Republicans in the United States charged loudly that President Truman's Administration had 'lost' China. To most policymakers in Washington, it was unthinkable that the United States should even talk to the leader from what they called 'Red China'.

But Richard Nixon brought unique credentials to the Presidency which allowed and led him to travel to China for discussions with its leaders. He had an undeniable reputation as an anti-communist, dating back to his days as an influential Congressman in the 1940s and 1950s who searched out communists in the American government. That reputation gave Nixon more freedom than a liberal, Democratic President would have had in reaching out to China without being politically damaged by the predictable conservative charges of 'selling out' the people of China by talking with the communist leadership there. Also, Nixon understood that China had long since dropped its alliance with its giant communist neighbour, the Soviet Union. By pursuing better diplomatic relations with both China and the USSR, each of the mutually hostile communist countries was kept on guard about American relations with the other.[46]

Nixon's trip to China was a dramatic success. It went over well with the voters back home in the 1972 election, which Nixon won in a landslide. It solidified his standing as a world leader as well. And in terms of sheer logic, it made enormous sense for two of the world's most populous countries, the United States and China, to recognise the existence of each other and start negotiations. Similarly, Nixon pursued a policy of détente with the Soviet Union. After two decades of a tense Cold War, both Nixon and the Soviet leadership recognised the need for dispassionate negotiations leading to a more stable management of the rivalry of the world's two most powerful nations. Détente did not mean friendship, exactly. (That word would only start being used in reference to the Soviet government in the late 1980s by President Bush.) But it did mean at least limited cooperation between governments, and talks about such crucial problems as a burgeoning nuclear arms race and serious differences on issues such as human rights and revolutions in Third World countries. One product of these negotiations were the first Strategic Arms Limitation Treaty (SALT I) talks, which placed limits on the growth of strategic nuclear arms stockpiles.

The Nixon Administration did not care much about Third World countries, unless they showed signs of moving towards friendlier relations with the Soviet Union. Then, the Administration would show a good deal of attention. Nixon took socialist Salvador Allende's election as President of Chile in 1973 as a personal affront, signifying the 'loss' of Chile under his watch.[47] Though not proven, many have suspected that the CIA, urged on by Nixon, played a central role in the subsequent overthrow of Allende by a group of military plotters.

In non-crisis times, however, Kissinger and Nixon treated countries of Africa, Latin America, and other parts of the Third World with benign neglect. This attitude reflected the *realpolitik* philosophy of international affairs which Nixon and Henry Kissinger shared, emphasising the importance of power as the main determinant in international relations. Since Third World countries were not powerful themselves, they counted for little.

Finally, for the Nixon Administration (and the Ford Administration, which completed Nixon's term of office), there was the problem of Vietnam. Nixon was in the unenviable position of taking over a war he had not started, one which had already polarised and dispirited the American people, and one with little prospect for a successful conclusion. Nixon rejected the idea of a quick American withdrawal from Vietnam. Indeed, his Administration expanded the war into Cambodia and indulged in massive bombing of North Vietnam. However, he did practise 'Vietnamisation' – slowly withdrawing American troops, while turning over their combat duties to soldiers of the government of South Vietnam. In retrospect, Nixon's Vietnam policies (like those of the Democratic and Republican Presidents who preceded him) are widely considered a failure. The recognition that the United States was fighting not just communism, but a very strong brand of Vietnamese nationalism, never took hold in his or preceding Administrations. Therefore, Nixon and Kissinger wasted tens of thousands of lives and billions of dollars on a venture which ended only in 1975, with the creation of a unified communist Vietnam.

(b) *Carter*   Jimmy Carter (1977–81) was elected President during an era of American citizens' revulsion over the apparent lies of preceding Administrations about Vietnam and Watergate. Recalling the idealistic approach to international affairs of Woodrow Wilson, Carter asserted as a Presidential candidate that American idealism should be at the heart of foreign policy. In his 1976 campaign autobiography, Carter wrote that in 'such areas as Pakistan, Chile, Cambodia, and Vietnam, our government's foreign policy has not exemplified any commitment to moral principles'.[48] President Carter, therefore, made concern for human rights a top priority during his four years of office. While he enjoyed some success in at least putting human rights on the agenda during international negotiations and in America's own policy deliberations, he also met some embarrassing setbacks.

Carter's approach is best understood in contrast to the Nixon–Kissinger–Ford foreign policy era. While Congress pushed increasingly hard during the Nixon era for human rights criteria to be employed in dealing with America's allies, such efforts were largely resisted by the Administration. The usual response was that 'quiet diplomacy' was more effective in prodding other countries to treat its citizens humanely than would be a 'sledgehammer' approach of threatening to cut off American foreign aid or publicly labelling such countries serious violators of human rights.

A major shift occurred in the Carter Administration, with the President's frequent rhetoric about human rights supported by institutionalisation of that concern. One scholar has written:

> A network of offices and personnel had been created within the government whose business was human rights. The position of 'Coordinator for Human Rights and Humanitarian Affairs' in the State Department was upgraded by Congress at the request of the administration to that of Assistant Secretary. The Bureau of Human Rights and Humanitarian Affairs was created to replace what had merely been an 'office' for human rights.[49]

Each year, the State Department issued a 'report card' assessing how well or poorly countries around the world performed in respecting human rights.

In Latin America, the Carter Administration's campaign for human rights was most noticeable in its impact. The Argentinian government, for example, was 'disappearing' many hundreds of citizens. Publicly and privately, Carter and his top foreign policy advisers subjected that government to severe pressure, eventually cutting off military aid to the country.[50] Since Argentina's return to a democratic system, Carter has been credited with saving the lives of some Argentinians during that country's years under military rule. Guatemala faced similar sanctions during the Carter Administration. Though determining precisely the effect of pressure from the United States is difficult, it is widely believed that Carter's campaign had some beneficial effect.

Critics point out, however, that Carter was inconsistent in applying human rights standards to other countries. They charge he was willing to overlook the human rights abuses by despotic governments which were useful to America's military position in the world, such as that of the Shah of Iran and Ferdinand Marcos of the Philippines. For instance, Carter complimented the Shah on his government's progress as an 'island of stability' because of the 'love which your people give to you'.[51] Soon thereafter, the Shah was forced to leave Iran due to a revolution against his rule. Also, many Western Europeans such as West German Chancellor Helmut Schmidt were irritated by Carter's alleged inconsistencies in applying human rights standards. Certainly, the leadership of the Soviet Union found Carter hard to understand. When all is said and done, however, Carter's emphasis on human rights struck a responsive chord with millions of people in the United States and around the world. It also set precedents which subsequent Presidents have not been able to ignore entirely.

The most spectacular success of the Carter Administration was the Camp David Accords, which brought about peace between Israel and Egypt. Carter himself could take much personal credit for the peace agreement, as he personally negotiated between Israel's Menachem Begin and Egypt's Anwar Sadat, who strongly disliked each other. By inviting Sadat and Begin to the Presidential retreat at Camp David and trying to forge a peace agreement between two countries which were long-time enemies, Carter took a big gamble. There were moments during the thirteen days of negotiations when collapse appeared imminent. But historic agreements resulted, even if they did not solve all of the problems of the Middle East. Begin and Sadat later were awarded the Nobel Peace Prize, but many thought Carter should have shared in the award for his remarkable venture into personal diplomacy.

Other successes during the Carter years included winning Senate approval of the Panama Canal Treaty, which provided for the eventual return of the Canal to the nation of Panama itself. This was an important step towards dis-associating the United States government from its past record and reputation as the imperialist 'neighbour' to the north. Also, the Carter Administration followed the lead set by Nixon for formalising the new relationship with China by extending full diplomatic relations with the People's Republic.

On other matters, Carter appeared inept. When the Iranian revolution occurred, some critics thought Carter was responsible for the downfall of the Shah of Iran. The charge is unfair, as the revolution was probably going to occur, with or without Carter's opposition. The President's problems were compounded when Iranian radicals raided the American embassy in Teheran and seized sixty-three Americans as hostages in November 1979. It was a remarkable incident, violating longstanding traditions of international law, but the kidnapping won the blessings of Iran's new leader, the Ayatol-lah Khomeini. Carter reacted sharply, imposing economic and military sanc-tions on the Iranian government, and for a while the American people rallied round their President. But frustration mounted, especially after an American attempt to rescue the hostages failed in the spring of 1980.

Another unfortunate episode also dominated the news in the last year of the Carter Presidency – the invasion of Afghanistan by the Soviet Union. The USSR sent over 80,000 troops into Afghanistan to show its displeasure with the government in power. Ultimately, a new leader took office, supported by the Soviets, but most of the governments of the world condemned the inva-sion. Carter's early public reaction was that his 'opinion' of the Soviet lead-ership changed 'drastically' because of the incursion.[52] In part, Carter's remark reflected his frustration with the uneven progress of the preceding two and a half years in improving relations with the Soviet Union. At a time when the agonising process of negotiating SALT II with the Soviet Union had been completed, it was clear that Afghanistan would destroy the treaty's chances for ratification by the United States Senate. Still, Carter's comments sounded naïve to many. Soon, he responded forcefully, though: an embargo on American grains being sold to the Soviet Union, limitation of high tech-nology sales to the Soviets, and a request (ultimately honoured) that Ameri-can athletes not participate in the 1980 Olympics, which were to be hosted by the Soviet government.[53] Nonetheless, these reverses in foreign policy, plus high energy costs and interest rates – caused in large part by policies of the Organisation of Petroleum Exporting Countries (OPEC) – ruined Carter's image with many voters. So did the obvious splits among his top

foreign policy advisers over how tough the United States should be in dealing with other countries.

The first anniversary of the taking of the hostages in Iran coincided with
the 1980 Presidential election. This seems to have contributed to Carter's
big loss to Republican challenger Ronald Reagan. In the long run, however,
Carter may come to be seen as a President who dealt successfully with many
of the extremely difficult foreign policy dilemmas facing the United States.[54]

(c) *Reagan*   Ronald Reagan (1981–89) assumed the Presidency insisting
that the Soviet Union's provocative foreign policies were behind 'all the
unrest that is going on. If they weren't engaged in this game of dominoes,
there wouldn't be any hot spots in the world.'[55] For this reason, Reagan
opposed previous arms control agreements which Republican and Democratic Presidents had made with the Soviets. The SALT II treaty, for instance,
was 'fatally flawed', he said. In Central America, Reagan saw a battleground
between the 'free world' and Soviet-Cuban adventurism. El Salvador's civil
war was, in the new President's words, 'a textbook case of indirect armed
aggression by Communist powers', while the socialist government of
Nicaragua was labelled a Soviet satellite and a threat to democracy in the rest
of Latin America.[56]

In the early years of his Administration, Reagan usually succeeded in persuading both the public and Congress to follow his militant anti-communist
lead in foreign policy. Defence spending, already on the rise in the latter part
of the Carter Administration, was sharply escalated to pay for an expansion
of American military power. In 1981, defence spending was approximately
$160 billion; five years later, it was almost double that amount.[57] When Pres-
ident Reagan heard of an idea of creating a 'nuclear shield' which would protect the United States from incoming nuclear missiles in the event of nuclear
war, he quickly made it his own. Soon, despite the scepticism of most of the
scientific community, the President convinced Congress to begin spending
hundreds of millions of dollars on the SDI project, which many others
simply called 'Star Wars'. Though the programme would be renamed and
scaled down in subsequent Presidencies, research and limited testing of missile defence technologies continued. Following through on a pledge by the
Carter Administration and its NATO partners, the Reagan Administration
also oversaw the deployment of intermediate-range nuclear missiles, despite
demonstrations by hundreds of thousands of Western Europeans and warnings of the Soviet Union. Temporarily, top-level meetings between Soviet
and American diplomats ceased.

In Reagan's second term, however, there was a dramatic change in the
American stance toward the Soviet Union, undoubtedly brought about by
the new policies and appealing image of Mikhail Gorbachev. The Soviet
leader met Reagan in Iceland, in the Soviet Union and in the United States.
A new treaty emerged between the United States and the Soviets, mandating

the removal of the very same Soviet and NATO intermediate-range missiles which had been the subject of such contention earlier in the decade. More importantly, there were dramatically new perceptions of the Soviet Union in the United States. These perceptions were shared by the public, the Congress and Reagan himself. Walking in Red Square in Moscow with Gorbachev, a reporter called out a question to Reagan, asking about his description in earlier years of the USSR as 'an evil empire'. The President paused a moment, then told the reporter that those comments were from 'another time, another era'.[58]

Even as relations with the Soviets began to improve from 1985 onward, Reagan and his advisers continued to see Central America in Cold War terms. When Congress stopped funding the Nicaraguan rebels (known as the Contras) who were attempting to overthrow the leftist government of Nicaragua, figures in the Reagan administration devised an ingenious but illegal plan to get funds to the rebels. These Reaganites, including Colonel Oliver North of the National Security Council staff, decided to deal with two foreign policy problems at once: in order to secure the release of Americans held hostage by Lebanese radicals who were loyal to Iran, the Administration would sell arms to the Iranians. The 'profits' from these sales would then be sent to the Contras without the knowledge of Congress. When the press learned of this Iran–Contra operation, Reagan entered a period of relative unpopularity with the public and a new low standing with Congress.

The President himself was inconsistent in his comments on the affair – denying at times that arms had been traded in return for the hoped-for release of hostages. Reagan also showed difficulty in remembering just how much he had known of the Iran–Contra decisions made in his White House. However, perhaps remembering that Richard Nixon's 'stonewalling' during the Watergate scandal ultimately got him nowhere, Reagan gave measured cooperation to those who wished to investigate the affair. For starters, he appointed a special Presidential commission, known as the Tower Commission, to investigate what happened. With the President's blessing, the Commission interviewed chief actors in the Reagan foreign policy system, including the President himself. The public report produced by the Commission was not flattering to Reagan. For instance, the Commission noted matter-of-factly that the President had admitted that 'he had not been advised at any time ... how the plan would be implemented'.[59] The picture emerging from the Tower Commission Report and other sources was of a President with a remarkable 'hands-off' style of management, leaving major decisions and implementation of those decisions to others. While finding no evidence that Reagan knew of the illegal plans to divert the arms profits to the Contras, the Commission found Reagan's usage of the NSC largely to blame for allowing his subordinates to attempt a swap of arms for hostages. The Commission noted that the advisory system of the NSC 'will not work unless the President makes it work ... By his actions, by his leadership, the

President therefore determines the quality of its performance.'[60] While Reagan himself emerged from the scandal without serious evidence that he broke the law, some Iran–Contra figures faced criminal legal action late in his Administration and during the Bush Administration. Meanwhile, the Nicaraguan government continued in power, while the Contras largely faded from the scene, and nine Americans were still held hostage in Lebanon. When the Iran–Contra affair began, there were only seven such hostages.

More than in the Carter Presidency, Reagan's foreign policymaking was subject to chronic bureaucratic politics.[61] Theorists of bureaucratic politics assert that policies do not emerge simply as the result of rationally devised *Presidential* decisions; rather they emerge from the *competition* of the various top policymakers in a President's Administration. But the usefulness of this theoretical framework varies – to the extent that a President is a 'hands-on' type manager, bureaucratic politics will be relatively limited and a President can, if not stop competition among his advisers, at least control major decision-making. To the extent that a President is a 'hands-off' manager, bureaucratic politics can run wild in an Administration and policies are often really not so much *Presidential* decisions as they are *resultants* of competition in the Administration. In the words of Reagan's Secretary of State George Shultz, there was such severe competition and infighting among Reagan's foreign policy advisers that it was like 'guerrilla warfare'.[62]

Unlike the Carter Administration, there was no dramatic breakthrough in the Middle East during the Reagan years (despite the presence of a US-led multinational force in Lebanon between 1982 and 1984). But there had been enough indications of American 'toughness' during the Reagan years – an American invasion of Grenada in 1983 to overthrow a leftist government, and bombings of Colonel Mu'ammer Gaddafi's Libya in 1986 – to match Reagan's campaign pledges that America would 'stand tall' during his Presidency.

(d) *Bush*   Though almost no one could have anticipated it, two remarkable events were to dominate US foreign policy during the Presidency of Republican George Bush (1989–93), who had previously served loyally for two terms as Ronald Reagan's Vice President. These historic events were the end of the Cold War (and the Soviet Union) and the brief but dramatic war in the Persian Gulf.

Taking the Presidency in January 1989, George Bush had an impressive list of credentials to his credit: besides being Vice-President under Reagan, he was also a former Director of the CIA, former American representative to China (this was before the United States had full diplomatic relations with China), a former Congressman, and one-time chairman of the Republican Party. Whatever problems Bush encountered, they were not because of inexperience. Still, it often takes a few years for a President to establish his style of management and to make choices about which initiatives he will take in foreign policy. In his early days as President, the most positive development of his foreign policy was the continuing decline in animosity between the United States and the Soviet Union. Bush was not primarily responsible for this; Mikhail Gorbachev and Ronald Reagan seized the initiative in improving relations before Bush took office. But Bush, after some initially hesitant and sceptical rhetoric, showed that he was ready to deal with Gorbachev in improving relations and effectively ending the Cold War.

It is not much of an overstatement to say that Bush, along with advisers including Secretary of State Baker and NSA Scowcroft, came to be *supporters* of Gorbachev as he tried to steer the Soviet government toward openness and reform of domestic and foreign policies. Bush recognised that, as rights of freedom of expression took hold in the USSR, this increased the odds that competing sectors and conflictual political forces could possibly lead the Soviet Union to civil war or anarchy. Bush and Gorbachev met often, in Malta in 1989, in Washington, Helsinki and Paris in 1990, and in London in 1991. Their productive relationship was reinforced by an unusually effective near-partnership between Secretary of State Baker and Soviet Foreign Minister Eduard Shevardnadze. Among the products of their negotiations were the signing of a Conventional Forces in Europe (CFE) Treaty, to reduce armaments and military personnel in Europe, and a Strategic Arms Reduction Treaty (START), to reduce the nuclear forces of the United States and USSR. Such progress made Bush and Baker somewhat fearful of the rise of Boris Yeltsin, who abandoned the Communist Party and headed the Russian Parliament in 1990 before being elected to the newly created Russian Presidency in 1991. Ultimately, they adjusted to the rise of Yeltsin and the decline of both Gorbachev and the Soviet Union itself.[63]

The final period of the USSR's existence overlapped with the other most significant event of Bush's Presidency, the Persian Gulf War. As briefly described earlier in this chapter, the President dominated policymaking in the United States in the aftermath of Saddam Hussein's invasion of Kuwait in the summer of 1990. Additionally, Secretary of State Baker enjoyed success in moving the leaders of diverse nations toward a working alliance in the United Nations, which condemned Iraq's invasion and ultimately authorised the allies to use military force to eject the Iraqis and restore the government of Kuwait to power. Certainly, the Bush Administration cannot be given sole credit for actions of the United Nations, yet few would deny that the US government was the most influential member of the UN in pushing for collective action. Baker travelled for ten weeks, holding over two hundred meetings with various leaders around the world, rounding up votes. One author described his strategy as:

[obtaining] ironclad assurance of support from the key UN countries before publicly acknowledging that the administration was even seeking a resolution

on the use of force. He had hedged, saying repeatedly that he was taking sound-
ings and that such a resolution was merely under consideration. Any one of the
five permanent members of the Security Council … could veto the resolution.
The Chinese turned out not to be much of a problem; early on, they agreed not
to veto. Britain's Prime Minister Thatcher was ready and willing to use force.
The French were a problem and required major effort, but Bush and Baker succeeded in bringing them on board. The Soviets were the big question mark.[64]

Eventually, the USSR's Shevardnadze agreed to a resolution permitting the
use of 'all necessary means' to push Iraqi forces out of Kuwait, and the resolution passed by twelve votes to two on 29 November 1990, with Cuba and
Yemen (two of the non-permanent Council members) voting no, and China
abstaining.

When the war began on 16 January 1991, it soon became evident that the
strategy was to pummel Iraqi installations and forces with aerial bombing,
then finish the job with ground forces. It turned out to be an effective military plan, achieving victory in forty-two days. Only during the last four of
those days was there significant ground combat. President Bush, recognising
that many members of the UN coalition did not wish to attempt an overthrow of Saddam Hussein and his government, ended US military attacks
when it was clear that Kuwait was liberated and that Iraq had suffered serious military losses. US combat deaths were just under 150. Iraq suffered far
greater losses of life, surely in the thousands, though the official accounts
vary.[65]

For all his apparent skill in managing diplomacy and war strategy after
Iraq invaded Kuwait, the picture of the Bush Administration's handling of
Saddam Hussein prior to that point is far less impressive. Obviously, events
from the Bush years are too recent for there to be a definitive account, but
there are clear indications that the US government misread Iraq and possi-
bly mishandled its relations with that country in the late 1980s and in 1990.
This can only be understood by recalling how hostile US relations were with
Iran in this same timespan. Ever since the Iranian revolution overthrew the
Shah in the late 1970s, the two governments had displayed open hostility.
Since Iran's and Iraq's own long war in the 1980s, the Bush Administration
(following the lead of Reagan) decided to 'tilt' American policy in favour of
the supposedly more responsible or reformable Iraq. This was observed in
various ways: in 1989, Bush signed a National Security Directive which
mandated economic and political incentives for Iraq to 'moderate its behaviour and to increase our influence' with that government; in 1990, the US
government provided $1 billion in agricultural credits to Iraq; in July 1990,
April Glaspie, US ambassador to Iraq, met with Saddam Hussein and apparently stressed a 'hands-off' US policy toward the brewing Iraqi–Kuwait dispute. Soon thereafter, the invasion occurred.[66] Such errors, if indeed they
can be so classified, provoke a defence from former President Bush and his
associates that hindsight is always clearer than what can be seen in dealing

with unfolding situations. It seems unlikely, though, that Bush will enjoy an unblemished record in history, given such US policies prior to the invasion of Kuwait.

Bush also faced dilemmas in dealing with the People's Republic of China earlier in his Presidency. In 1989, when the Chinese government cracked down on students and others demonstrating for democratisation of China's political system, the American President was restrained in his criticism of the Chinese political leadership. This displeased many Democrats and some Republicans, who noted that the Chinese students in Tiananmen Square raised a statue they called the 'Goddess of Liberty', modelled after the Statue of Liberty in the United States. When Bush sent his NSA and Deputy Secretary of State to meet Chinese leaders in Beijing in late 1989, many in Congress accused him of 'selling out' to pressure from the Chinese government. Democratic Senator George Mitchell, the Majority Leader of the Senate, condemned the visit as 'embarrassing kowtowing to the Chinese government'. But Bush defended his decision, noting 'I don't want to see ... China remain totally isolated'.[67] For the rest of his Presidency, he mostly succeeded in preventing the Congress from using trade restrictions to punish the Chinese government.

As to Central America, which gained daily attention from the Reagan Administration, its seeming importance to US policymakers declined as the Cold War was ending. However, in Bush's first year as President, the dictator of Panama, Manuel Noriega, came to be seen as threatening American lives and interests in the Panama Canal Zone and the surrounding area. (General Noriega, though a brutal, corrupt figure, had previously worked cooperatively with the CIA and other US government agencies.) A massive US military intervention in December 1989 overturned the dictatorship and arrested Noriega on drug-running charges. The democratically elected government which had been deposed by Noriega was returned to power.[68] And what of Nicaragua, which had been almost an obsession of the Reagan Administration? In 1990, the Nicaraguan government, controlled by the Sandinista Party, held free elections. Showing suspicions leftover from the Cold War, most Bush Administration officials thought the elections would be a sham. Democratic practices prevailed, however, delivering a stunning surprise to the White House: the hated Sandinistas lost. Soon thereafter, a peaceful change of government followed, and most American leaders stopped thinking about Central America.[69]

(e) *Clinton*   Though he gained much political and governmental experience as governor of the state of Arkansas for a decade, Bill Clinton had little background in international affairs. A product of the anti-Vietnam War student movement of the 1960s and 1970s, he had never served in the military and never reached what Americans call a 'comfort level' with military issues. By all accounts, he was the opposite of George Bush, in terms of his interests: Bush cared passionately about foreign affairs, but was mostly bored by domestic issues; as a candidate and early in his Presidency, Clinton struggled painfully (and sometimes resistantly) to gain depth in his understanding of foreign policy issues, while his ambitions had to do with domestic reform. Not surprisingly, as a candidate, he stressed that, if elected, he would focus 'like a laser beam' on the economy and other domestic issues. There was an implication that he would spend minimal time on foreign affairs. But, as he quickly learned in the White House, no President can avoid spending huge portions of his working days on the political, military and economic problems facing the United States in dealing with the rest of the world. He also learned that there can be rewards for performing effectively in foreign affairs.

Clinton was the first US President born after World War Two; he was also the first truly post-Cold War President. The overarching goals of US foreign policy which he and his top foreign policy advisers enunciated reflected the 'newness' of his Presidency and the political environment in which it functioned. What was not new, however, was an assumption that the United States should continue to be 'leader of the free world', even if there was no longer an enemy like the Soviet Union. Among the goals Clinton's Administration described was to promote the continued spread of democracy around the world, on the assumption that democracies rarely go to war with each other. Another goal with particular resonance to those thinking of domestic economic conditions was the promotion of free trade and other agreements which promoted export opportunities for US business. As well, Clinton and his Secretary of State Warren Christopher, and NSA Anthony Lake, committed the Administration to a continued engagement with those parties to long-term conflicts that were seeking peaceful resolutions, especially in the Middle East. Finally, the Clinton Administration committed itself to focusing on potential long-term threats including terrorism and proliferation of nuclear weapons.

In attempting to pursue such goals concretely during its first term, the Clinton Administration faced many reverses. In war-torn Somalia in Africa, President Bush had authorised a humanitarian US intervention to feed starving people. (This decision is considered at length in Chapter 8.) The new President Clinton authorised troops to use force in 1993 in dealing with competing Somalian warlords. Soon enough, though, American soldiers began dying, provoking outrage among the US public and Congress. Critics called the President dangerously amateurish for having allowed the US military's mission in Somalia to expand from a humanitarian one. In response, a chastened Clinton announced that the United States would soon withdraw from Somalia.

Similarly, in its early years, the Administration seemed unable to describe clear US goals concerning specific troubled nations including Bosnia and Haiti. As recounted earlier, the Administration did pursue vigorous, if controversial goals, to enunciate and pursue a more-or-less coherent policy. Not that *any* policy toward the fiercely violent three-way conflict between Serbians, Croatians and Muslims in that part of the former Yugoslavia could have been successfully pursued with ease. But, towards the end of Clinton's first term, even he and Secretary of State Warren Christopher admitted that their early Bosnian policies had been inadequate, especially in terms of forging a joint approach with the US NATO partners. In May 1993, Christopher went to Europe, offering a plan to exempt the militarily weak Bosnian government from an ongoing UN arms embargo. But US allies in Europe opposed it, fearing that a growing war would engulf thousands of European peacekeeping troops already stationed in Bosnia. Said Christopher in 1996: 'The way that I made the trip to Europe in 1993 was not consistent with global leadership'.[70] Eventually, Clinton decided that the United States had to play a leading role in attempting a Bosnia settlement, and that part of the solution would rest in using American troops alongside the Europeans as peacekeepers, if a settlement could be negotiated. Such a treaty was achieved in 1995 in an unusual diplomatic conference held in the out-of-the-way city of Dayton, Ohio. While peace mostly prevailed in 1996, with Bosnian elections held in September, the long-term prospects for Bosnia remained highly uncertain. For Clinton, though, there was a new, improved reputation with many European leaders. The Italian Minister Romano Prodi said of Clinton: 'He is playing foreign policy very strongly.'[71]

Regarding post-Cold War Russia, Clinton held firm to a pro-Yeltsin stance. The US President all but endorsed Yeltsin for re-election in the 1996 Russian Presidential campaign. To the great relief of the United States, Yeltsin won. Among the US–Russian advances during the Clinton years, early in 1996, the Senate ratified the START II Treaty, which was negotiated by the Bush Administration. The treaty provided for deeper cuts in the nuclear arsenals of both countries than those secured by the START I Treaty.

Much like his predecessor, Clinton also decided that economic sanctions against China for human rights abuses were ineffective. This, despite the fact that as a candidate in 1992, he had criticised Bush for putting trade ahead of humanitarian factors in dealing with China. This was Clinton's explanation in the summer of 1996 of his change of heart early in his Presidency:

> I concluded that if we were to revoke MFN [Most-favored-nation status, which permits countries to have extensive, low-tariff trade with the US], we might cause serious short-term damage to them economically, but that they would not change their human rights policies – if anything, they would become more repressive – and that we would risk creating a new, I hesitate to say, Cold War, but a very long-term fissure with a country that I think we still have some chance of influencing in a very positive way.[72]

Perhaps it is in dealing with the Middle East that Clinton's growing depth as a foreign policy leader became clearest. When the leaders of Israel and the

Palestine Liberation Organisation (PLO) gathered at the White House in 1994 to sign a peace agreement negotiated in Oslo, Norway, the drama and symbolism of a handshake with Yasir Arafat and Yitzhak Rabin was stunning. Yet, everyone knew that the Clinton Administration figured minimally in bringing that agreement to fruition. In the following two years, however, as the implementation of the PLO–Israeli accords was attempted, the United States became a central mediator. This was especially evident in late September 1996 when extensive violence broke out in Jerusalem and other parts of Israel, the West Bank and Gaza. The gravest sign of troubles was the fact that Israeli soldiers and Palestinian police officers traded gunfire. Secretary Christopher said that the 'peace process was plunged into what I feel was the most serious crisis' since the Oslo agreement.[73] Finding it impossible to persuade Arafat and the new Israeli Prime Minister Benjamin Netanyahu to meet in Israel, President Clinton acted boldly by inviting them and King Hussein of Jordan to the White House in October. Though no formal agreement emerged from the meeting, there was a commitment for the two sides to resume energetic negotiations back in Israel. Allowing for the dangers of further PLO–Israeli breakdowns, from a strictly US vantage point, Clinton showed himself adept at handling his Middle Eastern visitors and at explaining his efforts to the press.

All of this came just weeks after Clinton ordered limited bombing and increased the US military presence in the Persian Gulf, in reaction to a once-again assertive Saddam Hussein, who sent troops into an area of northern Iraq from which his government had been forbidden to send military forces. As with the Israel–PLO troubles, there were no guarantees for the future, but polls in the summer and early autumn of 1996 showed that the public viewed Clinton as being reasonably strong in handling such matters. In early September, for example, one respected poll showed 53 per cent of Americans approving of President Clinton's handling of foreign affairs. By contrast, a poll conducted two years earlier (shortly before the 1994 Republican victories in Congress) showed only 31 per cent of the public viewing Clinton's foreign policy leadership with favour.[74]

Of course, Clinton continued to have vocal critics. One prominent published critique held that the President had pursued 'social work' worldwide, rather than protecting American national interests. Others found fault with his recurring concern with economics in dealing with world affairs. A sign of this priority was the President's creation of a National Economic Council, to coordinate foreign and domestic economic policy. Mickey Kantor, one of Clinton's trade advisers, said: 'Clinton is the first president to really make trade the bridge between foreign and domestic policy.'[75] But in September 1996, the President was able to make a gesture with highly important symbolism, suggestive of statesmanship, rather than mere economic diplomacy: with the 1996 Presidential campaign against Republican nominee Bob Dole in full swing, the President was the first official to sign the Comprehensive

Test Ban Treaty in the company of other leaders from around the world. The Treaty, which called for a halt to all nuclear testing, represented ideas which had been discussed for over four decades.

Much to the surprise of critics and some supporters, Bill Clinton moved towards the end of his first term with a growing reputation as a President capable of dealing with the complexities of international affairs. Following the 1996 defeat of Bob Dole, Clinton announced a new foreign policy team. Madeleine Albright would replace Christopher at the State Department. In a bipartisan gesture, ex-Republican Senator William Cohen was nominated to head the Department of Defence. Samuel Berger became NSA, a post vacated by Anthony Lake, who moved to the CIA. The Albright–Cohen–Berger team appeared well endowed in the field of political skill, but perhaps less well qualified as moulders of a new strategic vision. Clinton's first term foreign policy has been ably defended as a 'best possible' internationalist response to the end of the Cold War. But, as former British Prime Minister Harold Macmillan once remarked: 'If you want a vision, consult a saint. I am a politician.'[76] As Clinton entered his second term, four main items appeared to dominate the agenda: restoration of good relations with the United Nations; expansion of NATO eastwards, without unduly upsetting Russia; promotion of the regional free trade strategy; and further integration of the United States in the Asian-Pacific community of nations.

8   Conclusion

Despite the Constitution's 'invitation to struggle' over the making of US foreign policy, American Presidents since the Truman era have had a decidedly upper hand in guiding that policy. Indeed, Congress, the Supreme Court and the American public *expect* modern Presidents to lead the way in foreign affairs, subject of course to occasional complaints from various quarters. There is a deeply rooted bipartisan expectation that the President will set the agenda for America in international affairs. Not even the trauma of Vietnam in the 1960s and 1970s, much less the strains produced by the Iranian hostage affair or the Iran–Contra scandal of the 1980s, could eliminate that expectation. Nor, so far, have the evolving post-Cold War international and domestic political environments. As long as Presidents have appeared to be managing foreign policy with at least moderate competence and success, the public has rallied behind Presidents. Only with long, drawn-out evidence of Presidential incapacity to deal with a foreign policy crisis have voters turned against a President's international stewardship. Such was the case with Lyndon Johnson and Vietnam and Jimmy Carter's hostage crisis. If they can avoid such 'endless' crises, Presidents have a good deal of power and freedom of manoeuvre in foreign policy.

Despite serious questions raised and investigations conducted by Congress and others during and after the Iran–Contra scandal, there has been almost no sentiment to diminish the significant foreign policy bureaucracy that attends to the President at the White House. The authors of the Tower Commission Report (two out of three of them former members of the US Senate) went out of their way to endorse the legitimacy and future necessity of the NSC system, despite its illegal misadventures during the Reagan era. If anything, the Clinton Presidency has increased White House capabilities to dominate policymaking by its creation of the previously mentioned National Economic Council which, at least towards the end of Clinton's first term, managed to coordinate its activities with those of the NSC, the NSA and NSC staff.

In describing the Presidency as a 'sole organ' of the federal government in the field of international relations, in the *Curtiss-Wright* case, Justice Sutherland and the Supreme Court gave a skewed interpretation of the Constitution. But as a prediction of the future – especially the Cold War era – their opinion was, for better or worse, only a modest overstatement. Whether this will change as the post-Cold War era further unfolds is a provocative question which cannot yet be answered.

Notes

1   See L. Gelb and R. Betts, *The Irony of Vietnam: The System Worked* (Washington, DC, Brookings, 1979).

2   The best treatment of this theme is in R. Berger, *Executive Privilege* (New York, Bantam Books, 1975).

3   Alexander Hamilton, *The Federalist* 69, quoted in H. Bailey and J. Shafritz, eds, *The American Presidency* (Chicago, Dorsey Press, 1988), p. 21. Emphasis in original.

4   James Madison, *Letters of Helvidius*, quoted in Berger, *Executive Privilege*, p. 77.

5   Hamilton, *The Federalist* 70, in Bailey and Shafritz, eds, *The American Presidency*, p. 25. See also Berger, *Executive Privilege*, ch. 4. A counter-argument may be found in K. M. Holland, 'The war powers resolution', in R. G. Hoxie, ed., *The Presidency and National Security Policy* (New York, Centre for the Study of the Presidency, 1984).

6   Cited in Berger, *Executive Privilege*, pp. 87–8. See also E. S. Corwin, *The President: Office and Powers, 1787–1957* (New York, New York University Press, 1957), p. 19. The great exception of the nineteenth century was the Presidency of Abraham Lincoln (1861–65), who dominated war decisions during the Civil War. But that was a national emergency of the highest order, uncharacteristic of the rest of the century.

7   Quoted in Corwin, *The President*, p. 26.

8   See J. T. Flexner, *Washington: The Indispensable Man* (New York, Little, Brown, 1969), chs. 4–6.

9   Quoted in Bailey and Shafritz, eds, *The American Presidency*, p. 35.

10   R. Sherwood, *Roosevelt and Hopkins* (New York, Harpers, 1948), pp. 262–3.

11   H. S. Truman, *Memoirs*, vol. 2 (New York, Doubleday, 1956), p. 333;

M. Miller, *Plain Speaking: An Oral Biography of Harry Truman* (New York, Berkeley Publishing, 1974), pp. 273, 280–4.

12   Berger, *Executive Privilege*, pp. 84, 92; T. Eagleton, *War and Presidential Power* (New York, Liveright, 1974), p. 71.

13   See H. Levine and J. Smith, eds, *The Conduct of American Foreign Policy Debated* (New York, McGraw Hill, 1990), p. 19; *US v. Curtiss-Wright Export Corp.*, 299 US 304 (1936).

14   See R. Pious, *The American Presidency* (New York, Basic Books, 1979), pp. 16, 394–5.

15   See A. D. Sandler, *A Staff for the President* (Westport, Greenwood, 1989), chs. 8, 9, 11.

16   See O. R. Holsti and J. N. Rosenau, 'A leadership divided: the foreign policy beliefs of American leaders, 1976–84', in C. W. Kegley and E. R. Wittkopf, eds, *The Domestic Sources of American Foreign Policy* (New York, St Martin's, 1988), p. 30.

17   See Gelb and Betts, *The Irony of Vietnam*, pp. 68–74.

18   See D. Shapley, *Promise and Power: The Life and Times of Robert McNamara* (Boston, Little, Brown, 1993), pp. 92–4.

19   See G. R. Hess, 'Commitment in the age of counter-insurgency: Kennedy and Vietnam', in D. L. Anderson, ed., *Shadow on the White House* (Lawrence, University of Kansas Press, 1993).

20   See Y. F. Khong, *Analogies of War: Korea, Munich, Dien Bien Phu, and the Vietnam Decisions of 1965* (Princeton, Princeton University Press, 1992).

21   Some analysts think Johnson and/or Secretary of Defence Robert McNamara lied about the second attack in order to persuade Congress to vote the President a wide grant of war-making powers in Southeast Asia. Others write that the commanders in Vietnam and the decision-makers in Washington *thought* there had been a second attack at the time. See Gelb and Betts, *The Irony of Vietnam*, pp. 100–5; G. McT. Kahin, *Intervention* (New York, Knopf, 1986), pp. 219–25; E. D. Moise, *Tonkin Gulf and the Escalation of the Gulf War* (Chapel Hill, University of North Carolina Press, 1996).

22   See R. J. McMahon, ed., *Major Problems in the History of the Vietnam War* (2nd edn, Lexington, Heath, 1995), pp. 209–10.

23   See D. M. Barrett, 'The mythology surrounding Lyndon Johnson, his Vietnam advisers', *Political Science Quarterly*, 103 (1988–89), pp. 736–63; D. M. Barrett, *Uncertain Warriors: Lyndon Johnson and his Vietnam Advisers* (Lawrence, University of Kansas Press, 1993).

24   L. B. Johnson, *The Vantage Point* (New York, Holt, Rinehart and Winston, 1971), p. 153.

25   According to *The Gallup Poll Index*, April 1968, in late 1968 only 28 per cent of Americans polled approved of Johnson's 'handling of the situation in Vietnam'. See Gelb and Betts, *The Irony of Vietnam*, pp. 91–197.

26   See L. Fisher, *Presidential War Power* (Lawrence, University of Kansas Press, 1995), pp. 128–33; P. D. Robbins, 'The war powers resolution after fifteen years', *American University Law Review*, 38 (1988), pp. 171–92.

27   See Corwin, *The President*, p. 171.

28   See B. Woodward, *The Commanders* (New York, Simon and Schuster, 1991), pp. 337–58; J. Dumbrell, 'The US Congress and the Gulf War', in J. Walsh, ed.,

The Gulf War Did Not Happen (Aldershot, Arena, 1995).

29   *Public Papers of the Presidents of the United States: George Bush, 1991* (Washington DC, US Government Printing Office, 1992), p. 20.

30   *Congressional Record*, 19 Jan. 1991, 146.

31   *Ibid.*, 14 Sept. 1994, 12886. Cohen became Defence Secretary in Clinton's second term.

32   *Weekly Compilation of Presidential Documents* (Washington, DC, Office of the Federal Register), vol. 30, no. 31, p. 1616.

33   *Congressional Quarterly Almanac*, 1994, p. 451.

34   See L. Berman and E. Goldman, 'Clinton's foreign policy at midterm', in C. Campbell and B. Rockman, eds, *The Clinton Presidency: First Appraisals* (Chatham, Chatham House, 1996).

35   H. Kissinger, *White House Years* (Boston, Little, Brown, 1979), p. 11.

36   *Ibid.*, p. 28.

37   C. Vance, *Hard Choices* (New York, Simon and Schuster, 1983); G. Shultz, *Turmoil and Triumph* (New York, Scribner's, 1993).

38   See S. Sarkesian, *US National Security: Policymakers, Processes, and Politics* (Boulder, Lynne Rienner, 1995), p. 161; on Chirac, see E. Sciolino, 'Bosnia policy', *New York Times News Service* (internet), 29 July 1996.

39   See E. Redford and R. McCulley, *White House Operations: The Johnson Presidency* (Austin, University of Texas Press, 1986), pp. 69–75.

40   See S. Erlanger and D. Singer, 'On global stage' and 'The President's brain trust', in *New York Times News Service* (internet), 21 July and 29 July 1996.

41   See Barrett, *Uncertain Warriors*.

42   G. Ford, *A Time for Healing* (New York, Berkeley Books, 1980), pp. 268–72.

43   A. George, *Presidential Decisionmaking in Foreign Policy* (Boulder, Westview, 1980).

44   Of these Presidents, Eisenhower relied the most on formal NSC meetings, but even he depended on a triumvirate of his Secretaries of State, Defence and Treasury to review important foreign policy plans. See P. G. Henderson, *Managing the Presidency: The Eisenhower Legacy* (Boulder, Westview, 1988), ch. 3.

45   J. Mayer and D. McManus, *Landslide* (Boston, Houghton-Mifflin, 1989), p. 187.

46   T. G. Paterson, *Meeting the Communist Threat* (New York, Oxford University Press, 1988), p. 222.

47   See R. Nixon, *RN: The Memoirs of Richard Nixon* (New York, Grosset and Dunlap, 1978), p. 490.

48   J. Carter, *Why Not the Best?* (Nashville, Broadman Press, 1975), pp. 140–41.

49   J. Muravchik, *The Uncertain Crusade* (Lanham, Hamilton Press, 1986), p. 40.

50   *Ibid.*, pp. 29, 43.

51   See Z. Brzezinski, *Power and Principle* (London, Weidenfeld and Nicolson, 1983), pp. 124–9.

52   *President Carter, 1979* (Washington DC, Congressional Quarterly Press, 1980), p. 41.

53   E. C. Hargrove, *Jimmy Carter as President* (Baton Rouge, Louisiana State University Press, 1988), pp. 155, 158.

54   See J. Dumbrell, *The Carter Presidency: A Re-evaluation* (Manchester, Manchester University Press, 1995); D. Brinkley, 'The rising stock of Jimmy Carter',

Diplomatic History, 20 (1996), pp. 505–29.

55 Quoted in Paterson, *Meeting the Communist Threat*, p. 256.

56 *Ibid.*, p. 257.

57 See A. Yoder, *The Conduct of American Foreign Policy since World War II* (New York, Pergamon, 1986), p. 168.

58 Mayer and McManus, *Landslide*, p. 387.

59 *The Tower Commission Report* (New York, Times Books, 1987), p. 231.

60 *Ibid.*, pp. 71, 79.

61 See C. Menges, *Inside the National Security Council* (New York, Simon and Schuster, 1988); A. M. Haig, *Caveat* (New York, Macmillan, 1984), ch. 14.

62 Quoted in A. Cigler and B. Loomis, *American Politics* (Boston, Houghton-Mifflin, 1989), p. 655.

63 See M. Beschloss and S. Talbott, *At the Highest Levels: The Inside Story of the End of the Cold War* (Boston, Little, Brown, 1993).

64 Woodward, *The Commanders*, p. 333.

65 See J. Heidenrich, 'The Gulf War: how many Iraqis died?', *Foreign Policy*, 90 (1993), pp. 108–25.

66 See B. Jentleson, *With Friends Like These: Reagan, Bush, and Saddam, 1982–1990* (New York, Norton, 1994); J. A. Baker, *The Politics of Diplomacy* (New York, Putnam's Sons, 1995), chs. 15–16.

67 *New York Times*, 12 Dec. 1989.

68 See Woodward, *The Commanders*, chs. 11–15.

69 See R. A. Pastor, *Whirlpool: US Foreign Policy toward Latin America and the Caribbean* (Princeton, Princeton University Press, 1992), pp. 90–101.

70 Sciolino, 'Bosnia policy', *New York Times News Service* (internet), 29 July 1996.

71 *Ibid.*

72 'Clinton's three big objectives', interview transcript, *New York Times News Service* (internet), 29 July 1996.

73 'Press briefing by Secretary of State Christopher', press release by office of the White House Secretary, 2 Oct. 1996.

74 *New York Times News Service* (internet), 6 Sept. 1996; J. Rielly, ed., *American Public Opinion and US Foreign Policy, 1995* (Chicago, Chicago Council on Foreign Relations, 1995).

75 See M. Mandelbaum, 'Foreign policy as social work', *Foreign Affairs*, 75 (1996), pp. 16–32; Kantor, quoted in Erlanger and Sanger, 'On global stage', *New York Times News Service* (internet), 29 July 1996.

76 Quoted in F. Zakaria, 'Groping for a vision', *Newsweek*, 16 Dec. 1996, p. 15. See also M. Cox, *US Foreign Policy after the Cold War: Superpower without a mission?* (London, Pinter/Royal Institute of International Affairs, 1995).

4

Executive branch foreign policy

A large range of executive branch agencies has long been involved in the making of foreign policy. The Treasury Department, for example, has interests in all foreign economic issues, especially those involving the value of the dollar. The Agriculture Department is closely involved in foreign aid issues and the – frequently highly sensitive – politics of US grain sales. The US Trade Representative, elevated to Cabinet status during the Ford Administration, attempts to coordinate diplomacy relevant to his or her office. With the end of the Cold War, and the redefinition of 'national security' to emphasise 'economic security', the role of these economic agencies expanded. The Commerce Department, headed in the early Clinton years by Ron Brown, became a vigorous champion of America's economic diplomacy. President Clinton set up the National Economic Council partly to ensure that 'foreign', 'economic' and 'domestic' decisions would not be damagingly separated. However, we should not accept too uncritically the view that all had changed with the end of the Cold War. Clinton's agenda, especially after 1994, reverted in some degree to security concerns – in Bosnia for example – which related to traditional agencies of American diplomatic and military capability.

1 National Security Adviser and Secretary of State

The case for locating foreign policymaking firmly in the Secretary and Department of State has been frequently made, and has been accorded lipservice even by its most conspicuous bureaucratic opponents. Henry Kissinger, the most powerful of all NSAs, later wrote of his conversion to the view that 'a president should make the secretary of state his principal adviser', with the NSA primarily a senior administrator and coordinator.[1] Zbigniew Brzezinski, President Carter's NSA, declared in December 1976: 'I don't envisage my job as a policymaking job. I see my job essentially as heading the operational staff of the president, helping him integrate policy, but above all, helping to facilitate the process of decision-making in which he will consult closely with his principal cabinet members.'[2] Brzezinski never attained Kissinger's eminence, later writing that he knew Carter would never countenance this.[3] Nevertheless, his rapid advance to the status of policymaker and policy advocate made nonsense of his 1976 promise.

This lip-service acknowledges the fact that the Secretary of State is, in formal terms, the leading Cabinet officer. He heads a department with unmatched expertise and potential for taking the long-term perspective on international questions. In a sense, it was the State Department, or at least George Kennan and its Policy Planning staff who 'invented' the modern world in the early years of the Cold War.

The NSA's organisational origins derive from the NSC system set up in 1947, and from the putative need for Presidents to have on their staff a manager and coordinator for foreign policy. The emergence of the NSA (otherwise 'assistant', 'NSC staff director' or 'special assistant') as a potential rival or counterweight to the Secretary of State occurred under Presidents Kennedy and Johnson. As John Prados writes, the very phrase, 'National Security Council', changed its meaning during this period:

> [It] no longer means what it did in Eisenhower's time. Today most people asked about the NSC would think of the national security adviser and his small *staff* of aides in the West Wing and Old Executive Office Building. In Ike's day the NSC was the President in council or, at a minimum, a reference to the NSC principals – the Vice President and secretaries of state and defense.[4]

McGeorge Bundy, JFK's Special Assistant for National Security Affairs made clear his view that the NSC staff should transcend the distinction made in the Eisenhower Administration between 'planning' and 'operations': 'It seems to us best that the NSC staff, which is essentially a Presidential instrument, should be composed of men who can serve equally well in the process of planning and in the operational follow-up.'[5] In the person of W. W. Rostow, who took over from Bundy in 1966, the NSA became a staunch, and highly public policy advocate.

Since the Johnson years, the NSA and the Secretary of State have generally been perceived as natural adversaries. As David Barrett indicated in the previous chapter, communication between NSA Kissinger and Secretary of State William Rogers during the Nixon years was minimal. Kissinger apparently often directed his staff: 'Don't tell Rogers'.[6] Kissinger himself occupied both posts between 1973 and 1976. President Ford's appointment of Brent Scowcroft (Kissinger's former NSC staff deputy) as NSA in 1976 did not represent a threat to Secretary Kissinger. However, the relationship between NSA Brzezinski and Secretary of State Cyrus Vance during Carter's Presidency was acrimonious and deeply damaging to the conduct of policy in this period. The two clashed publicly over substantive policy: for example, over approaches to the Horn of Africa conflict, and over the extent to which

Soviet behaviour in such areas should be linked to the US stance on arms control. Carter's tendency to back Brzezinski's harder line in the period following the 1979 Soviet invasion of Afghanistan, served to isolate Vance, who resigned in 1980.[7]

Reagan's first Secretary of State, Alexander Haig, experienced severe problems of gaining access to the President. He also tended, as a former Kissinger associate and a bureaucratic defender of his departmental interests, to be distrusted by Reagan insiders. Haig later accused William Clark, Reagan's second NSA, of 'conducting a second foreign policy' in the Middle East.[8] Conflict with Clark, and more especially with the White House 'troika' of James Baker, Ed Meese and Michael Deaver, precipitated Haig's 1982 resignation. Reagan later recalled of Haig: 'He didn't even want me as the president to be involved in setting foreign policy – he regarded it as his turf.'[9] Despite William Clark's close friendship with Reagan, none of Reagan's NSAs (Richard Allen, Clark, Robert McFarlane, John Poindexter, Frank Carlucci and Colin Powell) was a particularly powerful figure. It is one of the ironies of the Reagan Presidency that an Administration which became notorious for the unaccountable irresponsibility of its NSC staff (in the Iran–Contra affair) actually encompassed a substantial downgrading of the NSA post. Allen did not even have direct access to the President. At least before Carlucci's appointment, little effort appeared to be expended upon recruiting competent and experienced personnel; Clark was appointed largely as a means of checking Haig (he held the NSA and Under-Secretary of State positions simultaneously). According to Reagan's press spokesman, the 'President and his top aides' held the NSA post in low esteem, and paid 'little attention to those who held the post'.[10] The resultant situation was summarised by Spanier and Uslaner:

> while the secretary of state was not ... given the authority to be Reagan's spokesman and number one policy maker, the president's lack of interest and competence in foreign policy meant that the conflicts that naturally erupt in any administration were usually not resolved. The result was that the secretary of state, secretary of defense, CIA director ... and others were continuously feuding. Instead of a battle between the secretary of state and NSA, the Reagan administration ended up with a confused melee.[11]

Conflicts between Reagan's NSAs and his Secretaries of State – notably between Haig and Allen, Haig and Clark, between Secretary George Shultz and Clark, and between Shultz and Carlucci – were frequently made public. In his memoirs, Shultz wrote that the NSC staff 'improperly used the power of the White House while escaping the accountability of the rest of the executive branch'. The blame, according to Shultz, was Reagan's. The President 'frustrated' his Secretary of State by 'his unwillingness to come to grips with the debilitating acrimony among his national security advisers', and by his 'over-reliance on his immediate staff'.[12]

As indicated in the previous chapter, President Bush's NSC system worked far more successfully and harmoniously than its equivalent under Carter or Reagan. Yet the system, structured around its Principals Committee (centred on NSA Brent Scowcroft, Secretary of State James Baker and Defence Secretary Richard Cheney), regularly failed to deliver policy. Key decisions were made by *ad hoc* groups chaired by Bush, rather than by the Principals Committee. Baker worked through a tight inner circle at the State Department. Scowcroft assumed the role of foreign policy coordinator, manager, adviser *and* operator. However, Baker and Scowcroft shared a pragmatically conservative outlook, and avoided confrontation, although not differences of emphasis (for example, Scowcroft tended to be more cautious on Soviet issues than Baker, while the latter tended toward a more moderate position in the early stages of the Gulf crisis in 1990). James Baker later wrote:

> our differences never took the form of the backbiting of the Kissinger–Rogers, Vance–Brzezinski eras, or the slugfests of our national security teams during the Reagan years. There was no trashing of colleagues at the upper levels, and very little leaking to the press.[13]

The harmony of the Baker–Scowcroft relationship actually led some observers to raise the spectre of a dangerously uncritical 'groupthink'.

President Clinton committed himself – as Carter had before him – to a State Department which would implement policy, and a White House which would formulate it. Predictably, the division between 'thinking' and 'doing' broke down, as it had under Carter. NSA Anthony Lake, though a slightly diffident figure very much not in the mould of a Kissinger or a Brzezinski, became an activist operator on issues such as the growing Administration involvement in the politics of Northern Ireland. Secretary of State Warren Christopher, a veteran of the Carter-era rivalries, and Lake – a former Kissinger staffer, as well as a Carter employee (he resigned from Kissinger's staff in 1970 in protest at the Cambodian invasion) – undertook to avoid past mistakes. Yet, by July 1994, the *Washington Post* was reporting 'bitter tension' between the White House and the State Department. The transferral of White House counsellor David Gergen to State, reportedly to provide it with 'political reality checks in the foreign policy arena', illustrated this tension.[14] The Haitian invasion of September 1994 was undertaken with a minimum of State Department involvement. Throughout much of 1994, Christopher seemed to be on a kind of 'probation', which was only lifted in January 1995. The bureaucratic eminence of Assistant Secretary of State Richard Holbrooke during 1994 and 1995 was also interpreted as a rebuff both for Christopher *and* Lake.[15]

Bureaucratic and career rivalries are endemic in all organisational politics. Unless carefully policed and monitored by Presidents, however, the NSA–Secretary of State rivalry can destroy any purposive coherence within the Administration. The influence and status of the NSA in particular depends ultimately on the will of the President. He will rarely confine him-self – or be confined by the President – to 'neutral' managerial tasks. Many Presidents quickly see the advantage of using the NSA to promote particular positions within the foreign policy bureaucracy. The NSA and NSC staffers also regularly strengthen their bureaucratic positions by developing their own informational sources and 'back channels'. A common temptation is to highlight these sources at the expense of information emanating from the State Department.

Most controversial of all is the involvement of the NSA or the NSC staff in actual foreign policy operations. In a study published in 1984, Anthony Lake (along with I. M. Destler and Leslie Gelb) insisted that the NSA should be 'strictly an inside operator' with no public or even diplomatic function.[16] As noted above, Lake's own conduct as Clinton's NSA did not always reflect this self-denying ordinance. Most recent Presidents have used NSAs as free-wheeling, high-level diplomats and, indeed, as actual negotiators. Carter employed Brzezinski, over Cyrus Vance's protest, to negotiate the process whereby US relations with mainland China were to be normalised. In December 1989, Brent Scowcroft (serving his second stint as an NSA) was dispatched by President Bush to Beijing to re-open US–Chinese relations after the Tiananmen Square massacres. A clear distinction should be made between this public (or at least quasi-public) activity and NSC covert opera-tions. The Tower Commission report on Iran–Contra noted: 'As a general matter, the NSC staff should not engage in the implementation of policy or the conduct of operations. This compromises their oversight role and usurps the responsibilities of the departments and agencies.'[17] There may, of course, be a very fine line between flexibility and irresponsibility. From the Presi-dent's point of view, NSC operations are inescapably high-risk. Failures cannot plausibly be laid at any door other than the Chief Executive's. Ulti-mately, the case against NSC covert operations is a legal one. Congress does not appropriate funds for such operations. If they belong anywhere, their natural bureaucratic lodging is in the CIA.

Why do Presidents tend, sometimes despite their original intentions, to turn away from the State Department and towards the NSA and NSC staff? The answer lies partially in simple proximity. In most Administrations, the Secretary of State – despite his participation in the NSC and some kind of Principals Committee – is not part, nor does he partake in the developing experiential group identity, of the inner White House. He is a departmental 'baron' rather than a Presidential 'courtier'.[18] The NSA and NSC staff tend to be seen as flexible, responsive, relatively free of bureaucratic baggage, and sensitive to the President's political and electoral interests. As Leslie Gelb writes: 'Once a president comes to believe that Foggy Bottom (i.e., the State Department) is not attuned to politics, they are doomed to being ignored. Once he concludes that his staff has political savvy, that staff is on its way to dominating policymaking.'[19] 'Staff' in this context refers to domestic White

House, as well as NSC, staff. Friction between the NSA and the domestic White House political staff is not uncommon. President Ford's political aides, for example, saw Kissinger's public stature as potentially undermining the President's authority; stories were leaked to demonstrate that Ford was capable of overruling Kissinger.[20] The foreign policy staff, unlike the Secretary of State, are also non-confirmable appointees, and are regarded by Presidents as relatively removed from Congressional oversight. In B. A. Rockman's terms, the NSA and NSC staff are 'irregulars': similar to the 'high-flyers of the British civil service', but without 'the latter's attachment to the civil service system'.[21] It is commonly observed that several of the most influential of recent Secretaries of State – John Foster Dulles (1953–59), Kissinger (1973–77) and James Baker (1989–92) – have also made light of their departmental responsibilities.

George Shultz (1982–89) demonstrated that it is not impossible to combine departmental commitment with effective policy advocacy. Generally, however, any Secretary of State who attempts scrupulously to derive policy from the various segments of the State Department runs the risk of self-imposed paralysis. Conversely, as Snow and Brown conclude: 'A strong secretary of state ... does not necessarily mean a strengthened role for the Department of State. As often as not, it leads to precisely the opposite: a leaderless, ignored, and demoralized institution.'[22]

2 The State Department

Created in 1789, the State Department in 1994 employed approximately 26,500 people, 16,000 of them posted abroad. The Department has primary responsibility for forming, implementing and articulating US foreign policy. It is organised as a hierarchy, headed by the Secretary of State and centred around various geographic and functional bureaux. Each of the regional bureaux is divided into a number of country or area 'desks'. Long-range planning is, in theory, concentrated in the Policy Planning staff, located in the Policy Planning Council. The Department has many virtues which any NSC staff would find it impossible to emulate. By definition, the NSA and his staff, as Presidential creatures, lack continuity and institutional memory. The flexibility of the NSA/NSC staff system may allow it to short-circuit bureaucratic procedures. It may also, in the words of Christopher Shoemaker, 'allow impractical or silly ideas to surface' that would have been 'properly squelched' if they had surfaced in the State Department.[23] Upon being appointed to head the Department in 1977, Cyrus Vance noted that, although 'small in number of personnel and budget', it contained 'probably the most able and dedicated professional group in the federal government'.[24]

Yet even Vance felt that 'the department was haunted by widespread doubt concerning its primacy and role in the management of foreign affairs'. The problem was not only the Nixon–Kissinger legacy. Vance found a

'labyrinthine hierarchy of geographic and functional offices' lacking coordination and purpose.[25] A 1989 article in the *Foreign Service Journal* by a
former director of the executive development staff of the Foreign Services
Institute began: 'The Department of State has qualities of a second-rate
organisation: a poorly articulated mission, ill-defined goals, unhappy
employees ... and an apparent indifference to developing effective executives.'[26] A piece in the same edition of the *Journal*, written by a Foreign Service Officer (FSO), elaborated on the Department's image problem:

> State ... has been tarred with several negative stereotypes. Some of these, such
> as the perception that FSOs defend the interests of foreign countries better than
> those of our own country, are difficult to avoid. Others, such as the label 'elit-
> ist' or 'arrogant' seem unfair and are carried over from another era. The image
> of a secretive Foreign Service trying to keep a meddling Congress out of our
> business may be the most difficult stereotype to overcome.[27]

State's image problem is to some extent the product of sniping by White
House officials. President Nixon and his close associates made no secret of
their antipathy towards an organisation which they saw as dominated by
East coast Democrats. Kissinger later recorded Nixon's contempt for the
State Department, tracing it to the disdain shown him by FSOs when Nixon
had been Vice-President under Eisenhower.[28] In the early Reagan years, FSO
promotions were monitored by the White House political staff, who sought
thereby to promote Reaganite ideology in this supposedly hostile environment.[29] Incoming Secretaries of State also invariably express astonishment at
the Department's complex organisation and its inability to integrate its routine functions with its policy formulation responsibilities. In 1993, Warren
Christopher realigned the top management of the Department, naming five
Under-Secretaries – for political affairs; economics, business and agriculture;
arms control and international security; global affairs; and management – as
his major advisers. Secretaries of State, seen by the White House as potential bureaucratic co-optees, tend to be perceived by their own career staff as
insufficiently protective of the Department's interests. Warren Christopher
faced considerable criticism from his own ranks for his supposed lack of
imagination in facing post-1994 Congressional budget-cutters.[30]

All these tensions feed into and magnify negative perceptions of State. The
end of the Cold War did seem to open new opportunities for the Policy Planning staff – even to recreate the conditions of its golden age. However, the
whole array of spending on foreign aid, embassies, public diplomacy,
exchange programmes and international budgets generally, soon came under
attack, especially after 1994 from the Congressional Republican majority.
Exchange programmes, for example, were attacked as 'middle-class pork'
and foreign aid as a 'rathole'.[31] Republican attacks on FSO elitism recalled
those of their forebears during the McCarthy era of the early 1950s. In
1995, Republican Senate Foreign Relations Committee chairman Jesse

Helms launched a plan designed to eliminate the Agency for International Development, the US Information Agency and the Arms Control and Disarmament Agency. Helms sought to collapse these quasi-independent agencies – administered by State – into the State Department, as a prelude to 'a major re-examination of attitudinal, procedural and management issues within the department itself'.[32] The Helms plan, which eventually succumbed to Presidential veto, was built on pre-emptive reorganisation initiatives advocated by Warren Christopher himself, but reportedly rejected by Vice-President Gore. The Vice-President's own 'reinventing government' report on the State Department, published in 1993, called for the integration of State's 'policy, program and resource management processes' to suit its post-Cold War role and its 'increasingly limited resources'.[33]

Throughout its recent history, the Department has been subjected to virtually constant reorganisation planning, with a consequent damage to employee morale. In 1996, former Secretary of State Lawrence Eagleburger and former Ambassador Robert Barry attacked 'Balkanization at the upper levels' and called for 'a radical reduction in the number of assistant secretaries'. The Eagleburger–Barry criticisms – along with Al Gore's report, several internal studies and a report produced by the Carnegie Endowment in 1992 – argued the need for State to reorganise for global interdependency, especially 'giving trade its due'.[34] The rise of interdependency has allowed rival bureaucratic players into State's traditional 'turf', an area which the Department has not been able successfully to redefine. The internal State Department report, *State 2000*, announced that 'we must integrate foreign and domestic policy. We must learn, in fact, to see them as two parts of one whole.'[35] Recent years have also seen an intensification of the tendency for interdepartmental networks of influence and loyalty to develop and cut across traditional institutional identifications. Economic and trade specialists within State may, for example, look for bureaucratic allies not to the Department, but to the Treasury, the Office of Management and Budget (in the President's Executive Office) and to relevant staffers in Congress.

Modern communications and the rise of the international economic agenda have also tended to damage the prestige of the institution at the heart of State's operational prerogative: the ambassador and embassy staff. In 1995, Frank McNeil (former ambassador to Costa Rica) attacked such traditional institutions as 'archaeological curiosities' in an age of new technology and the 'Third Wave'. According to McNeil: 'The next Kissinger will be a diplomancer, a surfer on the wave of virtual diplomacy.'[36]

Such sentiments, especially when voiced by a former diplomat, serve further to stimulate defensiveness in the culture of America's professional Foreign Service. Some empirical studies have shown FSOs to be quite responsive to public opinion and sensitive to demands of democratic accountability.[37] However, the tradition of 'up-or-out' cutthroat promotion schedules has fostered an introverted culture of competition and corridor survival. The

1980 Foreign Service Act was designed to strike a balance between excessive specialisation and excessive generalisation, as well as to ameliorate some of the worst excesses of the 'up-or-out' system. The Act gave each FSO twenty years to gain promotion – the 'corridor and water cooler struggle' – to the new Senior Foreign Service.[38] Rapidly, a premium developed upon managerial experience, at the expense of specialist – particularly linguistic – expertise. Various subsequent initiatives attempted, without obvious success, to reinvigorate the Foreign Service and to imbue it with a clear sense of purpose, while civilising career competition.

Meanwhile, traditional criticisms and misconceptions continue. One common accusation is that of FSO clientism – the close identification between diplomatic staff and host regimes and local interests. President Johnson is reported to have told the Indian ambassador in 1968 that the Indian leader ('Madame Gandhi') did not know how lucky she was: 'She's got two ambassadors working for her ... you here and [US ambassador Chester] Bowles out there.'[39] Warren Christopher contributed to such perceptions when he stated in 1994 that his job was to staff 'America's desk'.[40] Obviously, clientism does exist, and diplomats should remember that their job is to represent the United States in foreign countries, rather than vice versa. The Clinton Administration's emphasis on 'economic security' in foreign policy involved a new FSO training curriculum, designed to emphasise trade promotion and to leave diplomats in no doubt as to where their responsibilities lay. When James Cheek assumed the post of US Ambassador in Buenos Aires in 1993, he immediately announced his main purpose as being to lobby for US business in Argentina.[41] The job of embassies, however, should not be allowed to slide merely into trade promotion. They are the eyes and ears of US foreign policy. The historical record is littered with examples of astute ambassadorial warnings and assessments being either ignored or discounted.

Public misconceptions of US diplomacy and its costs were evident in polls taken in the mid-1990s. They revealed massive public overestimation of the amount of federal spending going to foreign affairs. Warren Christopher told Congress in 1996 that the US international budget had actually been cut by half in real dollars since 1984.[42] State Department employees began to display buttons bearing the slogan, 'JUST ONE PER CENT' – a reminder of the real proportion of federal tax dollars devoted to foreign and diplomatic spending. State's ability to counter misconceptions and hostility is actually diminished by its very lack of a huge budget, with consequent vested interests. Lacking natural domestic constituencies, State regularly loses out to the Department of Defence. Foreign policy and diplomacy is also, unlike defence, an area relatively lacking in inhibiting technical jargon. Its apparent openness to all, combined with State's reputation for caution, positively encourages bureaucratic invasions.

3   The Pentagon

Headquartered in the Pentagon – the world's largest office building, just over the Virginia perimeter of Washington DC, – the Defence Department was created as a unified body only in the wake of World War Two. At the conclusion of the Cold War, it employed approximately three million people, about two million of them in uniform. Around 70 per cent of all federal government employees worked for the Pentagon. The Department's spending accounted for over one quarter of all Congressionally appropriated dollars. The termination of the Cold War in a sense extinguished the Department's very *raison d'être*.

The use or threat of force has been a continuous theme within American foreign policy since 1945. Post-World War Two Presidents have presided over a 'warfare' or 'national security' state. The developing Cold War saw a blurring of the distinction between defence and foreign policy: a militarisation of diplomacy and a consequent endemic tension between the Pentagon and the State Department. Nonetheless, the United States has not developed a praetorian military on the Latin American model. Civilian–military relations have often been poor. Indeed, President Clinton had particular problems in this area, associated with his own record in the Vietnam War era and his early handling of the issue of gays in the services.[43] However, the United States remains a clear prototype of the liberal model of civilian control of the military.[44] President Truman's dismissal of General Douglas MacArthur in 1951 provided a positive reference point for the upholding of this principle.

The Pentagon is headed by the civilian Secretary of Defence, who is assisted by a group of functional agencies grouped under the Office of the Secretary of Defence (OSD). Below the OSD, each branch of the military has its own service department. Military representation is aggregated in the Joint Chiefs of Staff (JCS), serviced by a joint staff. Despite the tradition of civilian control, civilian–military conflicts have been a persistent theme within the Pentagon's bureaucratic politics. James Forrestal, the first chief of the Defence Department upon its creation in 1947, declared that the military's peacetime mission was to 'destroy the Secretary of Defense'.[45] With no direct authority to dismiss or promote serving officers, the Secretary frequently finds himself pitted against formidable military–Congressional alliances. James Schlesinger (Defence Secretary 1973–75) observed in 1983 that his office 'provides the Secretary simply with a license to persuade outside parties. Even within the [Pentagon] building, quite frankly, it's only a license to persuade.'[46] Numerous reorganisations, such as that undertaken by Secretary Les Aspin in 1993 in relation to the OSD, have attempted – with limited success – to strengthen the Secretarial hand *vis-à-vis* the services.

No Secretary of Defence since the 1960s has attained the position of foreign policy influence occupied by Robert McNamara in the years of the escalation of the Vietnam conflict. McNamara's activist management style and

determination to assert civilian control at the Pentagon both upset service
sensibilities and reinforced his position as policy adviser. Caspar Weinberger
certainly held an important position within Reagan's decision-making structure, at least prior to the flowering of the President's dialogue with Soviet
leader Mikhail Gorbachev in the late 1980s. (Weinberger quit the Reagan
Administration in 1987.) Weinberger's advice, despite his distrust of Gorbachev, was certainly not consistently hawkish. The Pentagon did develop its
own covert operations facility in the early 1980s. Yet in the developing tension between the Secretary of Defence and Secretary of State George Shultz,
it was very often the former who tended to counsel caution. Indeed the
Reagan experience illustrates the folly of automatically identifying the Pentagon with hard-line militarism and State with a more cautious, softer
approach. Shultz saw Weinberger as excessively affected by post-Vietnam
inhibitions on the use of force. Commenting on US military exercises off the
Nicaraguan coast in 1983, Shultz felt 'we had a Pentagon that seemed to take
any means to avoid the *actual use* of American military power but every
opportunity to *display* it'.[47] Tensions between the Bush State Department
and Pentagon became evident in 1989 when Defence Secretary Cheney told
a television audience that Gorbachev's reforms would 'ultimately fail'. Secretary of State James Baker called on the White House to 'dump on Dick
with all possible alacrity', and a statement was issued to the effect that
Cheney's personal opinions did not reflect Administration policy. Cheney's
doubts about the use of force in Panama were also overruled by Bush later
in the year.[48]

    The sheer size of the Pentagon's remit is often held to compound admin-
istrative inefficiency and debilitating intra-Department rivalries. According
to Fred Thompson and L. R. Jones, during the Cold War the Pentagon 'failed
to clarify administrative boundaries and roles and mission responsibilities
and to delegate authority accordingly'. Gigantic levels of spending were
'crucial to management's failure to make farsighted choices about defense
organization or to understand the needs for those choices'.[49] The Secretary
is not confronted by a unified military, but one riven by inter- and intra-service rivalries. In a 1989 manual written for Pentagon employees, Major General Perry Smith described such rivalries as almost the defining characteristic
of life at the Defence Department: 'each of the four services (Army, Navy,
Air Force and Marines) has its own separate history, culture, clan, uniforms,
training establishment, staff colleges, bases, and, with the exception of the
Marine Corps, service academy and war college.' In some bureaucratic battles, the joint staff – accountable to the chairman of the JCS – constitute
another power base, opening the way to five-way contests. Intra-service
rivalries regularly surface at the level of defence procurement: for example,
rivalry between the strategic and tactical air commands. Perry Smith commented: 'If you find someone pushing a new weapons system hard, you
might ask yourself what subcommunity that individual comes from.'[50]

Equally destructive of rationality in the procurement process has been inter-service logrolling (mutual project support on a quid pro quo basis). Despite numerous scandals in the procurement process, the Pentagon has traditionally maintained an arms-length, competitive procurement regime. Many proposals for reform of the process centre on the need for the Department to adapt to sound commercial practice. In the early 1990s, about 40 per cent of the Pentagon's acquisition budget went on management and control of the procurement process, compared to an average of about 10 per cent in commercial enterprise. It can be argued that arms-length procurement competitiveness actually encourages waste and corruption more than the 'French model' of close, nurturing relationships with suppliers. Admiral F. R. Inman and David Burton wrote in 1994:

> The dominant characteristics of the defense procurement system are cost-plus contracts, high overhead costs, quality control based on inspection rather than design, highly specialized product requirements, limited production runs, long cycle-times, and restricted markets. They stand in stark contrast to commercial industry's preoccupation with flexibility, total quality control, volume manufacturing expertise, lean production, rapid cycle-time, and access to many different markets.[51]

The paralysing effect of inter-service rivalry stimulated a major defence reorganisation in 1986. A Congressional staff report prepared for Senators Goldwater and Nunn in the previous year highlighted the problem, and argued for an enhanced role for the JCS chairman. The report also criticised the 'limited mission integration' at the Pentagon and the 'imbalance between modernisation and readiness': 'current warfighting capabilities are robbed to pay for hardware in the distant future'.[52] Military reforms movements point to the Pentagon's fetish for new technology. New weapons systems often originate in the interstices of bureaucratic compromise, inter-service pulling and hauling, and the coincidental development of particular technologies, rather than in any objective need. The 1986 Goldwater–Nichols reforms attempted to encourage more coherent planning by providing career incentives to those engaged in trans-service duties. By 1994, the US military had over 9,000 joint duty (or 'purple suit') billets. The Joint Chiefs themselves supported the reforms, which gave new powers to the JCS chairman. Colin Powell, JCS chairman during the Gulf War, became – in Richard Kohn's words – 'the most powerful military leader since George C. Marshall' and 'the most political since Douglas MacArthur'.[53] Yet Goldwater–Nichols did not give the JCS chairman direct command of combat forces in the field; nor did it elevate him to automatic membership of the NSC. The Goldwater–Nichols reorganisation decisively shaped the impact made by Colin Powell on Gulf War decisions.[54]

The central problem of American defence policy is not one of a hawkish, praetorian military. Rather, it is a problem of adjusting to new conditions, new budgetary constraints and a new balance between readiness and modernisation. John Shalikashvili, JCS chairman under Clinton, declared that the Administration's mission was to 'redefine the relationship between diplomacy and force in the post-Cold War era'.[55] The Cold War stimulated institutionalised, high and accelerating levels of defence spending in the name of 'national security'. The failure in Vietnam provoked a temporary setback for the 'warfare state'. In constant dollars, military budgets were cut by 22 per cent between 1968 and 1975. By the early 1980s, the party had resumed. A Pentagon official involved in the formulation of defence procurement requests in 1981 recalled: 'I was in the Office of the Secretary, working for the readiness accounts. Carter had given us a lot. The Weinberger team came in and said, Add more. Find room to add. Find places to put more money.'[56] During these years, the Pentagon became a bureaucratic machine for generating spending. Explaining the Pentagon's apparent antipathy to the testing of military technology, an Air Force colonel told journalist Hedrick Smith: 'The reason the Pentagon doesn't like testing is that testing may interrupt the money flow to its programs. That's the strategy in the Pentagon: Don't interrupt the money flow.'[57] The Department's mindset had become one of finessing the dialectic of spending feast and spending famine – while all the time keeping the dollars flowing. By the early 1990s, it was obvious that transformed geopolitical conditions, combined with high US deficits, required a transformation in the culture and expectations of the military and its bureaucratic (and Congressional) allies.

The Bush Administration's understanding of the new military stance for the United States was developed under the title of 'baseforce'. By 1992, the Pentagon had articulated a strategy for reducing 2.1 million active duty troops to 1.6 million. The Administration accepted that, as Stephen Cimbala put it, 'the kinds of forces required for future multilateral or unilateral US military intervention will be … more mobile, technically advanced and elitist'.[58] The new environment seemed to encourage new inter-service rivalries, as the Army contested with the Marine Corps for pre-eminence as America's expeditionary force. (The Haitian invasion of 1994, however, involved quite effective inter-service cooperation.) Bush's 'baseforce' was geared towards deflection of any new superpower and protection of the regional enemies of Russia, Iraq and North Korea. A major controversy raged at this time about the wisdom of US 'microinterventions': calculated uses of force, rather than the Desert Storm model of massive-scale military intervention in pursuit of big goals. Les Aspin in September 1993 issued his 'bottom-up review' of military capabilities. Announcements made at this time by the Clinton Administration indicated that defence spending as a percentage of GDP would, by 1998, be less than half what it was in 1970. Aspin's main assumption was that the United States should be capable of fighting two 'nearly simultaneous' major regional conflicts.[59] The Clinton strategy was criticised in some quarters for not producing a significant 'peace dividend'. Benjamin Schwarz wrote in 1996 that in 1993 the new Administration 'concluded that the defense of US global interests still demanded military spending of more than 1.3 trillion [dollars] over the following five years and the permanent commitment of more than 200,000 US soldiers in East Asia and Europe – in other words, a strategy remarkably similar to that which America pursued during the Cold War'.[60] Many observers noted that spending levels did not seem to match commitments (including the commitment to keep 100,000 troops in Europe) – either commitments needed to be moderated, or spending needed to be *increased*. In 1994, the Administration announced that it was thinking in terms of a 1.4 million duty-active force. Both Aspin and his successor, William Perry, acknowledged the gap between spending and commitments. Perry indicated in 1994 that there would soon have to be an upturn in Pentagon procurements. Shalikashvili argued that 'modernization is tomorrow's readiness'.[61] Failure to achieve a satisfactory balance between readiness and modernisation can only presage a reappearance of the feast–famine cycle. The Clinton Administration retained a 'core strategic force' of 500 nuclear weapons in Europe. The 1994 Republican victories opened up intense battles over military spending, reigniting old controversies such as those concerning B-2 bomber acquisition and anti-missile defence.

4   The intelligence community

(a) *The community*   Although discussion of the US intelligence community inevitably focuses on the CIA, it must be remembered that the Pentagon is itself closely involved in intelligence gathering. Towards the end of the Cold War, it was estimated that the CIA had between 16,500 and 20,000 employees, with an annual budget of about one and a half billion dollars. Yet some estimates suggested that the CIA made up less than 15 per cent of the US intelligence community. Each of the armed services has its own intelligence arm, while the Defence Intelligence Agency – set up by Secretary of Defence Robert McNamara in 1961 – attempts a coordination role. However, the major portion of the Pentagon's Cold War intelligence budget went to the NSA – the 'puzzle palace', headquartered in Maryland. Principally concerned with signals intelligence, the NSA and its history are blanketed in secrecy. For the first five years of its life (1952–57), the NSA was in a kind of ontological limbo, its existence unacknowledged by the US government. Its enormous communications interception capabilities stimulated anxieties about domestic surveillance, an issue which the 1978 Foreign Intelligence Surveillance Act attempted to address. James Bamford wrote in the early 1980s that the NSA was 'free to pull into its massive vacuum cleaner every telephone call and message entering, leaving or transiting the country, as long as it is done by microwave interception'.[62] Especially when implicated in Iran–Contra, the NSA could not remain utterly immune from the 1990s debate about the proper role for post-Cold War intelligence.

Besides the CIA and the various Pentagon agencies, intelligence capabilities are located in various executive departments, including State and the Treasury, and in the Intelligence Division of the Federal Bureau of Investigation (FBI). The job of coordinating all this work falls ultimately, of course, to the President. Within the intelligence community itself, it is the CIA and its head (the Director of Central Intelligence or DCI) who try to lead and coordinate. The DCI chairs the National Foreign Intelligence Board and the National Intelligence Council: trans-agency bodies, designed to coordinate intelligence and to produce regular and specifically requested intelligence estimates on various parts of the world. The DCI's eminence has traditionally been based on deference, rather than direct control. Some Cold War DCIs, like James Schlesinger in 1973, tried consciously to take the reins. Others, tacitly acknowledging the quasi-federal structure of the whole operation, virtually admitted defeat.

(b) *The Cold War CIA*   The CIA was established under its first Director, R. H. Hillenkoettler, by the 1947 National Security Act. From its inception, the CIA embodied those Cold War concerns which elevated 'national security' over 'foreign policy'. Like the NSC itself, the CIA was an institutional embodiment of the 'trend towards non-accountable, subterranean policy-making and security operation'.[63] The early years of the CIA were concerned with the acquisition of a 'founding myth', derived in part from the those of the wartime Office of Strategic Services (OSS). (McGeorge Bundy later described the OSS as 'half cops-and-robbers and half faculty meeting'.)[64] The early CIA leadership also sought to establish bureaucratic standing. The 1949 Central Intelligence Act virtually exempted the Agency from normal oversight.

The very permissiveness of the founding Acts, especially the 1947 Act's mention of 'other functions' (besides intelligence-gathering) was to prove a double-edged sword. William Colby (DCI, 1973–76) later complained that the absence of a 'clear charter' had led to uncertainty and confusion.[65] What was clear, particularly in the 1949 Act, was that the CIA should not indulge in domestic intelligence. There should be no American Gestapo. Yet even this prohibition has not operated satisfactorily. On the one hand, it became evident by the late 1960s and early 1970s that the CIA had long been involved in domestic surveillance and in sponsoring domestic organisations. CIA funding of the National Student Association became a *cause célèbre* when revealed in *Ramparts* magazine in 1967. On the other hand, the domestic prohibition worked to the disadvantage of the CIA's strategic intelligence work. Cold War CIA estimates of Soviet military strength tended to lack an authoritative comparative element. The Agency rarely enjoyed access to raw Pentagon data on US military capabilities.

The early CIA turned to 'other functions' to secure its bureaucratic advancement. By 1953, major covert military and/or propaganda operations were under way in forty-eight countries. The CIA's buccaneering spirit and bureaucratic credibility were encouraged by the installation of pro-American regimes in Iran in 1953 and in Guatemala in 1954. The Cold War ethos encouraged irresponsibility. By the early 1960s, the Agency had acquired a reputation as a home for what former deputy DCI Ray Cline called 'romantic … "cowboy" types of covert action officers'.[66] The Agency's Cold War activism had enabled it to fend off McCarthyite attacks. However, it had also acquired a reputation on the right as a haven for Ivy League liberals inclined to underestimate Soviet strength. Recurring crises of 'intelligence failure' – what the CIA saw as the inability to predict the unpredictable – had also been experienced. Examples reverberated down the years, with the CIA being blamed for not anticipating riots attending the 1948 creation of the Organisation of American States in Bogota; the 1950 invasion from North Korea; the 1961 Bay of Pigs invasion fiasco in Cuba; the erection of the Berlin Wall in 1961; the Iranian revolution of 1979; and (more than a little unfairly) the eventual collapse of Soviet power in the early 1990s.

Despite President Kennedy's initial enthusiasm for the CIA, White House–agency relations deteriorated significantly during the era of the Vietnam War. President Nixon mounted a conscious campaign to politicise the CIA. According to Henry Kissinger, Nixon particularly distrusted DCI Richard Helms, seeing him as part of 'the liberal Georgetown set to which Nixon ascribed many of his difficulties'.[67] Using the NSC staff to double-check and interpret CIA raw data, Kissinger managed to establish a new control on intelligence.

The CIA's destabilisation of the Allende regime in Chile shocked liberal world opinion in the early 1970s. Within a few years, the Agency stood publicly accused of a range of acts of illegal intervention, murder and subversion: acts undertaken in the name of democracy, but actually contemptuous of the democratic process and of human rights. In 1973, James Schlesinger ordered the CIA bureaucracy to prepare a list of possibly illegal operations ('the family jewels'). Following revelations about the secret war in Laos by the CIA in the 1960s, Congress passed the Hughes–Ryan amendment (1974), requiring the reporting of covert operations to designated legislative committees. The Ford Administration, reacting to an anti-CIA gale, made efforts to tighten control of covert operations. Special committees in the Senate (under Frank Church) and the House (under Otis Pike) examined the CIA's record, coaxing DCI Colby to reveal some of the 'family jewels'.

Stansfield Turner, appointed DCI by President Carter in 1977 (after Carter had fired George Bush), committed himself to greater accountability. He publicly criticised the Agency's institutional culture. Yet Carter was ambivalent about the CIA: he was aware of past horrors, but increasingly anxious about impending effective intelligence. He was not prepared to condemn covert operations *per se*. On Capitol Hill also, as the Carter Presidency progressed, the concern became one of combining oversight with enhancement of CIA effectiveness. The 1980 Intelligence Oversight Act actually weakened the reporting requirements of the Hughes–Ryan amendment.

The frenetic atmosphere of the later Carter years, along with the 'intelligence failure' over Iran in 1979, provided the backdrop to President Reagan's appointment of William Casey as a Cabinet-level DCI in 1981. Reagan and Casey spoke of 'unleashing' the CIA. Under Casey, all the familiar CIA abuses were redoubled. The budget forged ahead, apparently uncontrollably, increasing at a probable compound rate of over 20 per cent annually. David McMichael, who quit the CIA in 1983, estimated that covert operations – the majority of which remained unreported to Congress – increased fivefold during the first Reagan Administration. The CIA became highly politicised, deeply implicated in 'secret' wars in Central America, in the Iran–Contra affair and in the administration of 'reprogrammed' funds to various anti-Soviet guerrilla forces throughout the world. An Executive Order, issued in 1981, actually set down conditions for CIA infiltration of private and academic institutions in the United States.[68]

Casey was frequently, and plausibly, accused of suppressing 'inconvenient' information, for example, concerning the Soviet shooting down of the aircraft KAL 007 in 1983. He was widely regarded as the most politicised DCI in history, regularly interweaving policy advocacy in his intelligence reports. (His successor, William Webster, was not accorded Cabinet status, nor enjoyed any great foreign policy influence.) Casey finessed information about Soviet economic weakness. Secretary of State Shultz considered him and his organisation 'as independent as a hog on ice'.[69] As his deputy Robert Gates later wrote: 'For Casey, the United States and the CIA were at war – just like when he was young and in the OSS – and speed and relevance to action were his benchmarks for effective analysis.' Nevertheless, CIA estimates of Soviet arms slowdown and economic difficulties did feed through, and had a major role in causing Reagan to ameliorate his 'evil empire' stance after 1983. By the late 1980s, as the Reagan–Gorbachev relationship developed, the CIA was – in the words of Deputy Director Gates – 'describing in considerable detail the failure of Gorbachev's reforms and the growing crisis in the Soviet Union'. Gates subsequently recorded that the inevitability of Soviet collapse was a CIA 'article of faith'. But 'the reluctance to forecast specific timing was born simply of uncertainty and political self-preservation. No one wanted to look the fool.'[70]

The central dilemma of Cold War intelligence revolved around the problem of objectivity. 'Pure' objectivity is probably a chimera. Lawrence Freedman thus described the position of the intelligence officer, attempting to estimate the military strength of a potential adversary:

> As an estimator is usually faced by a mass of confusing and contradictory data, in order to avoid a paralysing eclecticism he needs a 'point of view', a concep-

tual framework to enable him to select and organise the data and so create order out of chaos. This is why ... the conventional distinction between 'estimates of capabilities' and 'estimates of intentions' breaks down.

According to Freedman, the CIA's Cold War weaknesses included 'rigid adherence to professional norms and procedures, even when they inconvenience and irritate the clientele', and 'contempt for rivals who are considered less professional in their approach'. Yet Freedman found it 'hard ... to find examples where the CIA analyses have been distorted to satisfy the preconceived notions of its clientele'.[71] At various times during the Cold War, the CIA unquestionably did provide politicised, advocative intelligence. The Tower Commission investigation into Iran–Contra found evidence of this in connection with 1985 estimates on Iran. The (eventually successful) 1991 Senate confirmation hearings for Robert Gates's nomination as DCI centred on such charges.[72] Yet, as Freedman found, sustained CIA 'cooking' of intelligence is difficult to establish.

Besides the question of objectivity, critics and students of the Cold War CIA tended to concern themselves with covert operations. One strand of opinion favoured the formal distancing of operations from intelligence.[73] Various reforms over many years attempted to achieve this *within* the CIA, but intelligence and operations inevitably still came together at the Agency's highest levels. The option of removing operations completely from the CIA was not taken by any Cold War President (nor, indeed, in any Congressional statute). At another level, the debate on covert operations hinged upon the whole concept of Presidential control. The idea that the CIA provided a home for 'rogue elephants' figured prominently in the early deliberations of the Church Committee, although it was to some extent dropped in its final report. As a general theory, the 'rogue elephant' interpretation of the CIA is not very satisfactory. Certainly, the CIA frequently 'contracted out' operations to avoid oversight. During the Reagan years, a network of ex-CIA personnel and Cuban exiles operated in this manner, in an environment untouched by the law or democratic accountability. Nonetheless, the balance of the evidence suggests that the CIA has been an integral and consciously integrated arm of White House foreign policy. This was an important conclusion of the Pike Committee's study of covert operations between 1965 and 1975.[74] The 'rogue elephant' theory tends merely to strengthen the ability of Presidents plausibly to disclaim responsibility for failed, embarrassing or illegal projects.

Was there *any* justification in Cold War conditions for covert operations? After all, covert operations are scarcely an acceptable substitute for coherent foreign policy. They are inimical to the democratic process, and they antagonise world opinion. Their outcomes are difficult to predict or control. Former Secretary of State Dean Rusk once testified that the CIA needed to vie with the Soviets 'in the back alleys of the world'.[75] Richard Nixon in his memoirs wrote that CIA intervention against Salvador Allende in Chile had been justified by the fact that the Soviets also operated covertly.[76] These arguments affect an air of sad, world wisdom, but actually sail very close to a crassly relativistic view of the difference between democratic and totalitarian societies. It is also the case that the United States is party to a number of treaties and agreements (not least the United Nations charter) which are inimical to the kinds of operations undertaken by the CIA in Central America in the 1980s. There is also the question of from whom covert actions are meant to be concealed. The Reagan Administration's CIA interventions in Central America were scarcely even intended to be secret. As Gregory Treverton has argued, given that covert action is virtually a contradiction in terms, 'why not act openly?'.[77] However, few within America's Cold War political process wished to debar covert operations altogether, either within or outside the CIA. Senator James Abourezk's 1974 proposal to do so floundered, even in the anti-CIA context of the time. The Hughes–Ryan amendment countenanced covert action if 'important to national security'. Perhaps Cyrus Vance was right to argue that there are occasions 'when no other means will do'.[78] However, in a democratic system, decisions about covert actions must be resolved by the democratic process. In the American governmental context, this necessitates an important role for Congress.

(c) *After the Cold War*   The traditional Cold War attitude of Congress towards the CIA was summarised by Senator John Stennis, chairman of the Armed Services Committee in 1971: 'You have to make up your mind that you are going to have an intelligence agency and protect it as such, and shut your eyes and take what is coming.'[79] Efforts were made to demystify the Agency during the 'new oversight' era of the 1970s. Presidents were required to produce a 'finding' – a formal policy justification – for each covert action. Congress did eventually react to abuses of CIA authority under President Reagan.[80] Overall, however, the record of Congressional oversight of the CIA has been poor. Senator David Patrick Moynihan, leading Democrat on the Senate Intelligence Committee in the mid-1980s, remarked: 'Like other legislative committees, ours came to be an advocate for the agency it was overseeing.'[81]

The end of the Cold War stripped away the anti-communist basis of Congressional deference to the Agency. Renewed Congressional activism was signalled in November 1989 with the incorporation into the intelligence spending bill of a provision for a statutory CIA inspector-general, with a special duty to report to Congress. The provision was predictably criticised by former DCIs Richard Helms and James Schlesinger as 'micromanagement at its worst'.[82] Yet it became evident that blanket resistance to oversight was no longer an option. Where William Casey famously declared in 1984, 'the business of Congress is to stay out of my business', DCI William Webster was prepared to acknowledge the mutual value of oversight.[83] Congressional overseers could use the changed circumstances to acquire expertise (though, of course, in the process running the risk of the kind of clientism described by Moynihan). In 1994, Congress embarked on a thoroughgoing, unprecedented review of the Agency. Opening budgets and making sweeping organisational recommendations, Congress was – in the words of one commentator – 'forcing the CIA to become something like a company undergoing a court-supervised bankruptcy reorganization'.[84]

At Robert Gates's 1991 swearing-in ceremony, President Bush announced that the intelligence community needed to change 'as rapidly and profoundly as the world itself has changed'. The ensuing review of American intelligence emphasised the importance of nuclear weapons proliferation and instability in the former USSR as concerns for a reconstructed CIA. Various organisational reforms sought to enhance DCI coordination of intelligence, and to facilitate intelligence dissemination across the community, in particular to military consumers. In 1987, William Webster had inaugurated efforts, focused through the new Deputy Directorship for Planning and Coordination, to plan for intelligence in the new era. Gates developed these initiatives and also attempted to respond to accusations of politicisation during the Reagan years. Various procedures were instituted to investigate complaints and to liberalise the declassification process.[85]

What *was* to be the role for the intelligence community after the Cold War? In a sense, it had to be what it always was: investigating threats to America's security. President Clinton's first DCI, James Woolsey, declared in 1994: 'The Cold War has ended, but history has not, and neither has conflict.'[86] Perhaps the end of the Cold War might actually benefit the CIA by turning it away from 'other functions', and back to its true function of providing depoliticised intelligence? By the mid-1990s, covert operations accounted for less than 5 per cent of the budget of the CIA's Directorate of Operations. Paula Scalingi, staffer on the House of Representatives intelligence oversight panel, called on the CIA to seize the chance to undertake comprehensive, long-term planning. The Agency should resist the temptation to prioritise intelligence that 'really sells downtown' in terms of being tailored to immediate consumer concerns: 'US intelligence has increasingly been paying lip service to its responsibility to predict while in reality withstanding pressures to lean forward and postulate possible outcomes or assign percentage values to the likelihood of future developments.'[87] Budgetary restraint and Congressional oversight seemed to be sure features of the new environment. Perhaps now was the time to abolish the Directorate of Operations? Could the CIA turn its hand to economic forecasting, or was it unable to compete in this field? Maybe it could turn its attention to American industry, providing it with information about its competitors? (CIA agents seem to have been involved in a botched attempt in 1994 to steal commercial secrets from the French government.) Senator Daniel Patrick Moynihan actually gave his opinion that the Agency should be wound up altogether. Bruce

Berkowitz argued for an end to the notion of the 'intelligence cycle': the linear progress from requirement assessment to consumer dissemination. According to Berkowitz, the United States requires a 'dispersed intelligence network', an abandonment of the whole notion of centralised intelligence: 'the Information Age solution to the politicization of intelligence is to maintain as many competing centers of analysis as possible'.[88]

The 1990s debate on intelligence reform took place against the background of a new generation of CIA 'horrors'. At one level, there was the apparent failure of the CIA to predict the end of the Cold War, and to anticipate the 1990 Iraqi invasion of Kuwait. (On both counts, the CIA felt itself unfairly judged. One intelligence officer, who had questioned the Bush Administration's pre-invasion support for Saddam Hussein, commented: 'Sometimes we tell the policy level things that don't correspond with actual policy initiatives or thinking'.)[89] Allegations continued to surface about CIA involvement in Central American drug trafficking – some of it aimed at American cities – in the 1980s and early 1990s.

Above all, however, there was Aldrich Ames. In 1994, Ames, a counter-espionage officer, confessed to having sold information to Moscow between 1985 and 1992. Severe problems with counter-intelligence had been evident since the 1985 defection of CIA operations officer Edward Lee Howard. In 1994, the Senate Select Committee on Intelligence reported on the Ames case:

> [W]e found a bureaucracy which was excessively tolerant of serious personal
> and professional misconduct among its employees, where security was lax and
> ineffective. And we found a system and a culture unwilling and unable – par-
> ticularly in the early years of Ames' betrayal – to face, assess, and investigate the
> catastrophic blow Ames had dealt to the core of its operations.[90]

The Ames episode exposed deep rifts between the CIA and the FBI.[91] Evidence coming from the former East Germany suggested that many CIA agents there had actually been recruited as double agents by the East Berlin regime. A breakdown in radio security in Iran was also seen to have led, after 1988, to a new collapse of the US spy network there. In 1995, Congress 'discovered' billions of dollars in a fund relating to the National Reconnaissance Office. (Founded in 1960, this office for spy satellites had succeeded for many years in camouflaging its very existence.) During 1995 and 1996, new evidence emerged of CIA complicity in murder and human rights abuses in Guatemala. Republican Senator William Cohen repeated a complaint familiar from the Cold War era: 'The oversight committees have been misled and … may have been lied to.'[92] Accusations were also made about the Agency illegally funding Eastern European reconstruction in the Bush years.[93] In late 1996, Harold Nicholson – sometime head of station in Bucharest and CIA training specialist – was placed under federal investigation for selling secrets to Russia in the 1980s.

By the mid-1990s, the United States, victorious in the Cold and Gulf wars, found its intelligence services in a state of demoralisation. James Woolsey's unhappy tenure as DCI was terminated in 1995. President Clinton's difficulty in recruiting a successor exemplified the community's condition. Eventually, John Deutch, former scientific manager at the Pentagon, was persuaded to accept the job – pointedly, with Cabinet rank. Reports and reviews proliferated: from Congress; in-house; from the President's commission on intelligence (chaired by Les Aspin until his death, and subsequently by former Defence Secretary Harold Brown); and from various think-tanks. These reports tended to agree that America's intelligence needs had not ended with the Cold War, but had, rather, become more complex. Reforms promoted by Deutch and by Congress looked to giving the DCI more authority and to the streamlining and professionalisation of the CIA's workforce. Defence Secretary William Perry, who controlled a far larger proportion of the intelligence funding than did the DCI, cooperated with Deutch in achieving a consolidation of imagery intelligence. By mid-1996, it appeared that the number of people employed in intelligence work would have declined by about a quarter between 1990 and 2001; but that the annual intelligence budget was still running at around $29 billion. Clinton's late-1996 nomination of Anthony Lake as DCI raised yet more storms. The GOP leadership of the Senate Oversight Committee charged that Lake had been involved in an unreported 'covert action' – complicity in Iranian arms shipments to Muslims – in Bosnia.[94]

Notes

1   H. Kissinger, *The White House Years* (Boston, Little, Brown, 1979), p. 30. See also L. H. Gelb, 'Why not the State Department?', in C. W. Kegley and E. R. Wittkopf, eds, *Perspectives on American Foreign Policies* (New York, St. Martin's, 1983).

2   Cited in I. M. Destler, 'The rise of the national security assistant, 1961–1981', in Kegley and Wittkopf, eds, *Perspectives*, p. 268.

3   Z. Brzezinski, *Power and Principle* (London, Weidenfeld and Nicholson, 1983), p. 63.

4   J. Prados, *Keepers of the Keys* (New York, Morrow, 1991), p. 565.

5   Cited in J. A. Nathan and J. K. Oliver, *Foreign Policy Making and the American Political System* (Boston, Little, Brown, 1987), p. 48.

6   See B. H. Patterson, *The Ring of Power* (New York, Basic Books, 1988), p. 109.

7   See J. Dumbrell, *The Carter Presidency: A Reevaluation* (Manchester, Manchester University Press, 1995), pp. 194–200.

8   A. Haig, *Caveat* (New York, Macmillan, 1984), pp. 306, 352–8.

9   R. Reagan, *An American Life* (New York, Simon and Schuster, 1990), p. 284.

10 L. Speakes, *Speaking Out* (New York, Scribner's, 1984), p. 265.

11 J. Spanier and E. M. Uslaner, *American Foreign Policy and the Democratic Dilemmas* (Pacific Grove, Brooks Cole, 1989), pp. 55–6.

12   G. P. Shultz, *Turmoil and Triumph* (New York, Scribner's, 1993), pp. 275, 902, 1133. See also J. G. Bock, *The White House Staff and the National Security Assistant* (New York, Greenwood, 1987).

13   J. A. Baker, *The Politics of Diplomacy: Revolution, War and Peace, 1989–1992* (New York, Putnam's Sons, 1995), p. 22. See also J. M. Scolnik, 'The Bush approach to American foreign policy', in J. E. Winkates, J. R. Walsh and J. M. Scolnik, eds, *US Foreign Policy in Transition* (Chicago, Nelson-Hall, 1994); C.-P. David, 'Who was the real George Bush?', *Diplomacy and Statecraft*, 7 (1996), pp. 197–200.

14   See *Washington Post*, 3 July 1994 (A. Devroy, 'Christopher's job is said safe until end of year'); E. Drew, *On the Edge: The Clinton Presidency* (New York, Simon and Schuster, 1994), p. 144; L. Berman and E. O. Goldman, 'Clinton's foreign policy at midterm', in C. Campbell and B. A. Rockman, eds, *The Clinton Presidency: First Appraisals* (Chatham, Chatham House, 1996), pp. 299 ff.

15   See D. Kirschten, 'One for the books', *National Journal*, 6 Jan. 1996; *Washington Post*, 13 Jan. 1996 (D. Williams, 'Secretary of State gets vote of confidence').

16   I. M. Destler, L. H. Gelb and A. Lake, *Our Own Worst Enemy: The Unmaking of American Foreign Policy* (New York, Simon and Schuster, 1984), p. 277.

17   *The Tower Commission Report* (New York, New York Times Books, 1987), p. 94.

18   See Destler *et al.*, *Our Own Worst Enemy*.

19   Gelb, 'Why not the State Department?', p. 284. See also C. C. Shoemaker, *The NSC Staff: Counseling the Council* (Boulder, Westview, 1991), p. 43; G. Kemp, 'Presidential management of the executive bureaucracy', in E. R. Wittkopf, ed., *The Domestic Sources of American Foreign Policy* (New York, St. Martin's, 1994).

20   See Bock, *The White House Staff and the National Security Assistant*, p. 118.

21   B. A. Rockman, 'America's departments of state', in D. C. Kozak and J. M. Keagle, eds, *Bureaucratic Politics and National Security* (Boulder, Westview, 1988), p. 189.

22   D. M. Snow and E. Brown, *Puzzle Palaces and Foggy Bottom* (New York, St. Martin's, 1994), p. 90.

23   Shoemaker, *The NSC Staff*, p. 45.

24   C. Vance, *Hard Choices: Critical Years in America's Foreign Policy* (New York, Simon and Schuster, 1983), p. 39.

25   *Ibid.*, p. 40.

26   P. Bushnell, 'Leadership at State', *Foreign Service Journal*, Sept. 1989, pp. 30–1.

27   V. Huddleston, 'State's image on the Hill', *Foreign Service Journal*, Sept. 1989, p. 35.

28   Kissinger, *The White House Years*, p. 11.

29   Destler *et al.*, *Our Own Worst Enemy*, p. 100.

30   See J. Anderson, 'Singing the blues', *Foreign Service Journal*, Sept. 1995.

31   See *Congressional Quarterly Weekly Report*, 6 May 1995, p. 1249.

32   *Congressional Record*, 17 July 1995, S10086.

33   *Creating A Government that Works Better and Costs Less: National Performance Review: Department of State and US Information Agency* (Washington DC, US Government Printing Office, 1993), pp. 5, 14.

34   L. S. Eagleburger and R. L. Barry, 'Dollars and sense diplomacy', *Foreign Affairs*, 75 (1996), pp. 2–8: 3, 5. Also, US Department of State Management Task Force, *State 2000: A New Model for Managing Foreign Affairs* (Washington DC, State Department, 1992); Carnegie Endowment for New World, *Changing Our Ways: America and the New World* (Washington DC, Brookings, 1992); Memorandum to the President-Elect: *Harnessing Process to Purpose* (Washington, DC, Carnegie Endowment, 1992). See also A. Kanter, 'Adapting the executive branch to the post-Cold War World', in D. Yankelovich and I. M. Destler, eds, *Beyond the Beltway* (New York, Norton, 1994).

35   *State 2000*, p. 3.

36   F. McNeil, 'Focus', *Foreign Service Journal*, May 1995, pp. 53–4.

37   P. J. Powlick, 'The attitudinal bases for responsiveness to public opinion among American foreign policy officials', *Journal of Conflict Resolution*, 35 (1991), pp. 611–41.

38   Nathan and Oliver, *Foreign Policy Making*, p. 40.

39   Cited in R. Morris, 'Working for the other team: clientism in the foreign service', in C. Peters and J. Fallow, eds, *Inside the System* (New York, Praeger, 1976), p. 171.

40   *Washington Post*, 4 July 1994 (J. Hoagland, 'Needed at State: a show of confidence in Christopher').

41   See *Newsweek*, 6 March 1995.

42   See *The Economist*, 4 May 1996, p. 58; also, J. Muravchik, *The Imperative of American Leadership* (Washington DC, American Enterprise Institute, 1996).

43   See R. A. Kohn, 'Out of control', *The National Interest*, 35 (1994), pp. 3–17.

44   See E. Nordlinger, *Soldiers and Politics* (Englewood Cliffs, Prentice-Hall, 1977). M. S. Sherry's *In the Shadow of War* (New Haven, Yale University Press, 1996) surveys the militarisation of American life since the 1930s.

45   R. A. Stubbing, *The Defense Game* (New York, Harper and Row, 1986), p. 384.

46   *Ibid.*, p. 262.

47   Shultz, *Turmoil and Triumph*, p. 311.

48   See M. R. Beschloss and S. Talbott, *At the Highest Levels: The Inside Story of the End of the Cold War* (Boston, Little, Brown, 1993), pp. 47–9; David, 'Who was the real George Bush?', p. 205.

49   F. Thompson and L. R. Jones, *Reinventing the Pentagon* (San Francisco, Jossey-Bass, 1994), pp. 24, 26.

50   P. M. Smith, *Assignment: Pentagon* (Washington DC, Pergamon-Brassey's, 1989), pp. 157–9.

51   B. R. Inman and D. F. Burton, 'Breaking the adversarial tradition', in Yankelovich and Destler, eds, *Beyond the Beltway*, p. 178. See also E. B. Kapstein, ed., *Downsizing Defence* (Washington DC, Congressional Quarterly, 1995).

52   'The Goldwater–Nunn defense organization staff study', in Kozak and Keagle, eds, *Bureaucratic Politics*, p. 492.

53   Kohn, 'Out of control', p. 6. See also M. Perry, *Four Stars: the Joint Chiefs of Staff in the Post-War Era* (Boston, Houghton Mifflin, 1989).

54   See B. Woodward, *The Commanders* (New York, Simon and Schuster, 1991), p. 225.

55   Berman and Goldman, 'Clinton's foreign policy at midterm', p. 318.

56   Stubbing, *The Defense Game*, p. 391.

57   H. Smith, *The Power Game* (New York, Random House, 1988), pp. 166–7. See also T. Farrell, *Weapons without a Cause: The Politics of Weapons Acquisition in the United States* (Basingstoke, Macmillan, 1996).

58   See S. J. Cimbala, *US Military Strategy and the Cold War Endgame* (Ilford, Cass, 1995), p. 33.

59   See W. Q. Brown and D. H. Dunn, *American Security Policy in the 1990s: Beyond Containment* (Aldershot, Dartmouth, 1996), pp. 77–8.

60   B. Schwarz, 'Why America thinks it has to run the world', *The Atlantic Monthly*, June 1996, p. 92; 'So where's the peace dividend?', *The Bulletin of the Atomic Scientists*, 51 (1995), pp. 30–52. Also, A. Tonelson, 'Superpower without a sword', *Foreign Affairs*, 72 (1993), pp. 166–80; W. Y. Smith, 'US national security after the Cold War', in E. R. Wittkopf, ed., *The Future of American Foreign Policy* (New York, St. Martin's, 1994), pp. 291 ff.; H. Ullman and W. Getler, 'Common Sense defense', *Foreign Policy*, 105 (1996–97), pp. 21–33.

61   D. C. Morrison, 'Ready for what?', *National Journal*, 20 May 1995, p. 1218. See also R. K. Betts, *Military Readiness: Concepts, Choices, Consequences* (Washington DC, Brookings, 1995).

62   J. Bamford, *The Puzzle Palace* (New York, Penguin, 1983), p. 372.

63   G. W. Reichard, 'The domestic politics of national security', in N. A. Graebner, ed., *The National Security* (New York, Oxford University Press, 1986), p. 261. For a guide to academic writing on the CIA's Cold War history, see J. Ferris, 'Coming in from the cold: the historiography of American intelligence, 1945–1990', *Diplomatic History*, 19 (1995), pp. 87–116.

64   R. Winks, *Cloak and Gown* (New York, Morrow, 1987), p. 115.

65   W. Colby, *Honourable Men* (New York, Simon and Schuster, 1978), p. 201.

66   R. S. Cline, *The CIA under Reagan, Bush and Casey* (Washington DC, Acropolis, 1981), p. 211.

67   Kissinger, *The White House Years*, p. 169.

68   See S. D. Breckinridge, *The CIA and the US Intelligence System* (Boulder, Westview, 1986), p. 308. See also H. Sklar, *Washington's War on Nicaragua* (Boston, South End Press, 1988); B. Woodward, *Veil: The Secret Wars of the CIA, 1981–1987* (New York, Simon and Schuster, 1987).

69   Shultz, *Turmoil and Triumph*, p. 84.

70   R. Gates, *From the Shadows* (New York, Simon and Schuster, 1996), pp. 201, 415; C. Andrew, *For the President's Eyes Only* (London, Harper Collins, 1995), p. 495.

71   L. Freedman, *US Intelligence and the Soviet Strategic Threat* (London, Macmillan, 1986), pp. 187, 189. See also B. D. Berkowitz and A. E. Goodman, *Strategic Intelligence for American National Security* (Princeton, Princeton University Press, 1989); R. N. Lebow, 'Misconceptions in American strategic assessment', *Political Science Quarterly*, 97 (1982), pp. 187–206.

72   See C. W. Kegley and E. R. Wittkopf, *American Foreign Policy: Pattern and Process* (5th edn, New York, St. Martin's, 1996), p. 409; R. Jeffreys-Jones, *The CIA and American Democracy* (New Haven, Yale University Press, 1989), p. 251.

73   See A. E. Goodman, 'Dateline Langley', *Foreign Policy*, 57 (1984–85), pp.

160–79.

74   *CIA: The Pike Report* (Nottingham, 1977), pp. 186–8. This is also the argument advanced in Andrew, *For the President's Eyes Only*. See also R. Godson, *Dirty Tricks and Trump Cards: US Covert Action and Counterintelligence* (London, Brassey's, 1995).

75   Final Report of the Senate Select Committee to Study Governmental Operations with Respect to Intelligence Activities, 1976 (Church Committee Report), Book I, *Foreign and Military Intelligence* (Washington DC, US Government Printing Office, 1976), p. 9.

76   Richard M. Nixon, *RN: The Memoirs of Richard Nixon* (New York, Grossett and Dunlap, 1978), pp. 489–90.

77   G. F. Treverton, 'Covert action and open society', *Foreign Affairs*, 65 (1987), pp. 995–1014, 995. See also G. F. Treverton, *Covert Action: The Limits of Intervention in the Postwar World* (New York, Basic Books, 1987).

78   See S. Turner, *Secrecy and Democracy: The CIA in Transition* (Boston, Houghton Mifflin, 1985), p. 173; Treverton, 'Covert action', p. 1013.

79   Colby, *Honorable Men*, p. 18.

80   See L. K. Johnson, 'Legislative reform of intelligence policy', Polity, 17 (1985), pp. 549–73; also, F. J. Smist, *Congress Oversees the United States Intelligence Community, 1947–1989* (Knoxville, University of Tennessee Press, 1990), ch. 5.

81   T. G. Paterson, *Meeting the Communist Threat* (New York, Oxford University Press, 1988), p. 254.

82   R. Helms and J. Schlesinger, 'CIA watchdog – or mole?', *New York Times*, 22 Nov. 1989.

83   L. K. Johnson, 'Playing hardball with the CIA', in P. E. Peterson, ed., *The President, the Congress, and the Making of Foreign Policy* (Norman, University of Oklahoma Press, 1994), p. 71.

84   Tim Weiner, *New York Times*, 28 Sept. 1994 (cited in M. Cox, *US Foreign Policy after the Cold War: Superpower without a Mission* (London, Pinter, 1995), p. 18).

85   Andrew, *For the President's Eyes Only*, pp. 532–5. See also L. K. Johnson, 'New directions for US strategic intelligence', in Winkates, Walsh and Scolnik, eds, *US Foreign Policy in Transition*; J. Wilson, 'Thinking about reorganization', in R. Godson, E. R. May and G. Schmitt, eds, *US Intelligence at the Crossroads: Agendas for Reform* (London, Brassey's, 1995).

86   Andrew, *For the President's Eyes Only*, p. 541.

87   P. L. Scalingi, 'US intelligence in an age of uncertainty', in B. Roberts, ed., *US Foreign Policy after the Cold War* (Cambridge, Mass., MIT Press, 1992), p. 178.

88   B. D. Berkowitz, 'Information age intelligence', *Foreign Policy*, 103 (1996), pp. 35–50, 48. See also C. Lane, 'Why spy?', *The New Republic*, 27 March 1995; S. Turner, 'Intelligence for a new world order', *Foreign Affairs*, 70 (1991), pp. 151–66; D. DeConcini, 'The role of US intelligence in promoting economic interests', *Journal of International Affairs*, 48 (1994), pp. 39–58.

89   B. W. Jentleson, *With Friends Like These: Reagan, Bush, and Saddam, 1982–1990* (New York, Norton, 1994), p. 228. See also B. Berkowitz and J. Richelson, 'The CIA vindicated; the Soviet collapse was predicted', *The National Interest*, 41 (1995, pp. 76–91).

90   Report of the Senate Select Committee on Intelligence, *An Assessment of the Aldrich H. Ames Espionage Case*, Nov. 1994, p. 53.
91   See M. Riebling, *Wedge: The Secret War between the FBI and CIA* (New York, Knopf, 1994).
92   *Congressional Quarterly Weekly Report*, 15 April 1995, p. 1073.
93   See 'The CIA's darkest secrets', *US News and World Report*, 4 July 1994; J. Kitfield, 'Looking for trouble', *National Journal*, 18 May 1996.
94   See *Congressional Quarterly Weekly Report*, 21 Dec. 1996, p. 3442.

5

Congress

1 Legislative strengths

Key Administration witnesses in the Iran–Contra hearings clearly believed that foreign policy was, and should be, solely the concern of the executive. For Admiral John Poindexter, for example, the failure of Congress to appropriate funds for desired projects was unfortunate, but was not the final word. Poindexter and Colonel Oliver North seemed to regard it as self-evident that Congress was not to be taken seriously as an actor in the foreign policy process.[1]

In some respects, this attitude, although constitutionally alarming and absurd, is unsurprising. Denigration of Congress has a long history in American culture. References to Congress in American literature tend to be to a Senate of unrelieved windbaggery and cynical power-brokerage, and to a House of Representatives of mindless parochialism, venality and bad manners. Public perceptions of Congress as an institution, although not necessarily of individual members, are consistently negative. Presidents merrily add to the tradition of legislative denigration. When President George Bush was asked in 1992 why he could not 'bring the same kind of purpose to the domestic scene as you did in Desert Shield and Desert Storm', Bush replied: 'the answer is I didn't have to get permission from some old goat in the United States Congress to kick Saddam Hussein out of Kuwait!'.[2]

It is, therefore, especially important to remind ourselves of the impressive constitutional grant of power to Congress, even in foreign policy. As Harold Hongshu Koh wrote in 1990:

> At the Republic's birth, the Framers deliberately drafted a Constitution of shared powers and balanced institutional participation, fully aware of the risks that arrangement posed to the nation's international well-being. By mandating that separated institutions share power in foreign as well as in domestic affairs, the Framers determined that we must sacrifice some short-term gains from speed, secrecy and efficiency in favour of the longer-term consensus that derives from reasoned interbranch consultation and participatory decision-making.[3]

Congress alone has the power to declare war. It has important powers relating to the regulation of foreign commerce. Ultimately, it has the 'power of the purse', potentially as fundamental an influence on foreign as on domestic policy. This grant of power is not simply a constitutional obstacle, to be pushed aside by an executive which sees Congress as an irritant.

This is not to suggest that Congress is beyond criticism, nor that the case against Congressional foreign policy will disappear, even in the post-Cold War era. In no other policy area is there a stronger tradition of scepticism as to the desirability of a strong Congressional role as in the area of foreign affairs. These doubts rest to some extent on the Constitution. Clearly, as exemplified in his powers to negotiate treaties and to appoint Ambassadors, the President does enjoy a greater grant of foreign policy power than he does in the domestic arena. However, arguments for Presidential dominance rest primarily on pragmatic foundations. Writing as Pacificus in *The Federalist*, Alexander Hamilton held that the intrinsic demands of foreign policy placed it within the executive's purview.[4] Throughout American history, loud voices have held that successful foreign relations require secrecy, firm leadership and expeditious crisis-management, along with a transcendence of local and regional interests. Such qualities do not readily attach themselves to Congress. Rather, to cite John Lehman's 1976 catalogue of Congressional deficiency, legislative foreign policy has been hindered by 'multipolarity, diffuse authority, paucity of machinery, thinness of expertise and personnel, lack of intelligence sources, plodding and workaday character, freedom from secrecy, lack of continuity, and above all, localism and parochialism'.[5] Or, in the words of former Under-Secretary of State W. D. Rogers: 'Congress is beholden to every short-term swing of popular opinion. The temptation to pander to prejudice and emotion is overwhelming.'[6] Within this anti-Congress tradition, legislative 'micromanagement' of policy is especially castigated, primarily in the context of efforts to use the appropriations process to influence foreign and defence policies. Congress is regularly excoriated for undercutting the President in his relationship with other countries, causing conflicting signals and an impression of national irresolution to be sent, generally damaging the national interest.[7]

The case *for* Congressional foreign policy stresses the representational virtues of a decentralised legislature, the importance of airing policy alternatives, and the dangers of executive unaccountability. Congress may be said to 'represent' the United States in ways which the executive would find impossible. Members can, for example, attempt to balance the 'delegate' and 'trustee' aspects of representation: in other words, to combine the virtues of reflecting the views of the constituency with the freedom to weigh those views against other (national and party) considerations. Congress can, despite its traditional membership bias in favour of legally trained white males, present itself as far more of a nation-in-miniature than can the executive branch. Congress *is* likely to raise policy alternatives. Policy that is the product of a strong legislative input could also be the basis of a firmer and more democratically oriented consensus than one dictated by executive policy preferences. According to John Tierney, Congressional involvement causes foreign policy decisions to be 'shaped and tempered through consensus-forming procedures', making them 'more likely to enjoy popular legitimacy'.[8]

J. M. Lindsay has isolated three fallacies which characterise the perceived view of legislative foreign policy. The first fallacy is that Members are driven exclusively by re-election concerns. In fact, they concern themselves also with good public policy, as well as with intra-chamber influence. The second fallacy is that Congress is entirely a frivolous, politicised circus. Of course, Congress is utterly politicised. It is not a bureaucracy, equipped for rationality in the Weberian sense. Yet, to quote Lindsay: 'Far more than the critics acknowledge, members of Congress and their staff do engage in proactive and systematic review of bureaucratic behavior, or what political scientists are now fond of calling police-patrol oversight.' The third fallacy is that executive–legislative relations in foreign policy are always adversarial. Even as President Reagan clashed with Congress over Central America, executive and legislative branches were cooperating on Afghanistan, China, India, Libya and the Persian Gulf.[9]

If legislative consistency in policy is a contradiction in terms – itself a doubtful proposition[10] – then so is executive consistency. Intra-bureaucratic and inter-departmental rivalries, Presidential inconsistency and executive failures may, on a day-to-day basis, seem less deep-seated than defects in Congress; they do exist, however, and, in the long run, may be more dangerous, especially if not checked by Capitol Hill. Presidents find themselves undercut by members of their own Administration, as well as by Members of Congress. Also, as Lindsay argues: 'When presidents face pressure from members of Congress to compromise, they can blame foreign policy failures on congressional obstructionism, as Ronald Reagan frequently did.' Congress is 'a ready-made scapegoat'.[11] It is also important not to confuse activism with policy impact. Presidential invocations of the 'imperial Congress' or paralysing legislative micromanagement do not ring true. In 1987, President George Bush addressed the conservative lawyers' Federalist Society in the following terms: 'Over the last 20 years we have witnessed a departure from the way we have conducted foreign policy for nearly two centuries. Congress has asserted an increasingly influential role in the micromanagement of foreign policy – foreign operations if you will.'[12] In fact, the Pentagon spends less than 0.02 per cent of its budget on activities designed to respond to Congressional reporting requirements. The State Department similarly is not paralysed by legislative micromanagement.[13] Interestingly, Stephen Weissman finds micromanagement and reporting requirements an aspect of Congress's *deference* to the executive: 'Obsessive "micromanagement" thus appears not as a counterpoint to the culture of deference but rather as its ironic and perverse fulfilment.'[14] Robbed of real, substantive power, Congress turns to harmless detail.

Complaints about the 'omnipotent Congress'[15] are absurd. They reflect the impatience of the executive branch rather than anything more substantial. As J. B. Martin has written, the State Department 'thinks that the members of Congress engage in sordid politics and drink too much'.[16] The executive is constantly tempted to propagate the notion that it is being bullied by over-powerful legislators – country bumpkins who should really be put in their place. In fact, as Miroslav Nincic argues, neither 'the record of recent history' nor 'an examination of the various facets of competence in foreign policy suggest that Congress is as incapable of addressing international problems as is often assumed'.[17]

2   The foreign policy Congress

(a) *Committees and party leaders*   A former Reagan official in 1990 offered the following verdict on the Senate Foreign Relations and House Foreign Affairs Committees: 'One has died on the vine; the other has fragmented into little empires.'[18] Both committees are widely regarded as having lost influence, especially in the 1970s and 1980s. Since the mid-1980s, each committee has had problems in expediting its main legislative responsibility: the reporting out and passage of the annual foreign aid and foreign operations authorisations.

It is in the senior committee – Senate Foreign Relations, founded in 1816, and with particular responsibilities for considering treaties and foreign policy appointments – where decline has been most visible. As C. V. Crabb put it, in the early Cold War period, 'the voice of this committee' was 'usually the *voice of Congress* in foreign affairs'.[19] By the 1980s, membership of the Committee was actually regarded as an electoral liability. At one level, integration on the Committee was undermined by increasing subcommittee autonomy. The policy agenda of the late 1970s and 1980s also tended to undermine the authority of the full Committee. Multiple referrals for bills among several committees became increasingly common with the rise of the interdependency agenda. It became clear that some members of the Committee were paying an electoral price for becoming too identified with international, rather than constituency, concerns. Four such figures, including chairman Frank Church and ranking Republican Jacob Javits, were unseated in the Reaganite sweep of 1980. Charles Percy, the Illinois Republican who became chairman in 1981, was himself defeated in the 1984 elections. During the 100th Congress (1987–88), the Committee actually operated with one (Democratic) vacancy. James McCormick found in 1993 that 'turnover in membership means that Foreign Relations now tends to be composed of members with more limited service and less political influence within the institution' than traditionally. The Committee was also increasingly politicised – 'more sharply divided', with a consequent reduction in 'the prospect for compromise, and hence for effective decision making'.[20]

Partisanship on the Committee was increased by the presence of rightist Republican Jesse Helms, who eventually succeeded to the post of chairman after the 1994 elections. Richard Lugar, the Indiana Republican who became chairman in 1985, attempted to reinvigorate the Committee by embarking on a wide-ranging review of US foreign policy. His Democratic successor, Claiborne Pell of Rhode Island, proved to be a fair but ineffectual leader. During his chairmanship, no foreign aid bill was passed by the full Congress. Indeed, between 1985 and 1991, not one reported foreign aid authorisation bill even made it to the Senate floor. A series of reforms in 1991 further enhanced the power of subcommittees, with two functional subcommittees being given legislative responsibility. Helms proved a predictably combative chairman, and sought to reverse Pell's tendency to delegate. (Nevertheless, Helms did delegate management of the START II treaty, eventually approved by Congress in 1996, to Lugar's Subcommittee on European Affairs.)

Since the late 1980s, the House Foreign Affairs Committee has had greater success than its Senate counterpart in expediting its authorisations. Yet the House Committee also experienced increasing ideological polarisation. The growing incidence of multiple referring – more pronounced in the House even than in the Senate – tended to erode Committee authority. The House Committee (renamed the House International Relations Committee in the Republican Congress of 1995–96) also has a stronger tradition of subcommittee autonomy than its Senate counterpart. Democratic chairman Dante Fascell (Committee chairman, 1983–91) consciously encouraged subcommittee autonomy as a way of channelling and containing ideological divisions. The tactic was not without success, and some of the subcommittee chairs of this era – notably Stephen Solarz, the New York Democrat, who assumed chairmanship of the Asian and Pacific Affairs Subcommittee in 1983 – became highly effective foreign policy operators. Yet both Democrat Lee Hamilton (chairman, 1992–94) and Republican Benjamin Gilman (who became chairman of the International Relations panel in 1995) inherited highly decentralised committee structures. The Committee's failure to assert itself during the deployment of the US peacekeeping mission to Bosnia in 1995 was an indication of continuing weakness.

The problems of the two Foreign Policy Committees cleared the way, at least to some degree, for the House and Senate Armed Services Committees to expand their influence. During the 1980s and early 1990s, Armed Services Committee chief, Senator Sam Nunn of Georgia, became an effective foreign, as well as defence, policy leader. Since the early 1970s, the Armed Services Committees have greatly increased the Pentagon's requirement to seek annual authorisation and reauthorisation for weapons procurement (rather than relying on liberal, open-ended authorisations).[21] In 1995, the nonagenarian Senator Strom Thurmond (South Carolina Republican) assumed leadership of the Senate Committee. Both Thurmond and Floyd Spence (another South Carolina Republican, who became leader of the renamed House National Security Committee in 1995) allowed considerable leeway to their subcommittees.

The House and Senate defence policy panels tend to be much more successful than the foreign policy committees in seeing authorisations seamlessly converted into appropriations. The two-step, authorisation/appropriation process, though more regularly discussed in the context of domestic policy, can have considerable impact on international issues. Especially in an era of budget deficits, appropriations subcommittees in House and Senate have been able to make their mark. As Joseph White comments, most 'legislators care or know little about the details of each appropriations bills'. Disputes between appropriations subcommittees and the wider Congress generally occur only on high-profile issues. Yet battles between authorisers (on the foreign policy or armed services panels) and appropriators are more common. They are generally resolved in the context of executive–legislative relations. Appropriators, rather than authorisers, tend – in White's words – to 'gain more influence ... as the issue becomes more concrete (what is bought where) and less "strategic", easily related to policy goals'. Appropriations subcommittees tend to derive authority from their expertise in programme performance and management.[22]

The general picture of Congressional organisation since the 1970s has been one of decentralisation, succeeded by recentralisation. Explanations for these developments vary from those provided by rational choice theory – the desire of Members for constituency service opportunities, but also for legislative leadership – to those rooted in theories of party realignment and electoral change.[23] During the Reagan Presidency, the House Democratic leadership in particular developed distinct positions, and mobilised rank-and-file Members. Barbara Sinclair explains these changes in terms taken from rational choice theory, always emphasising that leaders function 'as agents of an active and involved membership not as independent policy entrepreneurs': Members 'expect their leaders to act as spokesmen, explaining party positions to the media, and thus to the public, thereby advancing their policy goals and often providing political protection'.[24] The reforms of the 1970s tended to weaken the position of committee chairmen, and party leaders stepped into the void. Increasing party cohesion was sustained by and reflected in the behaviour of leaders of both parties in Congress.[25] For the 100th Congress (1987–88), Barbara Sinclair calculated that 67 per cent of foreign and defence issues in the House pitted two-thirds or more of Democrats against the Republican President; this compared with 22 per cent in the 94th Congress (1975–76).[26] House Speaker Jim Wright's involvement in the Central American peace process during the late 1980s exemplified the partisan, activist leadership of the period. Intense partisanship mellowed somewhat during the first two years of Bush's Presidency – the years of Cold War victory and geopolitical shakeout – only to re-emerge in the 102nd Congress (1991–92).[27] The Republican Congressional victories of 1994 took partisanship into new directions.

(b) *Determinants and types of Congressional influence*   It is received wisdom that the making and conduct of foreign policy tends to be dominated by the executive. As the operating, rather than the enabling, branch, the executive finds it an easy matter to undercut or evade Congress. The legislative 'power of the purse' can be circumvented by executive decisions over the timing of spending or transfers between accounts (not to mention quasi-legal devices such as use of 'discretionary' or 'pipeline' money). Congress, despite its constitutional authority to oversee and investigate, also faces severe practical difficulties in obtaining access to information held by the executive. Such problems are magnified by the culture of hostility which frequently exists between the branches. Elliott Abrams, Assistant Secretary for Human Rights at the State Department under President Reagan, wrote in 1993:

> We were at war, we and the Democrats in Congress, or so we thought and they thought. There were sometimes hearings where they asked fair, decent, intelligence questions whose purpose was to find out the truth. Hearings on Haiti, Jamaica, earthquake aid, or religious freedom in Cuba. But on Central America, hearings were a form of combat. Questions were weapons, and answers were shields. So when I was asked for information that might help them, might give them more ammunition, I tried to deny it to them. I tried to figure out how I could give them the least information possible.[28]

Despite the general perception of executive dominance, the extent of Congressional influence over foreign policy clearly varies over time. The period from Pearl Harbor (1941) to the emergence of widespread legislative dissent over Presidential conduct of the Vietnam War (*c.*1968–71) unmistakably represented an extreme point of Congressional deference. Legislative pliancy was rooted in consensus over anti-communist foreign policy aims and in the relative and apparent success of Presidential initiatives. The consensus, with its implicit invocation of executive superiority in crisis management and in formulating consistent policy, was shattered by the early 1970s. In Alton Frye's words, the Vietnam War provoked the realisation in Congress that 'the constitutional system itself must be insulated from the perils of an overweening Presidency'.[29] Even in the years of Congressional passivity, however, it is worth noting that Presidents were not entirely immune from criticism in certain areas, and that the ability of Congress to initiate foreign policy was not entirely lost. So, while President Harry Truman was able to exploit Cold War certainties and his putative crisis powers to embark upon an undeclared war in Korea in 1950, he was soon exposed to violent

Congressional criticism regarding his handling of the war. During the Eisenhower Presidency, Congress still managed to initiate policy (one may cite the dominant legislative role in the creation of the International Development Association in 1958).

Most commentators accept that the increasingly intense Congressional foreign policy activism associated with the Vietnam War persisted until, and indeed beyond, the end of the Cold War. It was sustained, among other factors, by inter-branch disagreement on national security priorities, and by what J. M. Lindsay has called 'the demise of the textbook Congress': primarily, the post-Vietnam War reassertion of legislative power, the 1970s reform movement's assault on the power of committee chairmen, and the rise of assorted foreign policy interest groups.[30] The post-Vietnam War 'resurgent Congress' was characterised, as we have seen, by high levels of partisanship and by the rise of new, interdependency and 'intermestic' issues – energy concerns, the new salience of global trade, immigration and refugee policy.

Such generalisations about the 'resurgent Congress' are widely, though not universally, accepted. Researchers in this area face considerable difficulty in actually identifying, much less measuring, legislative activism. Many foreign policy issues never come to a vote. Presidents often act without Congress, either because they feel they enjoy legislative support or, conversely, because they fear inciting acrimonious debate. At the empirical level, research (for example, into hostile questioning by the foreign policy committees in Congress[31]) has not always found consistent evidence of 'resurgence'. As indicated above, it is also important to distinguish Congressional *participation* from Congressional *opposition* to Presidential priorities. After all, it is frequently argued that participation, and the acquisition of expertise, actually enhances inter-branch cooperation and collaboration. Significant arguments have also been made to the effect that Congressional criticisms of executive foreign policy generally amount to very little: that Congress, even after the Vietnam War, exhibited a debilitating 'culture of deference' on national security issues. Stephen Weissman, for example, sees both Democrats and Republicans in the Congress of the 1990s as still paralysed by the 'cultural heritage from the long Cold War'. According to Weissman – former Staff Director on the House Foreign Affairs Subcommittee on Africa – Members simply do not believe that Congress can make foreign policy. Barbara Hinckley contends that meaningful Congressional activity on foreign policy has actually *decreased* since the 1970s. The institution merely concerns itself with 'symbolic action' and the appearance of energetic involvement.[32]

In fact, whether Congress is overall adjudged to be activist or quiescent, the degree of legislative influence will tend to vary greatly across the spectrum of foreign and defence policy. To adopt the terminology used by Ripley and Franklin,[33] Congressional impact in the actual decision-making process is likely to be greatest in the 'structural' arena: the incremental administration of long-term commitments, most notably the defence budget, which Congress tends to handle in a decentralised fashion, in cooperation with executive and private sector personnel. 'Strategic' policy decisions, involving important departures in defence and foreign policy, tend to involve Congress in a less decentralised fashion, with the legislative inclining to defer to the executive. In the case of Ripley and Franklin's third category, 'crisis policy', the normal decision-making structure consists of the President and major executive advisers, with perhaps (as in the Grenada invasion of 1983) some peremptory and belated consultation with a few specially selected legislators.

It is inevitable that Congressional foreign policy will be shaped by local, domestic considerations. A common criticism is that legislators tend to see foreign policy as a slightly specialised branch of domestic policy. Where they exist, constituency concerns – for example, employment prospects at a local defence plant or military base – are almost bound to predominate. President Bush lambasted Congressional Democrats in 1990: 'Longstanding critics of defense spending should not turn around and block the closing of a base in their home districts'.[34] Some Members reflect particular ethnic identities in the constituency. Where there are no clear constituency concerns, Members' concern with foreign policy may be either absent or simply geared to empty position-taking. Constituency casework does not typically yield problems of international moment, although immigration issues may figure here.

In this context, Presidential policies which involve a relocation of resources away from or towards the domestic arena, or which have a major domestic impact, will tend to provoke an especially assertive legislative reaction. Historically, Congress has taken particular interest – initiating as well as reacting – in tariff and trading issues. While the increasing complexity and success of US trade inclined Congress to take a more passive role in the early Cold War, the reawakening of protectionist pressures in the late 1970s and 1980s was reflected in legislative activism. The 99th Congress (1985–86) saw the introduction of 782 trade bills, 248 with clear protectionist intent.[35] More generally, the perception of potential American vulnerability in a world of shrinking resources concentrated the legislative mind upon the domestic implications of international policies. As noted in Chapter 2, the centrality of economic foreign policy issues after the Cold War presaged a strong Congressional role. The early post-Cold War period saw the emergence of new coalitions relating to trade, to the politics of deficit reduction and to general interpretations of American internationalism.[36]

The legislature's various oversight, law-making, investigative and funding powers yield a range of opportunities to make and influence policy. Lindsay and Ripley draw particular attention to four avenues of influence: substantive legislation, anticipated reactions, procedural legislation and framing opinion.[37] It is often inappropriate to legislate foreign policy, and substantive legislation in this field is usually hedged around by significant qualifications and delegations of authority to the executive. On anticipated reactions, Lindsay and Ripley comment: 'As Presidents look to Capitol Hill, their reading of the congressional mood tells them what policies are not politically feasible. But the mood in Congress seldom compels the president to pursue specific policies.'[38] Congress rarely achieves an oppositional consensus; even if it does, such a consensus can usually be resisted, at least in the short term. Procedural legislation encompasses efforts, increasingly common since the 1970s, to enhance influence over executive conduct. An important example is the legislative veto, which allows Congress a second bite at the executive cherry. The executive is permitted to take certain action (for example, the purchase of certain weapons systems) subject to veto by the whole Congress, by one chamber, or even by one committee. Over two hundred legislative vetoes were enacted between 1983 and 1991; many were willingly accepted by the executive (despite the Supreme Court's denial of constitutionality in 1983) as the necessary price of receiving the delegation of authority.[39] Other types of procedural legislation include: the imposition of reporting requirements; placing other conditions on the executive's conduct of policy; and creating new institutions, or encouraging new actors, to participate in decision-making. Lindsay and Ripley offer various examples: Pentagon reorganisation, the setting of human rights standards in foreign aid legislation, the incorporation of formal legislative consultation over international policy on illegal drugs. The recent history of military base closure yields various procedural means whereby the Armed Services Committees have insinuated Congress into the decision-making and adjudication process. Members, either in groups or as individual entrepreneurs, also try to shape public opinion. (Such activity, notably by Republican Senator Richard Lugar and Democratic Representative Stephen Solarz, was important in turning the Reagan Administration away from support of the Marcos regime in the Philippines in 1986,)

3   Congress and foreign policy during the late Cold War, 1973–89

The Nixon Presidency (1969–74) was an era of transition towards greater Congressional impact on foreign policy. By 1976, Henry Kissinger was accusing the Congress of having dangerously hamstrung the White House, depriving it of 'indispensable flexibility'.[40] The threat to cut off funds, and Congressional activism generally, was an important factor in ending US military involvement in Vietnam in 1973. During the next seven years, legislative reassertion was most obvious in a series of Congressional conflicts with the executive, and in new techniques intended to enhance control over executive discretion. The Ford Administration (1974–77) found its policies successfully opposed not only in Southeast Asia – Congress effectively prevented resumption of US military operations there in 1975, – but also in

Cyprus (where Congress imposed an arms embargo after the Turkish invasion of 1974) and Angola. Everywhere loomed the memory of Vietnam and
the remembered nightmare of uncontrolled Presidential discretion.
Although, as T. M. Franck and E. W. Weisband noted, often 'maddeningly
inconsistent' in ideology,[41] Congress tended to oppose the interventionist
conservatism of the Ford Administration and to lead the 'human rights' orientation of the early Carter Presidency. However, increasing Congressional
conservatism in the late 1970s engendered fierce inter-branch conflicts over
the Administration's policy to relinquish ownership of the Panama Canal,
and over normalisation of relations with mainland China. Above all, the
Senate appeared poised to reject SALT II, before Carter abandoned it in the
wake of the 1979 Soviet invasion of Afghanistan.

The Carter Presidency (1977–81) inherited the 'new oversight' on Capitol Hill. Central to this was the technique of legislative veto, incorporated
into the 1974 War Powers Act. Many initiatives of these years, such as the
requiring of reports on arms control, were met by successful Presidential
evasion. Carter succeeded in exporting nuclear fuels to India in 1978 despite
prior restrictions upon his power in this area. The 1970s witnessed, not the
growth of Congressional dominance, but – as S. J. Baker described it – a
newly 'complex pattern of interaction' between the branches.[42] The 'new
oversight' also intersected with post-reform decentralisation, some effects of
which were to weaken Congressional abilities to oppose and criticise the
executive. Reviewing the period, ex-Congressman C. W. Whalen complained that the newly assertive House of Representatives was operating as
'a flotilla of 147 sub-committee vessels ... without a compass'.[43]

In October 1980, Presidential candidate Ronald Reagan promised to
'restore leadership to US foreign policy'.[44] Though primarily an attack on the
Carter Administration's failure to speak with one voice, the promise also
implied the need for a newly firm direction of Congress. In the first two
years of the Presidency, Congress was largely content to allow Reagan new
flexibility. At one level, Congressional leaders seemed to accept that executive discretion had become unduly fettered. Senator Charles Percy, the new
(Republican) Foreign Relations Committee chairman, spoke of the need to
restore bipartisanship – a clear invocation of the need for strong Presidential
direction.[45] In addition, Reagan's 1980 victory combined with the institutionalised weakness of oppositional leadership in Congress to promote
docility. Highly questionable measures, such as the 'reprogramming' of
funds to aid the government of El Salvador, were accepted with little protest.
With a Republican majority in the Senate, executive policymakers seemed in
a stronger position than any White House team since the mid-1960s.

Problems did, however, begin to surface in the Democratic House. Even
in 1981, the House rejected Reagan's plans to sell Airborne Warning and
Control System (AWAC) radar planes to Saudi Arabia. In December 1982,
the House adopted the first Boland amendment, disallowing covert US mil-

itary aid to the anti-government Contra forces in Nicaragua; and, in May 1983, the House adopted a resolution for a nuclear freeze. All these measures were reversed or killed in the Senate, and, indeed, the AWAC sale was trumpeted as a greater Administration victory. Nonetheless, the stage was set for the major foreign policy battles of Reagan's Presidency: especially over Contra aid and funding for the MX missile. Respectable Democratic performances in the 1982, 1984 and 1986 Congressional elections also tended to alter legislative perceptions of Reagan's mandate. The Administration began to adopt the tactic of moving to meet anticipated legislative action: for example, in removing marines from the Lebanon in February 1984, and in switching policy in the Philippines in 1986.

It would, therefore, be a gross exaggeration to depict the period between Reagan's inauguration and the onset of the Iran–Contra crisis (November–December, 1986) as one of unremitting executive domination. In 1985, for example, Congress forced the abandonment of proposed arms sales to Jordan and some modest changes in the Administration's stance towards South Africa. The overriding, in October 1986, of Reagan's veto of the South African sanctions bill was a major White House defeat. The final two years of Reagan's Presidency, after the eruption of the Iran–Contra affair and with a Senate Democratic majority, were inevitably difficult for the Administration. In September 1987, the Senate hindered the advance of the SDI by effectively disallowing Administration interpretations of the 1972 Anti-Ballistic Missile Treaty. In February 1988, the House rejected the President's request for new Contra aid. Nonetheless, attempts to invoke the War Powers Act over US action in the Persian Gulf failed. The Senate voted in May 1988 to accept, with certain provisos, the Intermediate Nuclear Force Treaty. Throughout the Reagan Presidency, the conduct of USA–Soviet relations remained firmly in the White House.

4   The Bush and Clinton years

(a) *Bush, 1989–93*   The Bush Administration's attitude towards legislative foreign policy was well summarised in a 1989 message from the Justice Department to the Congressional Armed Services Committees. The 'president', proclaimed Attorney General Dick Thornburgh, 'has exclusive authority to conduct and manage our relations with foreign nations.'[46] In July 1989, Bush declared the need to 'draw the line' between executive and legislative branches, accusing Congress of trespassing 'into areas entrusted by the Constitution exclusively to the executive'.[47]

The Bush years saw many examples of Administration high-handedness towards Congress. The invasion of Panama in December 1989 proceeded with a minimum of Congressional involvement. It commenced while Congress was out of session. In February 1990, the House passed a resolution stating that the President had acted 'decisively and appropriately in ordering

United States forces to intervene in Panama after making substantial efforts to resolve the crisis in Panama by political, economic, and diplomatic means in order to avoid resorting to military action'.[48] Policy towards Iraq before the Gulf War was expedited through unilateral National Security Directives, with Congress largely excluded. Subsequent legislative investigations into US support for Saddam Hussein were met by familiar executive tactics of blocking and evasion.[49] As argued in Chapter 3, the Gulf War did not see substantial legislative involvement.[50] In July 1991, Bush announced that he was unilaterally lifting the sanctions imposed on South Africa by Congress in 1986. The President held that South Africa had made sufficient democratic progress to enable sanctions to be removed, and Congress acquiesced amid grumbles about Presidential impropriety. As discussed in Chapter 8, Bush was equally successful in obtaining legislative backing for his commitment of troops to Somalia in December 1992.[51] In virtually his last act as President, George Bush issued 'midnight pardons' to key players in the Iran–Contra affair. Promulgated by a lame-duck President and without reference to Congress, the pardons were – in the opinion of Samuel Dash, former Chief Counsel to the Senate Watergate committee – 'the final acts of coverup'.[52]

In many of its actions towards Congress, the Bush Administration seemed consciously to be setting precedents for a new era of legislative–executive relations. Although Congress was kept at arms length in Washington's dealings with Moscow, the Administration was increasingly aware of legislative demands for a 'peace dividend' – and even for a turn towards isolationism. At one level, Bush's New World Order represented a means to deflect domestic isolationism by articulating a new, responsible version of US internationalism. The Administration's unwillingness to share information with Congress – even to the point of resurrecting Nixon's doctrine of unreviewable 'executive privilege' – seemed to serve notice that the White House intended to dominate post-Cold War foreign policy. A 1991 National Security Directive ordered the Administration's legal counsels to 'review and inventorise all requests' from Congress 'to determine which, if any, raise issues of executive privilege (deliberative process, foreign relations, national security, and so on)'.[53] The White House took also to issuing 'signing statements' to legislation, indicating that the law would be implemented according to the Administration's own interpretation. Congressional action in the field of foreign aid, notably to Central America, was undermined in this way. To the Administration, these 'signing statements' were a way of quashing, at the eleventh hour, procedural conditions and other manifestations of legislative 'micromanagement'.[54]

Despite White House high-handedness and desire to establish precedents, it was during the Bush years that many of the implications of the Cold War's end for executive–legislative relations became evident. Jeremy Rosner put the point clearly: 'Presidential power in foreign affairs is a function of national danger. Relative peace on earth will tend to mean relatively less peace down the length of Pennsylvania Avenue.'[55] During the Cold War, legislative assertiveness tended to ebb and flow with changing perceptions of the Soviet threat. By the mid-point of Bush's Presidency, differing perceptions of how to react to communist expansionism – a major Cold War theme – had virtually disappeared from the executive–legislative agenda. Opposition to communism began to mingle inextricably with the issue of human rights. Thus, Congressional criticisms of Bush's efforts to repair relations with communist China, in the wake of the 1989 Tiananmen Square massacre, were intense and widespread. Various Members sought to impose trade sanctions and to heighten public awareness of the issue. Yet, even here, the thrust of White House policy was not fundamentally altered. (Congressional policy on China also neatly illustrated linkages between foreign and domestic agendas. As James Lindsay notes: 'Stories of the Senate's failure in 1992 to muster enough votes to override a threatened presidential veto of legislation ending China's most-favoured-nation trade status ... highlighted the support President Bush received from farm state Democrats. These senators feared China would retaliate by buying fewer American farm products'[56].)

By the early 1990s, it was evident that US involvement in international peacekeeping had become a key issue. Between 1974 and 1989, peacekeeping figured in only 2 per cent of contested defence or foreign policy votes in Congress; in the period 1992–94, the figure rose to 12 per cent. Nevertheless, where issues could still be framed in 'national security' terms, Bush tended to score higher than when executive–legislative contests revolved around strictly defined 'foreign policy'. (Rosner calculates that, during his Presidency, George Bush won 70 per cent of contested 'defence policy' votes, but only 45 per cent on 'foreign policy'.) In 1992, with the post-Cold War agenda now clearly in place, Bush won only 49 per cent of contested defence and foreign policy votes in the Democratic Congress.[57]

(b) *Clinton, 1993–96*   President Clinton's major early successes with Congress related to the post-Cold War free trade agenda: the surprisingly clear victory (234–200 in the House; 61–38 in the Senate) on the North American Free Trade Agreement (NAFTA) in 1993; and Congressional acceptance, with some compromises, of the General Agreement on Tariffs and Trade (GATT) (Uruguay Round) in November 1994. Disputes with the Democratic Congress during Clinton's first year centred on UN peacekeeping, the Somalia operation and the conflict in Bosnia. The Administration's budget request of $642 million, constituting the American contribution to UN peacekeeping funds, was cut to $402 million. Congressional pressure led to a not altogether unwilling Presidential undertaking to withdraw from Somalia by 31 March 1994. The explicit Congressional undertaking to end funding for the Somalia mission amounted to an assertion of the legislative 'power of the purse' not seen since the Vietnam War. (Congressional action over the very limited humanitarian intervention in Rwanda represented a second such example.) Congress in 1993 adopted non-binding language requiring the White House to refrain from sending any US forces to Bosnia without explicit legislative approval. Rumblings over a legislative cancellation of the arms embargo on Bosnian Muslims came to little in 1993–94. In 1993, the White House also succeeded in gaining significant aid for Russia. During 1994, Clinton found legislative support forthcoming for huge troop deployments along the Iraqi border. Pressure, orchestrated by Senate Minority Leader Bob Dole, caused the Administration to stop using US military personnel to enforce the Bosnian embargo. The (virtually bloodless) Haitian invasion of September 1994 was mounted against a background of conflicting Congressional demands. Some liberal Members, especially in the Congressional Black Caucus, had urged the Administration to take military action to reinstate President Jean-Bertrand Aristide. Yet large sections of Congress resisted the military action and protested the President's usurpation of Congressional war powers. House Foreign Affairs Committee chairman Lee Hamilton commented: 'We have not approved of the policy, we have not disapproved of the policy. We simply default.'[58] Like the Bush Administration before it, the Clinton White House in 1994 failed to achieve its desired reform of the foreign aid process.

Executive–legislative ground rules for the post-Cold War era were emerging. Senator Sam Nunn remarked in 1993: 'Today, the time element is not the same as it was during the cold war. There is the perception that there's more time for decision-making, more time for debate, and that inevitably means that Congress is going to be much more involved than in the past.'[59] The key test for developing executive–legislative relations emerged in the form of the post-1994 Republican Congress. The 1994 GOP victories opened the way for intense Congressional attacks on a wide range of Administration policies: over defence spending, normalisation of relations with Vietnam, attitudes towards Cuba, support for the UN and especially for UN peacekeeping, over most-favoured-nation trading status for China, foreign aid, State Department reorganisation, Bosnia, Haiti, issues of free trade versus protectionism, the role of the CIA, and so on. Many commentators drew attention to the attitudes being adopted by (especially Republican) freshmen. The 1992 and 1994 Congressional elections saw the largest inflow of new Members since the elections of 1946 and 1948. By 1995, over half the House's membership had arrived since 1989. The new Members were not necessarily all foreign policy tiros, but they seemed unlikely to be willing to accept the deferential cultural heritage of the Cold War. First-term Representative David Funderburk (who had served as Ambassador to Romania under President Reagan) spoke for his fellows: 'We're not saying we're protectionist or isolationist. We're just looking to put the interests of our districts first. We represent the latest expression of populist feeling in this country.' As for the GOP leadership: 'Maybe Dole and Gingrich have been inside the Beltway too long.'[60]

The foreign policy provisions of the Republicans' Contract with America concentrated on the supposed need to cut funds for international peace-keeping, to prevent US troops from serving under UN or foreign command, and on the need for strong defence. The Contract, and the National Security Restoration Act which was extrapolated from it, made commitments to extended anti-missile defences and to eastwards extension of NATO. Any defence savings that could be made were to 'be used to reduce the deficit and the tax burden on families', rather than 'to continually fund more domestic social programs'. The Contract looked also to the creation of 'a blue-ribbon panel of military experts' to review national security policy and to 'ensure that we are getting good value for our defense dollars'.[61]

The Administration managed to contain and channel the threatened Republican foreign policy revolution in 1995–96. At its heart, this success rested on the executive's ability – even after the Cold War – to mould foreign policy agendas, and to carry public opinion along with it. The ability of Republican revolutionaries to re-set the national security compass was inhibited by the continual threat of the Presidential veto – and the enormous problem of mustering a two-thirds override when the veto was used. It was also constrained by the intra-GOP divisions. Some House Republicans, in particular, did represent a position of extreme unilateralism, hostility to free trade – of, in effect, *de facto* isolationism. Congressman Joe Scarborough of Florida introduced legislation on 24 October 1995 (the UN's fiftieth anniversary), calling on the United States to leave the United Nations. Representative Dana Rohabacher of California declared: 'Everything done through the United Nations can be better accomplished on a bilateral basis.'[62] In this environment, Speaker Newt Gingrich actually emerged as a force for moderation. Far more exercised over domestic than foreign issues, Gingrich – as noted in Chapter 1 – expressed support for US international engagement (albeit primarily in a unilateralist context). He persuaded John Kasich, chairman of the House Budget Committee, to reduce proposed foreign operations spending cuts by $2 billion in 1995.[63] In the Senate, Majority Leader Bob Dole, prior to his 1996 resignation to fight the Presidential election, resisted assaults on free trade and internationalism.[64] Tensions within the GOP surfaced early in 1995 in floor opposition to Clinton's loan guarantee plan – endorsed by House and Senate Republican leaders – for the Mexican currency.[65] Veteran GOP internationalists, like House Foreign Affairs Committee chairman Benjamin Gilman and Senator Lugar, had to make compromises with the new Republican surge, but also continued to insist that theirs remained an internationalist party committed to free trade. As with the Contract as a whole, the evolutionary push from the House tended to be dissipated in the Senate. The Administration waged a largely successful attack on Republican proposals, notably the National Security Restoration Act. Clinton condemned 'the most isolationist proposals ... in the last 50 years'.[66] Warren Christopher and Defence Secretary William Perry argued that the unilateralist National Security Restoration Act would 'leave the President with an unacceptable option whenever an emergency occurs: act alone or do nothing'.[67] During 1995 and 1996, it seemed that the foreign policy provisions of the Contract with America had no prospect of Senate passage.

A series of other factors intended to mitigate the force of the GOP foreign policy revolution. Most Republicans, like Gingrich, were primarily concerned with domestic issues. During Clinton's first two years in office, the President had actually enjoyed a measure of Republican support on foreign policy. Despite high degrees of partisanship, Republican support for Clinton on foreign affairs was about twice as high as on domestic issues in both chambers.[68] To some extent, this reflected the degree to which post-Cold War Republican realism coincided with the selective engagement priorities of the Administration. Since the ending of the Cold War, Republicans in Congress had been far more likely to berate the executive for excessive globalism than for neglecting strategies of preponderant power. If this left the Administration open to a neo-isolationist assault, at least – as Robert Kagan lamented in 1995[69] – the voters in 1994 clearly had not elected to reinstall the policies of the first Reagan Administration. Post-1994 Republicans wished to, and did, increase defence spending. But they tended to be constrained also by awareness of the deficit and of financial constraints – in the terminology of the times, they were 'cheap hawks'. In addition, the new Republican majority in Congress was heir to a foreign policy tradition which for so many years had exalted executive power and criticised the Congressional meddling. In a GOP discussion journal published in summer 1995, two former Reagan Administration officials attacked any Republican efforts to limit the President's authority: 'we are all too familiar with the imposition of ... micromanagement ... We believed then that such certifications detracted from the President's proper constitutional authority and did so in full view of our enemies. Our views on such fundamental matters cannot change because of the changing constellation of power in Washington.'[70] Both Gingrich and Dole remained committed to repeal of the War Powers Act. During the February 1995 floor debate on US involvement in UN peacekeeping, Republican Congressman Jim Leach of Iowa declared: 'Congress simply can't be relied upon to share executive authority.'[71]

None of this is to deny that the Republican Congress had an important impact. Defence and foreign aid spending patterns were deeply affected. The 1995 House and Senate votes against the Bosnian arms embargo were hedged around by qualifications, and in any case swiftly became irrelevant as conditions developed on the ground. Yet these highly publicised votes certainly were instrumental in provoking new Administration activism in Bosnia. (When it came to actual deployment of troops in Bosnia – a move which only a minority in Congress actually supported – the legislature was presented with a *fait accompli*). During 1996, slightly paradoxically, Congress began investigations into the Administration's policy of permitting Iran to break the arms embargo in Bosnia. The Helms–Burton sanctions on Cuba went further than was countenanced by the White House. However, by the latter part of 1996, with the likelihood of China being yet again granted most-favoured-nation trading status, it did not seem that the underlying dynamics of Presidential direction of foreign policy had been seriously disturbed. In 1996, Clinton won eight out of ten House defence and foreign policy votes on which he took a position. The Senate figures were seven and twelve.

5   War powers, advice and consent

(a) *War powers*   The 1974 War Powers Act emerged against the background of perceived Presidential abuse of his 'Commander-in-Chief' power. Only Congress has the constitutional authority to declare war, and has done so on five occasions: in 1812, 1846, 1898, 1917 and 1941.[72] (Congress, of course, has a long history – for example, regarding Tripoli in 1802 – of authorising limited military action without resort to a declaration of war.) Yet the 1974 Act specifically addressed itself to police actions, limited conflicts and other hostilities where Presidents were seen to be usurping the legislative prerogative. Under the legislation, Presidents must report to Congress the involvement of US troops in 'hostilities' within forty-eight hours. Unless Congress specifically authorises the troops to stay, the President must withdraw them in sixty – or, in especially difficult circumstances, within ninety – days. The Act, taking its language from the War Powers Resolution of 1973, instructed the President to consult Congress 'in every possible instance'.

The war powers legislation has conspicuously failed in its objective of giving Congress a controlling voice in crisis situations. Presidents have been able to exploit the existence of putative crises, requiring swift and secretive action, as well as the rather patchy nature of Members' interest in and knowledge of foreign affairs. The legislative language is also unsatisfactory. It is not clear exactly with whom the President is supposed to consult. The whole Congress? The party leaders? The relevant committees? The word, 'hostilities', is far too vague and positively invites executive dissimulation. Senator Eagleton also noticed at the time of passage that the war powers provisions effectively allow the President 'an open-ended blank cheque for ninety days of war-making'.[73] The Act's constitutionality has repeatedly been questioned. Issuing his veto on the original measure, President Nixon declared it a breach in separation of powers: an attempt 'to take away, by a mere legislative act, authority which the President has properly exercised for almost 200 years'.[74] The legislation incorporates a legislative veto, the propriety of which was cast into severe doubt by the Supreme Court's *Chadha* decision of 1983.[75] In the last resort, Congress is reluctant to challenge the

President in times of perceived (even of Presidentially manufactured) national emergency. As Senator Jacob Javits put it in 1985: 'The overwhelming temptation is to wait and see, to let the dust settle' before trying to assert Congressional war powers.[76] Congress will, seemingly, always allow Presidents consequent leeway in defining 'hostilities'. Senator Sam Nunn gave his verdict on the war powers legislation in 1993: 'It's never going to work. It's never worked in the past ... That automatic trigger makes any president reluctant to acknowledge that hostilities are imminent.'[77]

Recent experience bears out Nunn's verdict. Congress has only occasionally even tried to assert its war powers – usually when public opinion is exercised on a particular issue or where there are significant underlying political quarrels between White House and Capitol Hill.[78] Under President Reagan, actions in Lebanon and in Grenada violated the spirit and the letter of the law. The War Powers Act was invoked in connection with US involvement in Lebanon, but only with the proviso that the President be allowed to keep troops there for eighteen months. (US forces withdrew in February 1984.) Military assistance in Central America was successfully finessed so as to avoid invocation of the legislation. (In April 1983, for example, Defence Secretary Weinberger assured Senator Edward Kennedy that US forces in Central America were not involved in 'combat activities within the meaning of the War Powers Resolution'[79].) In 1987, 110 Members of the House unsuccessfully brought a lawsuit seeking to initiate the war powers procedure in relation to US action in the Persian Gulf.

The Panamanian invasion of 1989 was prosecuted without reference to the War Powers Act, although Bush's announced timetable for the troop deployments did seem to recognise the importance of the sixty- to ninety-day timescale.[80] In 1989, Senator Nunn led an unsuccessful bipartisan effort to amend the legislation in order to give Congress greater flexibility, essentially dismantling the sixty-day clock. President Bush's handling of the Gulf crisis was also challenged in court by more than 100 Members; the federal district court declared that it would only proceed if a majority in Congress were involved against the President.[81] Bush made his thinking plain when he requested legislative support for military action in January 1991:

> As I made clear to congressional leaders at the outset, my request for congressional support did not ... constitute any change in the long-standing positions of the executive branch on either the President's constitutional authority to use the Armed Forces to defend vital US interests or the constitutionality of the War Powers Resolution.[82]

In June 1993, President Bill Clinton failed to consult with Congress prior to the launching of a missile attack on Baghdad. He informed the legislature subsequently that he had acted 'pursuant to my constitutional authority with respect to the conduct of foreign relations and as Commander in Chief'.[83] Congressional activism over Somalia essentially concerned use of legislative funding rather than war powers. Both House and Senate passed measures in September 1994, criticising the President for sending troops to Haiti without due legislative authorisation and consultation. Clinton issued reports on the Haitian situation which were, in his phrase, 'consistent' with the law, but which did not concede its constitutionality. As noted above, by 1995 the leadership in Congress was itself committed to revoking the War Powers Act. Abolition formed one aspect of Senator Dole's 1995 Peace Powers Act. It soon became obvious that Congress would repeal the War Powers Act only as part of a general package, restricting US involvement with UN peace-keeping. Clinton's successful deployment of troops in Bosnia in late 1995 (albeit within a NATO rather than a UN command structure) illustrated the ironies of this position. The troops were despatched despite intense bipartisan opposition. In ways familiar from earlier conflicts, Congressional leaders responded to appeals based on the need to maintain US credibility, and to protect the integrity of troops already being sent. Republican Senator John McCain declared in November 1995: 'Our friends and enemies don't discriminate between Republican and Democratic presidents when the word of an American president is given.'[84] In a sense, even after the Cold War, politics still seemed to stop at the water's edge.

(b) *Treaties*   The powers of Congress regarding treaties provide another example of a potentially impressive grant of constitutional authority, which has to a considerable extent been abdicated to Presidential discretion. According to Article II, Section 2 of the Constitution, the President 'shall have Power, by and with the Advice and Consent of the Senate, to make Treaties, provided two thirds of the Senators present concur'. A report commissioned by the Senate Foreign Relations Committee in 1977 held that the 'original concept' of the Senate's role was that it 'would share fully in the process', rather 'as a council sitting to make decisions on treaty problems presented by the President'. It is also at least eminently arguable that the 'original concept' included a significant role for the House of Representatives.[85]

In modern times, the 'original concept' has become moribund. Certainly, some Presidents have sought the aid of important Senators in negotiating treaties. Congressional 'advisers' participated in the 1978 SALT II talks; during the Panama Canal treaty negotiations of 1977–78, a group of Republican Senators, led by Howard Baker, virtually conducted their own treaty-making process with General Torrijos of Panama. As Franck and Weisband pointed out in 1979, however, Cold War Presidential dominance in treaty negotiation was actually enhanced by the 'facade of selective senatorial participation'.[86]

The impact of Cold War consensus on the treaty ratification process is evident in the fact that only two out of over five hundred treaties signed in the period 1945–85 were defeated in Senate votes. Congress has tried to revive the process by use of its appropriations power. Thus, in 1987, the Congress responded to the Reagan Administration's controversial interpretation of the 1972 Anti-Ballistic Missile Treaty by adjusting allocations to the Pentagon. (Money was made available to fund only those tests of the SDI which fell under the more restrictive interpretation of the 1972 treaty.)[87] Such tactics have not been very successful. The Supreme Court has tended to favour the executive. In *Goldwater* v. *Carter* (1979), it was declared that Presidents could unilaterally abrogate treaties (the case at issue was the support agreement with Taiwan).[88] The Court has also held that Congress cannot cut off specific executive salaries in order to punish officials for treaty non-compliance, or indeed any other disregard of legislative intent.[89] Congress can, of course, use the treaty ratification power (as Senator Helms used the START II ratification process in 1995–96) as a lever against Presidents. Key treaty votes (like the NAFTA vote of 1993) can also still provide occasions for testing Presidential authority.

It has been the use of executive agreements – treaties in all but name, not requiring advice and consent – which has most decisively altered the treaty process as envisioned in the Constitution. White House preference for executive agreements has increased enormously since 1945. Between the end of World War Two and the early 1990s, the ratio of US executive agreements to treaties was approximately 7:1. The Reagan Administration between 1985 and 1989 entered into 1,271 international agreements, of which only 47 were regular treaties.[90] The constitutional case for executive agreements rests on Supreme Court interpretation (notably *Curtiss-Wright* (1936) and *Belmont* (1937)[91]), and on invocation of 'inherent' Presidential authority. Many executive agreements are, in a formal sense, authorised by statute. Nonetheless, the scale of contemporary executive agreement-making really does seem at variance with the constitutional intent. Yet, and certainly since the failure of the Bricker amendment in 1954, Congress has not been sufficiently united to address this problem satisfactorily. The 1972 Case Act dealt only with the question of executive secrecy, and related only to the *reporting* of executive agreements. The Act could not even prevent the 1973 Vietnam peace document being promulgated without advice and consent. Even the reporting provisions of the Case Act have been evaded and undermined by persistent executive delay.[92]

The entire treaty process in fact is vitiated by practices and precedents which tend to destroy significant legislative participation. In the case of measures actually submitted for advice and consent, Presidents often argue that they must either be accepted or rejected *in toto*. Tinkering or amending would, as Carter argued over SALT II for example, undercut the delicately negotiated balance of the treaty. Congress often accepts these arguments. (In the case of the 1993 NAFTA vote, Congress was bound by a prior undertaking to consider the measure under fast-track procedure, disallowing amendments.) Yet, in fact, the Senate does have a very strong case for a limiting and amending power: 'amendment, reservation, understanding, interpretations, declaration, and statement'.[93] As with war powers, circumstances generally conspire to ensure that this authority is not used. Presidents also often use executive agreements to amend and alter treaties which *have* been accepted by the Senate *in toto*. 'Side deals' – for example, over Japanese whaling in the Reagan era – can negate the force of treaties. Sometimes this can be achieved simply by unilateral executive action. (Nathan and Oliver cite the way in which, during the Clinton Administration, the US Coast Guard effectively cancelled part of a refugee asylum treaty by rejecting Haitian migrants[94].)

(c) *Appointments*   Senate advice and consent regarding Presidential appointments involve, in a way parallel to treaty consideration, the examination of nominees rather than prior consultation. The importance of the confirming power is tied to expectations that the President will consider anticipated Senate reactions before making the nomination. As noted above, likely problems with Senate confirmation of new appointees after the 1994 Republican victories effectively constrained President Clinton's freedom of choice in this period.

   Most appointments are subject to a simple majority vote on the Senate floor, and are confirmed without difficulty. Confirmation hearings can provide a forum for the articulation of Senate criticism of Administration foreign policy. The rejection of John Tower as Defence Secretary in 1989 was a major setback for the incoming Bush Administration. It was the first time in American history that a President's Cabinet-level nominee had been rejected at the start of his first term. It was only the second time that the Senate had turned down an ex-Senator nominated to the Cabinet. (The debate on Tower, of course, hinged not only on his hawkish defence record, but also on his personality and private life. The personality and prestige of his chief adversary, Senator Nunn, were also important factors.)

   The potency of the confirmation power is severely limited by the immunity from the process enjoyed by NSC and other White House staff. For most Senators, the appointment confirmation process is valued less for the opportunity to exercise a veto, than for providing chances (especially during the confirmation hearings) to initiate relationships with appointees, to acquire information and to publicise grievances.[95] Even within its limits, the 'advice and consent' appointment power is widely regarded as unsatisfactory. The 'sale' of ambassadorships in return for Presidential campaign assistance has long been recognised as an abuse of executive authority. Yet the Senate has generally not been prepared to use the confirmation power to remedy it. (Senator Jesse Helms's 1995 refusal to confirm ambassadorial appointments was an aspect of his war with the White House over State Department reorganisation, rather than an objection to the appointments *per se*.)

6   Foreign aid and defence budgeting

(a) *Foreign aid*   In many areas of foreign policy, Congress tends to lose the initiative because it has no 'handle': no ongoing process, specifically designed to develop new approaches. Rather, it reacts to crises, which are themselves defined by the executive. In the case of foreign aid, however, there is such a process: the annual foreign aid authorisation and foreign assistance appropriations measures. Since the early 1980s, Congress has frequently failed to pass coherent foreign aid authorisations, often relying instead on stopgap continuing resolutions. By the early 1990s, virtually no one on Capitol Hill denied that the foreign aid process had lost its focus and sense of purpose. As (then) House Foreign Affairs Committee chairman Lee Hamilton commented in 1994: 'Everyone in the Congress wants reform of foreign aid. The problem is that everyone wants to reform it in a different way.'[96] The Clinton Administration's 1994 reform proposals would have scrapped the 1961 legislative basis for foreign aid and substituted key new objectives: 'promoting democracy, promoting peace, providing humanitarian aid, promoting growth through trade and investment, advancing diplomacy and promoting sustainable development'. Old Congressional mandates for aid – known as 'earmarks' – would be abandoned. The reform collapsed amid Congressional uncertainty about the particular impacts of the new aid objectives, and their associated opportunities for oversight.[97]

During the Cold War, the lack – except in some exceptional cases like Israel – of any obvious domestic constituency for the bulk of foreign aid tended to orient Congress towards a confrontational budget-cutting role *vis-à-vis* the executive. Reluctance to go on record as supporting foreign aid contributed to the recurrent failure to pass an authorisation. A Congressman interviewed by C. W. Whalen said that he had opposed every foreign aid bill for twenty years: 'It is unpopular in my district, which is very poor. Had I voted for it, it would have become a campaign issue.'[98] Among Congressional liberals, the use of aid – particularly security assistance – to further military objectives in the developing world raised particular questions. Increasingly during the late 1970s and 1980s, Congress sought to tie aid to human rights agendas. The legislature also sometimes used the lever of aid to force specific courses of action on foreign countries. (For example, a 1984 Senate rider to an aid appropriation prevented Turkey receiving $215 million unless part of the city of Famagusta was returned to Cypriot government control[99].)

By the end of the Cold War, the United States – though the largest aggregate giver of aid – was still only giving out relatively small proportions of its national wealth in this way. By the early 1990s, despite widespread public perceptions to the contrary, foreign aid took less than 1 per cent of the federal budget (compared with around 20 per cent for defence). By 1994, the aid budget had already been cut by approximately half since its 1985 peak of $26 billion. Nonetheless, attacks on aid became an important feature of the post-Cold War Congress. To conservative Republicans, the end of the Cold War offered the chance to privatise aid and thus combat 'one world-ism'. In 1995, Republican attacks on foreign aid were sparing only in the cases of Israel, Egypt (whose aid has been tied to Israel's since the late 1970s) and Ireland. Senator Helms's campaign to dismantle the Agency for International Development (AID) sparked a major debate about post-Cold War internationalism.

Brian Attwood, head of the AID, accused Congressional 'isolationists' of being blind to the 'usefulness of development as a strategic weapon'.[100] Threatening to veto the foreign aid bill in May 1995, Clinton argued: 'We did not win the Cold War to walk away and blow the opportunities of the peace on shortsighted, scattershotted budget cuts.'[101] Attwood estimated that around 70 per cent of 'foreign' aid is actually spent on US goods and services, provided to the recipient countries. Despite the success of bureaucratic defenders of the AID in 1996, there could be no doubting the difficulty of mounting a generalised case *for* foreign aid on Capitol Hill.

(b) *Military budgeting*   As with foreign aid, annual consideration of defence spending provides Congress with the opportunity to develop policy on a coherent basis. The legislature moved to a more activist position on military budgeting after the Vietnam War. Between 1960 and 1968, there were only three examples of Congress making changes of over 5 per cent in the procurement, research, developing, testing and evaluation titles of the President's defence budget. The years 1969–77 saw seventeen such changes.[102] In this period Congress also grew in defence expertise, with the creation of the Military Reform Caucus in 1981 an important symbol of the developing climate.

Despite increasing assertiveness, most judgements on Congressional defence budgeting in the late Cold War period were negative. With the proliferation of reporting requirements and annual authorisations, the executive raised the familiar complaint of 'micromanagement'. Congress was being tempted 'to intrude too deeply in the national security policy-making process'.[103] The whole process reeked – so opponents of 'micromanagement' held – of centrifugalism and parochialism, not to mention the 'pork barrel'. The defence budget in Congress typically has over twenty stages at which votes are taken. Individuals and sub-groups compete to gain lucrative contracts for states and districts. The final House-passed authorisation bill for fiscal year 1981 actually provided a job-creating defence project for every single member of the Armed Services Committee. Congress is lobbied by defence contractors and by the military itself. Members who consistently support high defence spending very often receive substantial defence contracting Political Action Committee (PAC) contributions. (In 1988, Philip Stern cited the case of Senator Dan Quayle, before his elevation to the Vice-Presidency under George Bush. Quayle, chairman of a military procurement sub-committee which enacted a defence cost reporting measure in 1985, reversed his position after receiving contractors' PAC money[104].) In this environment, causes like arms control, with little obvious centrifugal benefit, often took second place. The long lead time of weapons systems research has also tended to militate against effective Congressional action. Barry Blechman summarised the late Cold War case against Congressional defence budgeting in 1990: 'Congress continues to get lost in the "trees" of detailed defense programs, losing sight of the "forest" of broader issues in defense planning and military strategy.'[105]

Unquestionably, much of this critique was accurate, and significant elements of a flawed defence-budgeting process – at once too deferential and too oriented to narrow, constituency concerns – continued after the Cold War. Yet, as noted at the beginning of this chapter, the case against 'micromanagement' always tended to be overstated. The Pentagon resents rather than suffers under-reporting and reauthorisation requirements. Members' incentives in the defence policy area are not always centrifugal; career development can be achieved with the acquisition of generalised policy expertise and articulation.[106] At the empirical level, James Lindsay has found that political ideology, rather than constituency interest, best explains legislative voting patterns on strategic weapons.[107]

The ending of the Cold War also seemed to push Congress away from detail, and towards wider, strategic issues. During the Bush Presidency in particular, Congressman Les Aspin and Senator Nunn were actually the leaders of American efforts to re-think strategic defence commitments. Paul Stockton concluded in 1995: 'Congress has moved beyond micromanagement into the realm of strategy. Although legislators continue to manipulate the details of the defense budget, broad policy concerns now affect individual and committee behavior, with important implications for the nature of the budgeting process and assessments of Congress itself.'[108]

By 1996, Republicans in Congress were able to point to an additional $7 billion which they had added to Clinton's defence budget. Significant and substantive conflicts, over fighter and bomber aircraft procurement, over anti-missile defences and force levels, demonstrated that Congress was challenging executive priorities, rather than merely 'micromanaging' them. The post-1994 Republican stance on defence was, of course, intensely partisan, and also riven by intra-GOP tensions between 'deficit hawks' and 'defence hawks'. Senator John McCain (Republican of Arizona) emerged as a key defence policy specialist on the Armed Services Committee, attempting to strike some kind of a balance between attacking 'pork' in the defence budget and following Republican policies on strong defence.[110] The difficulties in achieving a defence authorisation bill in 1995 illustrated Paul Stockton's point: 'even the most concerted efforts at top-down budgeting will always be suffused with politics'.[111] The Republican House sustained Clinton's veto of the fiscal 1996 defence authorisation. GOP leaders were forced to remove provisions regarding anti-missile defence systems. The post-1994 Republican leadership was certainly not able to impose any 'top down' rationality. Congress simply does not work that way; its democratic strengths lie elsewhere. As former Under-Secretary of State David Newsom wrote, in a discussion of Congress and public opinion: 'Congress speaks with many voices and listens to many more'.[112]

Notes

1 See L. Fisher, 'Foreign policy powers of the President and Congress', *Annals of the American Academy*, 500 (1988), pp. 148–62.
2 *Congressional Quarterly Almanac*, 1992, p. 533.
3 H. H. Koh, *The National Security Constitution* (New Haven, Yale University Press, 1990), p. 211. See also L. Henkin, 'Foreign affairs and the Constitution', *Foreign Affairs*, 66 (1987–88), pp. 286–90.
4 *Federalist Paper*, no. 70 (A. Hamilton *et al.*, *The Federalist Papers* (New York, Mentor, 1961)).
5 J. Lehman, *The Executive, Congress and Foreign Policy* (New York, Praeger, 1976), p. 30.
6 Cited in J. M. Lindsay, *Congress and the Politics of US Foreign Policy* (Baltimore, Johns Hopkins University Press, 1994), pp. 3–4. See also J. G. Tower, 'Congress versus the President', *Foreign Affairs*, 60 (1981–82), pp. 229–46.
7 See R. Cheney, 'Congressional overreaching in foreign policy', in R. A. Goodwin and R. A. Licht, eds, *Foreign Policy and the Constitution* (Washington DC, American Enterprise Institute, 1991).
8 J. T. Tierney, 'Congressional activism in foreign policy', in D. A. Deese, ed., *The New Politics of American Foreign Policy* (New York, St. Martin's, 1994), p. 126.
9 Lindsay, *Congress and the Politics of US Foreign Policy*, pp. 3–8.
10 See S. J. Baker, 'Evaluating Congress' foreign policy performance', in H. Purvis and S. J. Baker, eds, *Legislating Foreign Policy* (Boulder, Westview, 1984).
11 J. M. Lindsay, 'Congress and diplomacy', in R. B. Ripley and J. M. Lindsay, eds, *Congress Resurgent: Foreign and Defense Policy on Capitol Hill* (Ann Arbor, University of Michigan Press, 1993), p. 280.
12 *Congressional Quarterly Weekly Report*, 3 Feb. 1990, p. 293.
13 See Lindsay, 'Congress and diplomacy', pp. 276–7. See also L. Fisher, 'Micromanagement by Congress: myth and reality', in L. Gordon Crovitz and J. A. Rabkin, eds, *The Fettered Presidency* (Washington DC, American Enterprise Institute, 1989).
14 S. R. Weissman, *A Culture of Deference: Congress's Failure of Leadership in Foreign Policy* (New York, Basic Books, 1995), p. 184. See also B. Hinckley, *Less Than Meets the Eye: Policymaking and the Myth of the Assertive Congress* (Chicago, University of Chicago Press, 1994).
15 See E. V. Rostow, *President, Prime Minister, or Constitutional Monarch?* (Washington DC, National Defence University, 1989) (cited in Lindsay, 'Congress and diplomacy', p. 276). See also P. W. Rodman, 'The imperial Congress', *The National Interest*, 1 (1985), pp. 26–35.
16 J. B. Martin, *US Policy in the Caribbean* (Boulder, Westview, 1978), p. 123.

17 M. Nincic, *Democracy and Foreign Policy: The Fallacy of Political Realism* (New York, Columbia University Press, 1992), p. 89.

18 Cited in J. M. McCormick, 'Decision making in the Foreign Affairs and Foreign Relations committees', in Ripley and Lindsay, eds, *Congress Resurgent*, p.116.

19 C. V. Crabb, *American Foreign Policy in the Nuclear Age* (New York, Harper and Row, 1988), p. 181. See also J. M. McCormick, 'The changing role of the House Foreign Affairs Committee in the 1970s and 1980s', *Congress and the Presidency*, 12 (1985), pp. 1–20.

20 McCormick, 'Decision making', pp. 131, 133.

21 See C. J. Deering, 'Decision making in the Armed Services committees', in Ripley and Lindsay, eds, *Congress Resurgent*.

22 J. White, 'Decision making in the Appropriations subcommittees on defense and foreign operations', in Ripley and Lindsay, eds, *Congress Resurgent*, pp. 194, 199. See also B. M. Blechman, *The Politics of National Security: Congress and US Defense Policy* (New York, Oxford University Press, 1990), pp. 38–40.

23 See D. W. Rohde, *Parties and Leaders in the Postreform House* (Chicago, University of Chicago Press, 1991); R. H. Davidson, ed., *The Postreform Congress* (New York, St. Martin's, 1992); B. Sinclair, *Legislators, Leaders and Lawmaking: The US House of Representatives in the Postreform Era* (Baltimore, Johns Hopkins University Press, 1995).

24 B. Sinclair, 'Congressional party leaders in the foreign and defense policy arena', in Ripley and Lindsay, eds, *Congress Resurgent*, p. 217.

25 See S. S. Smith, 'Congressional party leaders', in P. E. Peterson, ed., *The President, the Congress, and the Making of Foreign Policy* (Norman, University of Oklahoma Press, 1994). See also J. M. McCormick and E. R. Wittkopf, 'Bipartisanship, partisanship, and ideology in congressional–executive foreign policy relations, 1947–1988', *Journal of Politics*, 52 (1990), pp. 1077–100.

26 Sinclair, 'Congressional party leaders', p. 216.

27 See D. W. Rohde, 'Partisanship leadership and Congressional assertiveness in foreign and defense policy', in Deese, ed., *The New Politics of American Foreign Policy*, p. 99.

28 E. Abrams, *Undue Process* (New York, Free Press, 1993), p. 171. See also R. G. Sutter, *The China Quandary* (Epping, Bowker, 1983), pp. 103–7.

29 A. Frye, *A Responsible Congress* (New York, McGraw-Hill, 1975), p. 225.

30 Lindsay, *Congress and the Politics of US Foreign Policy*, pp. 26–9.

31 See P. E. Petersen and J. P. Greene, 'Questioning by foreign policy committees', in Petersen, ed., *The President, the Congress*. See generally J. M. Lindsay and W. P. Steger, 'The "Two Presidencies" in Future Research', *Congress and the Presidency*, 20 (1993), pp. 103–17; J. M. Lindsay, 'Congress, foreign policy and the new institutionalism', *International Studies Quarterly*, 38 (1994), pp. 281–304.

32 Weissman, *A Culture of Deference*, pp. 17, 31; Hinckley, *Less Than Meets the Eye*, pp. 173–4.

33 R. B. Ripley and G. A. Franklin, *Congress, the Bureaucracy and Public Policy* (Pacific Grove, Brooks Cole, 1991), pp. 21–5.

34 *American Foreign Policy Current Documents: 1990* (Washington DC, Department of State, 1990), p. 34.

35 *Congressional Digest*, 1987, p. 298.

36 See N. J. Ornstein, 'Congress in the post-Cold War World', in D. Yankelovich

and I. M. Destler, eds, *Beyond the Beltway* (New York, Norton, 1994).

37 J. M. Lindsay and R. B. Ripley, 'How Congress influences foreign and defence policy', in Ripley and Lindsay, eds, *Congress Resurgent*.

38 *Ibid.*, p. 27.

39 See L. Fisher, *The Politics of Shared Power: Congress and the Executive* (Washington DC, Congressional Quarterly, 1993), p. 83.

40 See S. Brown, *The Faces of Power* (New York, Columbia University Press, 1983), p. 436.

41 T. M. Franck and E. Weisband, *Foreign Policy by Congress* (New York, Oxford University Press, 1979), p. 35.

42 Baker, 'Evaluating Congress' foreign policy performance', p. 15.

43 C. W. Whalen, *The House and Foreign Policy* (Chapel Hill, University of North Carolina Press, 1982), p. 80.

44 Cited in I. M. Destler, 'The evolution of Reagan's foreign policy', in F. I. Greenstein, ed., *The Reagan Presidency: An Early Assessment* (Baltimore, Johns Hopkins University Press, 1983), p. 118.

45 C. H. Percy, 'The partisan gap', *Foreign Policy*, 45 (1981–82), pp. 82–103.

46 *Congressional Quarterly Weekly Report*, 3 Feb. 1990, pp. 293–4.

47 *Ibid.*

48 L. Fisher, *Presidential War Power* (Lawrence, University Press of Kansas, 1995), pp. 145–6.

49 See B. W. Jentleson, *With Friends Like These* (New York, Norton, 1994), chs. 3, 4.

50 See *Congressional Quarterly Almanac, 1992*, p. 533; J. Dumbrell, 'The US Congress and the Gulf War', in J. Walsh, ed., *The Gulf War Did Not Happen* (Aldershot, Arena, 1995).

51 Fisher, *Presidential War Power*, p. 153.

52 S. Dash, 'Saturday night massacre II', *Foreign Policy*, 96 (1994), pp. 173–86, 186.

53 C. Tiefer, *The Semi-Sovereign Presidency: The Bush Administration's Strategy for Governing without Congress* (Boulder, Westview, 1994), p. 108.

54 *Ibid.*, p. 38.

55 J. D. Rosner, *The New Tug-of-War: Congress, the Executive Branch, and National Security* (Washington DC, Carnegie Endowment, 1995), p. 4.

56 Lindsay, *Congress and the Politics of US Foreign Policy*, p. 34.

57 Rosner, *The New Tug-of-War*, pp. 17, 39.

58 *Congressional Quarterly Almanac*, 1994, p. 451.

59 Cited in M. Small, *Democracy and Diplomacy: The Impact of Domestic Politics on US Foreign Policy, 1789–1994* (Baltimore, Johns Hopkins University Press, 1996), pp. 168–9.

60 *Congressional Quarterly Weekly Report*, 3 Feb. 1996, pp. 306, 309.

61 S. Moore, ed., *Restoring the Dream* (House Republicans) (New York, New York Times Books, 1995), p. 26.

62 *Congressional Quarterly Weekly Report*, 6 May 1995, p. 1249, and 27 May 1995, p. 1514.

63 See R. S. Greenberger, 'Dateline Capitol Hill: the new majority's foreign policy', *Foreign Policy*, 101 (1995–96), pp. 159–69: 166.

64 See R. Dole, 'Shaping America's global future', *Foreign Policy*, 98 (1995), pp.

29–43; C. Lane, 'Dole: the last interventionist', *New Republic*, 3 July 1995, pp. 19–25. See generally, E. Drew, *Showdown: The Struggle between the Gingrich Congress and the Clinton White House* (New York, Simon and Schuster, 1996).

65 See N. J. Ornstein and A. L. Schenkenberg, 'The 1995 Congress: the first 100 days and beyond', *Political Science Quarterly*, 110 (1995), pp. 183–262: 189.

66 Rosner, *The New Tug-of-War*, p. 2.

67 *New York Times*, 13 Feb. 1995.

68 See J. R. Bond and R. Fleisher, 'Clinton and Congress: a first-year assessment', *American Politics Quarterly*, 23 (1995), pp. 355–72.

69 R. Kagan, 'A retreat from power?', *Commentary* (July 1995), p. 21.

70 C. J. Cooper and J. O. McGinniss, 'The Republican Congress and the Constitution in foreign and military affairs', *Common Sense*, 2 (1995), pp. 75–88, 88.

71 *Congressional Record*, 16 Feb. 1995, H1859.

72 Robert Scigliano ('Politics, the Constitution, and the President's war power', in Deese, ed., *The New Politics of American Foreign Policy*, p. 151) holds that actually the United States 'has never *declared war* against anyone'. Technically, Congress has simply 'recognised' existing conflicts. See also J. H. Ely, *War and Responsibility: Constitutional Lessons of Vietnam and its Aftermath* (Princeton, Princeton University Press, 1993).

73 See J. L. Sundquist, *The Decline and Resurgence of Congress* (Washington DC, Brookings, 1981), p. 258.

74 R. D. Clark *et al.*, *The War Powers Resolution* (Washington DC, National Defense University, 1985), p. 1. See also R. A. Katzman, 'War powers: toward a new accommodation', in T. E. Mann, ed., *A Question of Balance* (Washington DC, Brookings, 1990).

75 *Immigration and Naturalization Service* v. *Chadha*, 103 S. Ct. 2764 (1983).

76 J. K. Javits, 'War powers reconsidered', *Foreign Affairs*, 64 (1985), pp. 130–40, 138.

77 *Congressional Quarterly Almanac*, 1993, p. 485.

78 See J. Meernik, 'Congress, the President, and the Commitment of the US military', *Legislative Studies Quarterly*, 20 (1995), pp. 377–92.

79 *Congressional Quarterly Almanac*, 1983, p. 1239.

80 See Fisher, *Presidential War Power*, p. 145.

81 *Dellums* v. *Bush*, 752, F. Supp. 1141 (DDC, 1990).

82 Fisher, *Presidential War Power*, pp. 150–1. See also L. Fisher, 'Congressional checks on military initiatives, *Political Science Quarterly*, 109 (1994–95), pp. 739–62.

83 Fisher, *Presidential War Power*, p. 152.

84 *Congressional Quarterly Weekly Report*, 2 Dec. 1995, p. 3668.

85 Staff Memorandum to the Senate Foreign Relations Committee, *The Role of the Senate in Treaty Ratification*, 1977, p. 28. See also L. Fisher, *The Constitution between Friends* (New York, St. Martin's 1978), pp. 197–204.

86 Franck and Weisband, *Foreign Policy by Congress*, p. 138.

87 See Lindsay, *Congress and the Politics of US Foreign Policy*, pp. 79, 87.

88 *Goldwater* v. *Carter*, 444 US 996 (1979).

89 See Lindsay, *Congress and the Politics of US Foreign Policy*, p. 88.

90 G. R. Berridge, *Diplomacy: Theory and Practice* (London, Prentice Hall, 1995), p. 166.

91 *US* v. *Curtiss-Wright Export Corporation*, 299 US 304 (1936); *US* v. *Belmont*, 301 US 324 (1937).

92 See J. M. McCormick, *American Foreign Policy and Process* (Ithaca, Peacock, 1992), p. 310.

93 1977 Staff Memorandum, *The Role of the Senate*, p. 3.

94 J. A. Nathan and J. K. Oliver, *Foreign Policy Making and the American Political System* (Baltimore, Johns Hopkins University Press, 1994), p. 103. See also A. Frye, 'Searching for arms control', in Peterson, ed., *The President, the Congress*.

95 See M. L. Mezey, *Congress, the President and Public Policy* (Boulder, Westview, 1987), p. 64.

96 *Congressional Quarterly Almanac*, 1994, p. 452.

97 *Ibid.*

98 Whalen, *The House and Foreign Policy*, p. 146.

99 See *Congressional Quarterly Weekly Report*, 28 April 1984, p. 959.

100 Speech, 26 Sept. 1995 (US Information Agency press release).

101 *Congressional Quarterly Weekly Report*, 27 May 1995, p. 1514.

102 See J. A. Nathan and J. K. Oliver, *The Future of United States Naval Power* (Bloomington, Indiana University Press, 1979), p. 136; P. N. Stockton, 'Congress and defense policy-making in the post-Cold War era', in Ripley and Lindsay, eds, *Congress Resurgent*; R. G. Carter, 'Budgeting for defense', in Peterson, ed., *The President, the Congress*.

103 L. J. Korb, *The Fall and Rise of the Pentagon* (Westport, Greenwood, 1979), p. 175.

104 P. Stern, *The Best Congress Money Can Buy* (New York, Pantheon Books, 1988), pp. 149–50.

105 Blechman, *The Politics of National Security*, pp. 27–8.

106 See J. M. Lindsay, 'Congressional oversight of the Department of Defense budget: reconsidering the conventional wisdom', *Armed Forces and Society*, 17 (1990), pp. 7–33.

107 J. M. Lindsay, 'Parochialism, policy and constituency constraints: Congressional voting on strategic weapons systems', *American Journal of Political Science*, 34 (1990), pp. 936–60.

108 P. N. Stockton, 'Beyond micromanagement: Congressional budgeting for a post-Cold War military', *Political Science Quarterly*, 110 (1995), pp. 233–59, 257.

109 See D. C. Morrison, 'Defense deadlock', *National Journal*, 4 Feb. 1995.

110 See J. Kitfield, 'The maverick,' *National Journal*, 25 Nov. 1995.

111 Stockton, 'Beyond micromanagement', p. 259.

112 D. D. Newsom, *The Public Dimension of Foreign Policy* (Bloomington, Indiana University Press, 1996), p. 202. See also F. R. Harris, *In Defense of Congress* (New York, St. Martin's, 1995).

6

Public opinion

Arguments against diverse and sustained public involvement in foreign policy-making are similar to those advanced against Congressional foreign policy. Speed, crisis management and informal judgements are held to be the exclusive province of the executive branch. Walter Lippmann famously argued that the 'people' had forced governments to be 'too late with too little ... too pacifist in peace and too bellicose in war, too neutralist or appeasing in negotiation or too intransigent'. In *The Public Philosophy* (1955), Lippmann argued that the executives of Western democracies had become enfeebled by the irrationality of mass opinion, and its natural allies in legislatures.[1]

Within American liberal democratic discourse, it is rather unusual to find doubts openly expressed about the wisdom of 'the people'. Such doubts reflect poorly on the nation's commitment to democracy – or at least summon up the characterisation of democracy given by George Kennan: 'similar to one of those prehistoric monsters with a body as long as this room and a brain the size of a pin'.[2] Yet hostility to meaningful public participation in (above all) foreign policy is implicit in a variety of ideological traditions: most obviously within realism and conservatism, but also in many liberal formulations. To some extent, sentiments of opposition to public partici-pation may be countered by the same arguments which support a strong legislative role in foreign policy. The historical record shows that un-accountable executive discretion – even when not driven by 'mass' public opinion – leads to irrationality and the abuse of power. Of course, democ-racy should not be equated with simple majoritarianism or 'tyranny of the majority'. Popular participation is partly exercised through representa-tive organs of government – notably the Congress – but also through organ-ised groups and vehicles for minority dissent. It is facilitated through the widest possible dissemination of information and high levels of public edu-cation.

1   Public opinion on foreign policy issues

Opponents of extensive public involvement in the foreign policy process have no difficulty in demonstrating high levels of public ignorance. In 1983, apparently only 8 per cent of the American public knew that the United States supported the government of El Salvador against guerrilla forces, but supported anti-government guerrillas in Nicaragua. In 1993, following extended conflict in the former Yugoslavia, only about one quarter of respondents were able correctly to identify the contending parties. Even people with some accurate information may have no opinion, even after long periods of public debate. Many public opinion scholars have also argued that US public opinion is beset by more or less irrational mood shifts: usually between the poles of internationalism and isolationism.[3]

Ignorance about foreign affairs is not the prerogative of the masses. (During his confirmation hearings in 1981, William Clark – as Under-Secretary of State designate – revealed a virtual absence of knowledge of European politics.) However, there is no question that the 'average' American, like the 'average' British citizen, is not well informed on foreign issues. For long periods, foreign affairs do not impinge on people's everyday lives. T. G. Paterson quotes a blue-collar worker interviewed in the late 1940s: 'Foreign affairs, that's for people who don't have to work for a living.'[4] People confronted with the problems of having to make a living, especially those facing economic hardship, may (understandably if not rationally) lack interest in 'remote' issues like elections and foreign policy.[5] Even as US troops prepared for the Gulf War in late 1990, only just over half of respondents surveyed by the Chicago Council on Foreign Relations declared themselves 'very interested' in foreign news.[6] It makes no sense to pretend that the public is consistently well informed, avid for information and self-consciously committed to specific foreign policy agendas. The case for public participation needs to be set in the context of a commitment to education. It also needs to take account of people's immediate priorities, and to avoid patronisation. (One is reminded of a 1970s British cartoon, querying the contemporary vogue for worker-directors and industrial democracy. A worker, clad in overalls and nervously handling a spanner, stands before a besuited panel of company directors. The chairman commands: 'For God's sake, Entwistle, participate!')

During the latter part of the Cold War, William Schneider argued that a majority of Americans wanted the United States to be the toughest kid on the block, but in a defensive sense, rather than as a global policeman. They wanted both peace and strength, with the stress on either one varying over time.[7] Late Cold War US public opinion on foreign policy was typically a product of countervailing forces: notably, suspicion of Soviet expansionism, anxiety about nuclear weapons, concern for foreign policy issues with domestic economic impact, and (especially following the Vietnam War) caution about committing troops abroad. Even during the 1980s, US distrust of Soviet intentions remained deep-seated. Americans typically perceived nuclear war as more likely than did other nations, and tended to harbour even more pessimistic notions about the survivability of such a war. Arms control and peace initiatives, at least during the later Cold War, tended to gain automatic support. Yet, notably in the late 1970s, nuclear anxieties also contributed to demands for higher military spending to gain advantages over the USSR.[8] Public concern for the impact of foreign policy on jobs is easily documented.[9] On troop commitments, public caution was evident even before the Vietnam War. In May 1961, for example, some 65 per cent of Americans appeared to oppose using troops against the Castro regime in Cuba.[10] After the Vietnam War, it was noticeable that the hardening of public attitudes towards the Soviet Union in the 1970s did not extend to enthusiasm for military intervention. In the 1980s, typically no more than one-third of Americans seemed to favour intervention in foreign wars.[11]

The view that public opinion is quixotic, capricious and unstable does not bear much examination. It is certainly the case that wars – and, above all, war casualties – do alter opinion dramatically, as was demonstrated in the Korean as well as the Vietnam conflict.[12] The Vietnam War occasioned a significant restructuring of US public opinion, provoking major fluctuations in support for military expenditure.[13] During the Cold War, the American public was preoccupied with external 'threat' in various forms.[14] Yet this preoccupation did not lead it into irresponsible bellicosity, or indeed into reactionary isolationism. Polls tended to rate the danger to US lives as the major criterion by which to judge the desirability of foreign interventions. Public support for internationalism – the view that the United Stats should take an active role in international affairs – did decline after the Vietnam War. Yet, by the early Reagan years, it had recovered to approximately 60 per cent.[15] Perusal of US public opinion over the entire Cold War led Nathan and Oliver to conclude: 'In the postwar period, Americans have usually rejected belligerency, rash solutions and quick fixes.'[16]

The problem for students of foreign policy public opinion is one of explaining change-within-stability, rather than fickleness. Even those theorists who do posit rather unpredictable shifts between internationalism and isolationism tend not to see public opinion as structureless. It is complex rather than formless. Various cyclical and generational theories have attempted precisely to establish structure within public opinion.[17] One particularly influential way of assessing public opinion has involved the separating out of opinion leaders and 'attentive publics' from mass opinion. In such formulations, 'attentive publics' – people interested in foreign policy, but not always enjoying direct access to policymakers – are held to constitute between one quarter and about 10 per cent of the population.[18] Various attempts have been made to map post-Vietnam opinion cleavages, both in terms of 'mass' and 'attentive publics'. For elite and non-elite opinion, the notion of the 'belief system' has been used to establish elements of coherence and pre-dictability. In 1984, for example, Holsti and Rosenau argued that the Viet-nam War had caused elite opinion to split into three sections: Cold War internationalists (largely unaffected by the War); post-Cold War internation-alists (looking to the interdependency agenda); and isolationists (on both left and right wings).[19] Writers such as Michael Mandelbaum and William Schnei-der traced these tendencies in general public opinion.[20] By the 1980s, consid-erable research supported the view that mass opinion was structured around fear belief systems: internationalists (favouring both force and diplomacy as means to advance and protect US interests); isolationists; hardliners (inter-ventionist opponents of détente and accommodation with communism); and accommodationists (favouring multilateralism and cooperation).[21]

An alternative approach – possibly an 'emerging new paradigm'[22] – is that encapsulated in the Shapiro and Page notion of the 'rational public'. This essentially turns Lippmann's view on his head. The debate is akin to that between the tradition set by the 1960 study of the American electorate, *The American Voter*, and the perspective embodied in V. O. Key's *The Responsi-ble Electorate*.[23] According to the 1960 study, voters form an ill-informed body, politically unsophisticated and basing choices largely upon leadership cues. Key, however, argued that voters are not fools. They exhibit ideologi-cal consistency and do concern themselves with candidates and issues, on the basis of such information as they have to hand. Similarly, Shapiro and Page, who associate their view with that of Key and use comprehensive data, hold that foreign policy preferences are mostly consistent. Changes are generally 'reasonable, given the unfolding of events … as reported and interpreted by the media and political leaders'.[24] 'At any particular moment in time, public opinion about foreign policy tends to be *differentiated*, that is, the American public makes sharp distinctions among policies, favoring some and opposing others.' Furthermore, 'these distinctions tend to be coherent and consistent with each other: they fall into regular patterns that make sense and fit with an overall system of values'.[25] Shapiro and Page cite consistent public atti-tudes towards arms sales to particular countries during the Cold War. Devel-oping attitudes are seen to follow a rational pattern. Thus, public attitudes towards the Middle East in the 1980s showed strong traces of traditional support for the state of Israel, but also 'sympathy for the Palestinians and a more critical view of Israeli foreign policy, later accentuated somewhat by revelations of the Israeli role in the Iran–*contra* affair'.[26] However, even Shapiro and Page acknowledge that opinion on foreign issues, especially those with a military dimension, tends to change quicker than domestic atti-tudes. Of course, adult members of the American public, no less than poli-cymakers, are conceptual consistency-seekers, capable of suppressing information which challenges established notions. Nonetheless, early politi-cal socialisation neither fixes adult opinions irrevocably, nor destroys the capacity for reasoned choice.[27]

2 After the Cold War

How did the 'rational public' react to the ending of the Cold War? Mass opinion generally backed accommodation and agreement with the USSR in the later stages of the Cold War. Both elite and mass opinion surveys gave weight to what O. R. Holsti has called the 'rational and events-driven' interpretation of public attitudes. Such research in the years of Cold War wind-down yielded little evidence of any non-rational need to locate new external enemies.[28]

Post-Cold War public opinion saw an evolution, rather than an extinction, of the various belief systems which were apparent in the period following the Vietnam War. Kegley and Wittkopf hold that militant and cooperative internationalist positions – themselves versions of realism and idealism – persisted into the new era, simply taking up new issues (like NATO extension and aid to Russia).[29] Attitudes to the use of force also continued to display the evolution of attitudes deriving from the Vietnam War. Bruce Jentleson argues that a 'new "post post-Vietnam" pattern has emerged in which public support for military force is neither as strong as during the "Cold War consensus" nor as generally weak as during the "Vietnam trauma"'. Examination of nine cases (Nicaragua and El Salvador during the 1980s; Lebanon in 1981–82; Grenada, 1983; Persian Gulf and Afghanistan policy in the late 1980s; Libya, 1986; Panama, 1989; and the Gulf War) led Jentleson to posit a 'pretty prudent' public, neither paralysed by fear of using force nor bellicose, 'boorish' and 'overreactive'.[30] Summarising opinion in the early 1990s, Catherine McArdle Kelleher discerned continued support for NATO (despite some polling indications that the level of support was reducing). There was also a willingness to protect Israel and South Korea. Elsewhere, however – and, of course, not allowing for any Presidential prompting – there was 'an overwhelming reluctance, if not a fundamental aversion to the use of force'.[31] In the case of the Gulf War, John Mueller concluded: 'the poll evidence suggests that Bush was unable really to persuade an increasing number of Americans that war was either desirable or necessary – though he did perhaps keep the percentage favoring war from declining notably.' In early November 1990, respondents were asked a stark question: 'Suppose that eventually we have to choose between compromise with Saddam Hussein or starting a war. Which would you choose: compromise or war?' Compromise was chosen by 58 per cent; 34 per cent chose war.[32]

Mueller's conclusions about Gulf War public opinion did not go unchallenged,[33] and polling data are notoriously slippery. Great care has to be taken over the wording of poll questions, over the size and type of samples, and with comparisons over time. Extrapolating from limited or unreliable data, some commentators in the early 1990s came to premature conclusions about the main issue concerning foreign policy public opinion: the extent to which

Americans were 'homeward bound', reaching to the end of the Cold War by turning to some form of neo-isolationism.

The early post-Cold War period did see some articulation of public support for positions which could be interpreted as neo-isolationist. A 1991 survey, for example, found 44 per cent of respondents endorsing the rather extreme proposition that 'the US should mind its own business internationally and let other countries get along as best they can on their own'. Polls showed overwhelmingly that Americans largely attributed the nation's economic problems to 'helping others' rather than putting 'America's needs first'. Chicago Council on Foreign Relations polling in 1994 revealed that public support for 'global altruism' had dived to its lowest point since the later Vietnam War years.[34] Pat Buchanan's early showing in the 1992 and 1996 Republican primaries stimulated commentary about the 'new populism': protectionist, 'America first' and unilateralist – if not actually isolationist. Bruce Jentleson concluded in 1992 that the American public was 'much more likely to support the use of force for the restraint rather than the remaking of other governments' in a liberal democratic mould.[35] A. J. Bacevich reiterated in 1996 that Americans were in no mood for crusades: 'Americans are becoming increasingly adamant in their insistence that the proper measure of effectiveness for US diplomacy is not whether a particular policy contributes to some larger or longer-term strategic or ideological agenda, but whether it delivers immediate and tangible benefits for the United States.'[36] Advocating a return to Reaganism in foreign policy, William Kristol and Robert Kagan in 1996 bemoaned the existence of an introverted US 'citizen population increasingly unaware of or indifferent to the importance of its military's efforts abroad'.[37]

The post-Cold War public mood seemed to be one of pragmatism, suspicion of open-ended internationalist activism and willingness to countenance 'America First' stances. There was some evidence of hostility to foreign aid (and, as noted in the previous chapter, a tendency hugely to overestimate the burdens placed by aid on the US economy). Despite worries about the impact on jobs, defence spending reductions tended to gain support in Chicago Council on Foreign Relations polling. The issue of US troops serving under UN command became an important campaign issue in some mid-1990s Congressional races. The ending of the Cold War also stimulated a major drop in the saliency and immediacy of foreign policy to the electorate; by the mid-1990s, Gallup polling suggested that only 2 per cent of voters saw any foreign policy issue as 'the most important problem facing this country today'.[38]

Yet public prudence or introverted suspicion did not prevent US action in the Gulf, Haiti or Bosnia, any more than it prevented the NAFTA and GATT ratifications in President Clinton's first year. Public unhappiness with the free trade agreements subsided noticeably as US domestic economic indicators improved after 1994. President Clinton acknowledged that the public 'don't want us to waste any money overseas'.[39] But neither he nor President Bush were faced by solid public opposition to their versions of internationalism. Polling taken in 1995, before the Bosnian troop commitments, actually revealed considerable *support* for peacekeeping operations. (During 1996, US public opinion was closely divided over Bosnian peacekeeping. In contrast, missile strikes on Iraq were overwhelmingly supported[40].) Research undertaken by the Program on International Policy Attitudes (PIPA) at the University of Maryland found continued support for internationalism, even for certain varieties of universalist liberalism. Slight changes in the wording of poll questions seem to elicit vastly different responses. Thus, in contrast to the 1991 poll which found Americans declaring that the 'US should mind its own business', a 1994 PIPA survey found only 14 per cent of respondents prepared to agree with the following proposition: 'the US should not make sacrifices in an effort to help the world as a whole'. Americans seemed to favour more assertive UN peacekeeping, rather than no peacekeeping (or US participation in peacekeeping) at all. Americans want the United States to be *able* to act alone, but – certainly in specific cases of military intervention – favour multilateralism. Even on foreign aid, public hostility tends to break down when the purpose and destination of aid is incorporated into poll questions. PIPA polling in June–July 1994 also found 75 per cent agreeing that 'whenever it can, the US should look beyond its own self interest and do what's best for the world as a whole, because in the long run this will probably help make the kind of world that is best for the US'.[41] Structural complexity and low foreign policy saliency seem to be major features of post-Cold War public opinion. The new era may also have opened up elite–mass divisions. (Chicago Council on Foreign Relations in the early 1990s, for example, found relative mass enthusiasm and elite scepticism regarding protectionist trade policy[42].) Generally, however, the appeal of the 'new populism' in foreign policy, at least during the period 1989–96, seems to have been exaggerated.

3 Policy and public opinion

Complexity, uncertainty and low levels of public information allow Presidents to lead and mould public opinion. The historical record yields many such examples: Truman's invocation of the Soviet threat;[43] Kennedy's public relations campaign on behalf of the Green Berets;[44] George Bush's demonisation of Saddam Hussein. David Gergen – communications adviser to Presidents Nixon, Ford, Reagan and Clinton – concluded that 'the chief lesson to emerge from the Gulf experience' was that 'a president's foreign policy need not be a creature of public opinion polls'.[45] In a sense, Presidents feed off public ignorance and confusion. As Graebner put it in 1983: 'The better informed the public, the more threatening it becomes.'[46] Crises become occasions to achieve a 'rally-round-the-flag' effect. Presidents take initiatives in the knowledge that they generate short-term enthusiasm, and that this may deflect public attention from failed or embarrassing policies. Such tactics are powerful, especially given the Presidential ability to control the flow of information. Yet they do not always work, and may be subject to a law of diminishing returns.[47]

In those instances where a clear and stable public preference exists, foreign policy leaders will – especially if apparent preference peaks coincide with the electoral cycle – find it difficult not to respond. Thomas Graham cites the case of public opposition to sharing nuclear secrets (even with international agencies, much less the USSR): this 'level of opinion was responsible for the policy reversal associated with the transformation of the utopian Acheson–Lilienthal plan into the almost non-negotiable Baruch plan' (1946).[48] Typically, public opinion may set limits to Presidential freedom of action. In the Reagan years, Defence Secretary Caspar Weinberger argued that no post-Vietnam leader could afford to take military action without support in the polls. It has plausibly been argued that public fear of 'another Vietnam' in Central America prevented a US invasion of Nicaragua in the early 1980s. Indeed, as indicated in Chapter 2, some scholars attribute almost entire trajectory of Reagan's later foreign policy to his Administration's response to public opinion.[49]

The balance of academic judgement on the relationship between policy and opinion has been inclined to shift in recent years. Bernard Cohen's influential study generally downplayed the influence of public opinion.[50] Some more recent accounts have tended to focus on the attentiveness of policy-making elites to polls, and to argue that policy often follows public opinion.[51] Shapiro and Page argue that this is not so much a matter of policymakers following the polls in any automatic fashion: 'The effect is very likely often a more subtle one, which occurs as political leaders attempt to use information about public opinion for the purpose of leading, persuading, or manipulating the public.'[52]

Empirical research is difficult in the field of opinion–policy linkages, because of the uncertainty of the relevant causation. Does policy respond to opinion, or does opinion respond to policy? In the case of defence spending, do policymaking elites tend to respond to public opinion, or do both the policymakers *and* the public respond to changes (real or imagined) in the external threat? Since the making of US foreign policy is complex, how do we isolate the responsiveness of Congress, of the bureaucracy and of Presidents? With foreign policy issues figuring so little in (especially post-Cold War) election campaigns, why *should* politicians bother with public opinion in this area at all? Despite these problems, various empirical investigations have found high levels of congruence between policy and opinion – and, crucially, between policy and opinion *shifts*. The Shapiro and Page 1983 investigation into over two hundred cases found a 66 per cent congruence between policy and opinion shifts.[53] Christopher Wlezien similarly traces high levels of con-

gruence between Congressional defence appropriations and public preferences.[54]

Crucial to this discussion is the question of linkage mechanisms. How is
public opinion communicated to policymakers? Philip Powlick suggests five
'paths of linkage': elites (including friends and associates of policymakers);
interest groups; the news media; elected representatives (especially Congress, often seen by executive policymakers as performing a fairly straightforward 'delegate' role); and the general public.[55] The last category includes
casual contacts on the campaign trail, but also institutionalised scrutiny of
(private and published) polls. The 'general public' linkage can also be con-
strued to encompass perceived electoral needs. (For example, Thomas Noer
has traced the Ford Administration's evolving African policy – from covert
operations in Angola to public diplomacy in Rhodesia – to the perceived
need 'to score a foreign policy victory' in connection with the 1976 Presidential election. President Nixon's orchestration of the Vietnam peace negotiations to chime in with the 1972 election had given Ford a precedent[56].)

The notion of 'linkage paths' is a very helpful one, but also raises new
research problems. What degree of autonomy is enjoyed by the mechanisms
of linkage? Elites, interest groups, news media and Congress all shape as well
as reflect public opinion. They are also, to varying degrees, independent
actors in the process. Even pollsters do not present 'raw' public opinion, but
rather refine, order and tidy it into perceivable and mediated categories. The
publication of a poll itself helps shape future public perceptions of issues.

The end of the Cold War caused academic and practitioner elites to recon-
sider the public role in foreign policy. Generally, this occurred in the context
of resisting 'new populism'. To some degree, however, it also reflected the
view that public opinion had become an insistent force in foreign policy, and
would remain so. Powlick argues that the US foreign policy bureaucracy
retains the institutional assumption it adopted following the Vietnam War:
public opinion must be heeded and fostered.[57] Low post-Cold War foreign
policy saliency might suggest more scope for executive discretion. Post-Cold
War Presidents have clearly seen it as part of their role to educate the public
in the virtues of internationalism. In the context of the 1996 Presidential
election, Clinton's foreign policy campaign adviser J. P. Rubin announced his
main task as instructing the public that international issues 'do come home
to America at some level or another'. (Neither the 1992 nor the 1996 Presidential elections, however, witnessed much serious discussion of foreign
policy choices.) Nonetheless – as noted in previous chapters – the more divisions between foreign and domestic policy are dissolved, the more the executive may have to countenance forces like foreign policy interest groups.[58]

4 Sensitised public opinion: pressure groups

The main focus of this section will be on citizens' and ethnic lobbies. Interest groups geared to elite representation will (along with the news media) be discussed in the following chapter.

(a) *Citizen lobbying*   Organised citizen lobbying in recent US history has varied from direct action, of the type associated with the anti-Vietnam War movement, to the activities of public interest lobbies. (Such groups, like Ralph Nader's Public Citizen or Common Cause tend to focus primarily, though not exclusively, on domestic issues.) Regarding direct action, efforts to measure its impact on policy, and on wider public opinion, tend to detect fairly minimal effects. Sometimes direct action is depicted as actually counter-productive. A major historiographical debate surrounds the policy impact of the anti-Vietnam War movement. Adam Garfinkle argues that anti-war protests actually prolonged the conflict. The Silent Majority was mobilised, US leaders found it difficult to make compromises, and America's enemy was encouraged.[59] However, far more positive interpretations of direct action in the Vietnam War era may be advanced. Marches, petitions, occupations and teach-ins shook complacency and slowly altered the decisional climate. The anti-war movement had an important role to play in presenting credible information on the war, slowly undermining the official version of events.[60]

The most influential foreign policy citizens' movement since the Vietnam War was the nuclear freeze campaign of the early 1980s. The movement sprang from the Massachusetts referendum proposals for a bilateral, verifiable moratorium on nuclear weapons acquisition and development, fostered by Randall Forsberg and Randy Kehler. The movement exploited modes of political activism, such as direct mailing, often associated in the 1980s with the New Right. A freeze petition acquired nearly two million signatures in a fifteen-month period. The June 1982 rally in New York City's Central Park attracted over half a million people. Eventually, in May 1983, the House of Representatives passed a joint resolution requiring the President to negotiate a mutual halt to the arms race with the Soviet Union. As indicated in Chapter 2, great claims have been made for the freeze movement's impact on Reagan Administration policies. However, the significance of the 1983 resolution should not be exaggerated. The proposal was for a mutual freeze. When the press scented a whiff of unilateralism at the 1983 freeze conference in St. Louis, it threatened to harm the movement. Moreover, the resolution had no chance of passing the Republican-controlled Senate. It was also subjected, prior to House passage, to significant amendment. In particular, the amendment proposed by Elliot Levitas made the freeze dependent on achieving negotiated arms reductions.[61]

Citizen lobbying is not confined to the left of the political spectrum. In the Carter era, the Emergency Coalition to Save the Panama Canal coordinated conservative citizens' group efforts to oppose Presidential policy on the Canal. Rightist groups, like Citizens for Reagan, emerged to lobby for

Nicaraguan Contra aid in the 1980s. Between 1982 and 1989, it has been estimated that over two hundred lobbying groups involved themselves in the debate for or against the Contras.[62] Intense citizens' group lobbying has occurred at various times in policy arenas such as human rights (especially in the context of foreign aid), environmental issues and certain population and development issues. Pro-life groups have become involved in debates about US stances towards world population growth.[63]

Mitchell Bard has pointed to 'a kind of Cartesian mentality latent in the literature in interest groups that seem to suggest that interest groups exist and therefore must have influence'.[64] As the environmental groups that opposed NAFTA ratification found, mere existence does not bring success. Individual citizens often find their loyalties and interests tugging in opposite directions. Proliferation of interest groups can conspire to dilute the influence of any one group. Like other non-domestic groups, foreign policy citizens' lobbies also suffer from the executive branch's privileged access to information. Domestic groups often manage to insinuate themselves in the policymaking process by providing specialised information to both executive and legislative branches of government. Few foreign policy groups are able to do this; (an exception is Amnesty International in the human rights field). Citizens' lobbies are, in particular, likely to prosper only when (as in the case of the nuclear freeze movement) they manage to excite wider public opinion.

(b) *Ethnic lobbies*   Although the contribution of ethnic group lobbying to the shaping of US foreign policy has probably been exaggerated in the voluminous literature on the subject, there is no doubting the potency of such pressure in certain policy areas.[65] Ethnic lobbies tend to succeed in situations where, because of poor organisation, funding or the nature of immigration patterns, there is an absence of countervailing organised ethnic interest. The role of the Greek-American lobby in orchestrating support for the post-1974 Turkish arms embargo is one such example. Greek-American activists were able to marshal and target information supportive to their cause, virtually unchallenged by any comparable Turkish-American activity.[66]

At times in American history, ethnic lobbying has stimulated nativism and raised contentious questions about American identity. Many of the best-known ethnic lobbies have been non-White Anglo-Saxon Protestant (WASP), and have seen themselves as consciously challenging elite WASP assumptions. WASP opinion has on occasion condemned ethnic lobbies as 'foreign fungus'.[67] (On the attitudes displayed by patrician leaders to more recently arrived 'fellow immigrants', one cannot resist quoting a letter written by President Franklin Roosevelt to FBI head J. Edgar Hoover in 1942: 'Have you pretty well cleaned out the alien waiters in the principal Washington hotels? Altogether too much conversation in the dining rooms!'[68]) Ethnic lobbying has, nevertheless, come to be recognised as an important and legitimate influence, especially on Capitol Hill. Congressman Lee Hamilton

remarked in 1979: 'American foreign policy at times has been an elitist operation, and it needs the counterbalance that ethnic groups can often give.'[69]

The academic debate over ethnic group lobbying has tended to divide
between 'assimilationists' and 'pluralists'. In the 1960s, Gabriel Almond
stood for the view that the American 'melting-pot' was gradually cancelling
the interests of hyphenated Americans in their lands of origin. Nathan
Glazer and D. P. Moynihan responded with the pluralist thesis of stubborn
ethnicity.[70] New patterns of immigration in the post-1965 period combined
with the influence of the Civil Rights Movement to effect what Alexander
DeConde calls an 'ethnoracial resurgence', and to strengthen the
Glazer–Moynihan position.[71] However, one of Almond's fundamental
points – that assimilation does tend to reduce concerns for country of origin
– is still persuasive. John Tierney argues that 'to be politically effective an
ethnic group must have reached a finely balanced point in the process of
assimilation into American society: the ethnics must be part of the mainstream of American life but still identify strongly enough with their "homeland" to be willing to take political action on its behalf.'[72]

In 1967, George Kennan drew attention to the impact on Congress of
'ethnic groups ... representing compact voting groups in large cities'.[73] Jour-
nalistic invocations of 'the Polish vote' or 'the Italian vote' overplay the
coherence of such blocks. Psephological studies tend to discredit the notion
of cohesive voting blocks, taking their cue from perceptions of US policy
towards the 'homeland'. Rare indeed is the voter who casts his or her ballot
purely on such issues. However, in swing voting situations, 'homeland' issues
do have their place. In February 1995, Dick Kirschten noted in the *National
Journal* that many East European ethnic voters had abandoned the Republican Party in 1992 in protest at President Bush's reluctance to recognise the
new Soviet republics. Central and East European hyphenated Americans
were concentrated in the Northeast and Midwest 'in sufficient numbers to
be a potential swing vote'.[74] Members of Congress often indulge in 'no lose'
policy stances designed to impress small, influential sections of constituency
opinion, provided that significant countervailing interests are not thereby
offended. Some leading Congressional figures position themselves as advocates of particular 'homeland' interests. Dan Rostenkowski, Democratic
chair of the House Ways and Means Committee in the 1980s and early
1990s, identified himself with Polish-American lobbies. Senator Claiborne
Pell used his chairmanship of the Senate Foreign Relations Committee to
advance policy positions favoured by Armenian-Americans (a small ethnic
group, but one heavily represented in Pell's Rhode Island constituency).
During 1996, two Cuban-American members of the House International
Relations Committee (Republican Ileana Ros-Lehtinen of Florida and
Democrat Robert Menendez of New Jersey) led the campaign to impose
sanctions on the Castro regime. In so doing, they were promoting the
agenda set by the Miami-based Cuban-American Foundation.

Presidential candidates regularly make symbolic gestures towards the ethnic lobbies. Clinton in 1992 attacked George Bush's 1991 'Chicken Kiev' speech, wherein the President had apparently opposed Ukraine's breakaway from the USSR. President Franklin Roosevelt once famously attempted to use ethnic pressure as a bargaining chip. He told Stalin at the 1943 Teheran conference that he could not accept Russia's interpretation of Polish border issues. Some six million Poles lived in the United States, and 'as a practical man' FDR 'did not wish to lose their votes'.[75] Before the 1972 election, Richard Nixon reportedly made (largely symbolic) foreign policy gestures towards Italian-, Cuban-, Polish-, and Mexican-Americans.[76] On the executive side, however, it is almost as easy to point to examples of the executive exploiting ethnic loyalties as to examples of ethnic influence. Thus, for example, Washington organised a campaign by Italian-Americans on behalf of non-communist candidates in the 1948 Italian elections.[77] The Assembly of Captive European Nations was, since its foundation in 1954, the most prominent ethnic organisation lobbying for a tougher US stance towards Soviet influence in Eastern Europe. Apart from symbolic achievements, like the establishment by Congress in the 1950s of Captive Nations Week, it is difficult to identify any real impact on policy made by the Assembly. Yet the CIA was able, during the Cold War, to use the Assembly to generate and orchestrate anti-Soviet feeling.[78]

During the Cold War, it became accepted wisdom that ethnic group preferences in foreign policy would succeed only if they coincided with overarching, anti-communist security interests as perceived in Washington. The smashing of the anti-Soviet compass after 1989 thus created some new opportunities for ethnic lobbies. African-American mobilisation over the issue of South African sanctions in the 1970s and the 1980s was impressive in terms of both extent and success. Organisations like TransAfrica, the Washington Office on Africa and the coalitional Free South Africa Movement (founded in 1984) succeeded in uniting African-American activism with a broader 'social conscience' constituency.[79] The main success centred on enactment, over Reagan's veto, of the Comprehensive Anti-Apartheid Act of 1986. During these years, an effective lobbying network was mobilised around the House Foreign Affairs Subcommittee on Africa. However, African-American influence on US African policy during the Cold War always tended to run up against the constraints of the anti-communist agenda. Some African-American lobbyists saw the ending of the Cold War as a chance to develop more rational strategies for African development. In the event, Congressional aid-cutting and the reduced security prominence of Africa combined (especially after the Somalian incursion of 1992–94) to disappoint such hopes. TransAfrica's main early post-Cold War success actually involved the awakening of public interest in the situation in Haiti. The hunger strike of Randall Robinson, President of TransAfrica, publicised US restrictions on Haitian immigration. TransAfrica and the Congressional

Black Caucus were important influences upon the action taken by President Clinton to reinstall President Jean-Bertrand Aristide in 1994.[80]

The post-Cold War policy environment also produced new actors. The Central and East European Coalition (CEEC) was formed in 1993 to coordinate the foreign policy concerns of hyphenated Americans from the old Soviet empire (including Eastern Europe). The CEEC protested the Bush–Clinton policy of treating Russia as the post-Soviet regional hegemon. It also attempted to persuade the Clinton Administration to support the eastwards expansion of NATO.[81]

The pro-Israeli lobby (especially AIPAC, the American Israeli Public Affairs Committee) is almost universally regarded as the most powerful ethnic foreign policy lobby. AIPAC was founded in 1954 to coordinate pressure on Congress for the pro-Israeli cause. By the mid-1990s, AIPAC had a staff of about one hundred and fifty with an annual budget of around $15 million. As John Tierney explains, the pro-Israeli lobby has thrived through 'the extraordinary issue attentiveness and high voting participation rates of American Jews'.[82] Pro-Israeli Political Action Committees make contributions to Congressional campaign funds (around $2.68 million in 1991).[83] In the past, AIPAC has demonstrated its strength by conspicuously opposing the re-election of candidates deemed to be unsympathetic to Israel's cause. Senator Charles Percy lost his seat in such circumstances in 1984, as had Republican Congressman Paul Findley in the same state of Illinois two years previously.[84]

Legislators with significant members of Jewish voters in their constituency – like New York's Benjamin Gilman – are especially vulnerable to AIPAC mobilisation. Yet Members without special Jewish constituency interests may be influenced by the efficiency of the information services offered by AIPAC; by the informal pro-Israeli networks on Capitol Hill; by sensitivity to charges of anti-Semitism; and by the fact that (traditionally at least) public opinion has tended to be either pro-Israeli or uniformedly neutral. M. C. Feuerweger quotes a member of the House Appropriations Subcommittee on Foreign Operations in the 1970s to the effect that Israel succeeds in Congress because 'two or three per cent of voters care intensely about it, and the rest are uninformed and don't care'.[85]

The pro-Israeli lobby's main focus has been on Congress. A Congressional source interviewed by Edward Tivnan in the mid-1980s indicated: 'AIPAC does not want an even-handed Congress because it sees Congress as a countervailing force to even-handedness in US policy.'[86] On many occasions, Congress certainly has delivered the goods, especially when voting aid to Israel. When Secretary of State George Shultz sought to restrain Israel after its 1982 invasion of Lebanon, he found Congress actually increasing military aid. Huge claims have been made for the potency of the domestic Jewish lobby in framing US Middle East policy.[87] While its influence in Congress is not in doubt, it is more difficult to establish direct influence over the executive. Especially during the period 1977–92, it would be a wild exaggeration to depict American Administrations as dancing to the domestic Jewish lobby's tune.[88] For one thing, Administrations have had to take account of some public sympathy for the Palestinian cause. However, there are subtle and powerful influences. One of Tivnan's State Department interviewees suggested that executive planning on the Middle East operated according to a law of anticipated Congressional reactions: 'As a result, a lot of real analysis is not even getting off peoples' desks for fear of what the lobby will do.'[89] State Department planners do not wish to provoke damaging legislative blocking, or retaliation across a range of issues.

AIPAC is not omnipotent. Any lobby will prosper when its prescriptions coincide with perceived US security interests, or when it is joined by other influential interests. Legislative attempts in the 1970s to force Moscow's hand on Jewish emigration saw domestic Jewish groups working alongside various labour, human rights, scientific and academic interests.[90] US Jewish opinion is not always as cohesive as is often imagined. The issue of Palestinian rights has opened divisions.[91] There have also been rifts between Israeli and American Jewish opinion. In 1992, Israeli Prime Minister Yitzhak Rabin actually attacked AIPAC for endangering relations between Israel and the White House.[92]

At the same time, AIPAC has to take account of America's pro-Arab lobby, which is not entirely without influence. I. L. Kenen, co-founder of AIPAC, always insisted that the lobby's main task was to counter the influence of Arab petrodollars on Capitol Hill.[93] Following the 1967 Arab–Israeli war, the four oil companies comprising the Arabian American Oil Company began a campaign to awaken public sympathy for the Arab cause. Inward Arab investment in the United States – possibly as much as $200 billion by the early 1990s – has generated vested domestic interests. The National Association of Arab-Americans was founded in 1972 in the image of AIPAC. It has had to contend not only with domestic Jewish lobbies, but also with divisions within Arab opinion and changing perceptions of Islam after the 1979 Iranian revolution. The Arab lobby has been able to reinforce US solidarity with oil-rich pro-Western Arab states like Saudi Arabia. It has tended, however, to devote its energies towards opposing pro-Israeli measures in Congress, rather than to developing its own agenda. Of considerable interest for the future is the projection that by the end of the twentieth century, Muslims in the United States will actually outnumber Jews. In the mid-1990s, the two communities were roughly equal in size: about six million each. Some implications of the rise in the domestic Muslim population were evident during the Clinton years. Ali Mazrui considered the Clinton Administration 'more pro-Israel than any other US administration since that of Lyndon Johnson'. Yet the Administration was also at pains to make more or less unprecedented gestures towards the domestic Muslim population: recognising the Ramadan fast in 1996, for example, and publicly consulting American Muslim Council members over the Bosnian crisis.[94]

An area of American ethnic politics of special interest to observers in Britain is the Irish lobby (a case-study of Clinton's policy towards Northern Ireland is included in Chapter 8). Around forty-four million Americans claim some sort of Irish ancestry. They are frequently portrayed in the British press as atavistic nationalists, whose 'emotions and loyalties' (in the words of former Prime Minister Margaret Thatcher) 'are manipulated by Irish Republican extremists'.[95] For James Prior (Mrs Thatcher's Secretary of State for Northern Ireland, 1981–84): 'The most difficult people are those congressmen and senators, like Senator Edward Kennedy, with large numbers of Irish constituents who still harbour views which originate from the potato famine of the 1840s and the ghastly oppression to which the British subjected them.'[96] In fact, the Irish lobby – even in its Catholic and nationalist incarnations – is quite complex. Various organisations have, over the years, attempted to enhance US governmental interest in Northern Ireland, generally in a direction favoured by nationalist interests. The traditionalist Ancient Order of Hibernians has embraced various republican positions. The Irish National Caucus emerged as a leading Congressional pressure group in the 1970s, and was instrumental in the 1977 establishment of the Congressional Ad Hoc Committee on Irish Affairs. Until its eclipse in the early 1990s, the Irish Northern Aid Committee (NORAID) raised money for the Provisional Irish Republican Army among the socially conservative, Irish-American Catholic working class. It had some limited influence in Congress and at state governmental level. It is, nevertheless, important not to overstate the power of the Irish-American nationalist lobby, even in terms of Democratic Party electoral politics. The assimilation and suburbanisation of Catholic Irish-America militates against activist interest in contemporary Northern Ireland. Over the course of the conflict there, Irish-American sympathy and interest has ebbed and flowed dramatically. It reached a high point with the early 1980s hunger strikes, but has been repelled by instances of republican terrorism.

Much of the recent history of elite Irish-American responses to the conflict is explicable more in terms of diplomatic initiatives from Dublin than of the domestic lobbies. Beginning in the mid-1970s, Iveagh House (the Irish Republic's Department of Foreign Affairs) followed a successful strategy of recruiting Irish-American opinion leaders to the cause of peaceful, constitutional nationalism. The Anglo-Irish Agreement of 1985 was, at least at one level, a fruit of this strategy. Many stereotypes of Irish-American political behaviour also tend to ignore the extent and impact of Irish *Protestant* immigration. In 1994, Congressman Joseph Kennedy (Democrat from Massachusetts, and son of Robert Kennedy) estimated that a quarter of Irish-American voters in his constituency were of Protestant stock.[97] There were signs of increased mobilisation amongst Irish-American Protestant opinion in the early 1990s. However, it is certainly the case that high levels of assimilation have tended to deny organised Irish-American loyalism the role of an effective countervailing lobby. Even in such circumstances, nation-alist Irish-America has not found it easy to influence policy. Certainly, before 1993, US Presidents and the State Department remained extremely cautious about intervening in Northern Irish issues, and about upsetting Anglo-American relations. Some battles were won, notably in connection with the MacBride fair employment proposals in connection with US investment in Northern Ireland. In 1990, President Bush signed into law a new immigration lottery system, allowing Irish applicants particularly generous terms. The law was widely accredited to Irish-American lobbying of Congress, especially by the New York-based Irish Reform Movement. However, the failure of nationalist lobbies to prevent the extradition from the United States of IRA personnel – notably Joe Doherty – indicated the limits of their influence.

5   American women and foreign policy

Wendy Brown argues that more 'than any other kind of human activity, *politics* has historically borne an explicitly masculine identity'.[98] If this is indeed the case, then the politics of foreign policy constitutes the very citadel of masculinism. Most studies of women and public policy concentrate almost entirely on domestic issues.[99] The foreign policy process has historically been dominated by men to an extraordinary degree. Jeane Kirkpatrick declared on the occasion of her departure from the post of Reagan's Ambassador to the UN: 'I was the only woman in our history, I think, who ever sat in regularly at top-level foreign policy meetings.' In 1985, she described seeing a mouse in the Situation Room: 'That mouse is no more surprising a creature to be [there] than I am.'[100] By 1990, only seven women had ever served on the House Armed Services Committee, thirteen on the Foreign Affairs Committee. The State Department has a well-documented history of discriminating against women in its employment practices. By the 1980s, a number of class actions suits began to force a change. In the early 1990s, female representation in the US foreign service stood at approximately one quarter. Yet women made up only about 5 per cent of top-level foreign service employees.[101] (Some high-ranking women in the State Department have noted the problems associated with securing a mentor. According to Michele George Markoff, 'men of stature who take on talented females … are often painted with the allegations of impropriety, no matter how false the perception'[102].)

Women have served with distinction in foreign policy bureaucracies. Eleanor Lansing Dulles (sister of Allen and John Foster Dulles) was in charge of State's Berlin desk from 1952 to 1959. Patricia Derian occupied the key role in the Carter Administration's human rights foreign policy initiatives. Rozanne Ridgway served as First Assistant Secretary for European Affairs in Reagan's State Department. The Bush Administration also saw women at senior levels at State (notably Assistant Secretaries Tutwiler and Mullins) and on Brent Scowcroft's NSC staff (notably Condoleeza Rice). The position of Madeleine Albright as leading foreign policy adviser to Presidential candidate Michael Dukakis in 1988 stimulated speculation about the prospects for a first female Secretary of State. Albright, who had served on Brzezinski's NSC staff in the Carter years, eventually became Clinton's Ambassador to the UN and was appointed Secretary of State for Clinton's second term. The Clinton Administration adopted a conscious strategy – the 'egg', or ethnicity, gender and geography test – for achieving balance in its appointments. Anthony Lake's NSC staff included some high-profile female members – for example, Nancy Soderberg, highly influential in developing the Administration's activism on Northern Ireland.

The 'gender gap' in recent Presidential and Congressional elections is a recognised phenomenon. There is some evidence that female preference for Democratic candidates is linked to defence and foreign policy issues. In 1980, 53 per cent of men declared themselves to be 'closer to Reagan' on defence spending, compared to 40 per cent of women. According to Rhodri Jeffreys-Jones, women 'have always been especially inclined to support peace'.[103] In the early 1980s, a range of women's groups took direct action to oppose the Reagan Administration's military build-up. Many of these activists linked their peace activities to feminist theory, and to the campaigns of European women, notably the Greenham Common peace camp in England. The peace cause was frequently linked to ecological imperatives, as, for example, in statements issued from the Puget Sound peace camp. Polls on Reagan's Central American policies tended to find women opposing them at levels (around 10 per cent) higher than men. The 1983 Grenada invasion also elicited a more enthusiastic response from men.[104] Such gender differences do not appear to have lessened with greater female participation in traditionally male-dominated areas of the labour market. John Mueller writes: 'To use old-fashioned terminology, women seem to have become liberated without losing their femininity in this respect.' Female support for the Gulf War was significantly below that expressed by male poll respondents. The ending of the Cold War does not seem to have altered these familiar patterns.[105]

The debate over enhancing the role of women in the foreign policy process centres not only on strategies to increase female involvement, but also on speculation as to the effect of a stronger feminine input. (It should be stressed that many of these points about female involvement apply equally to traditionally excluded ethnic minorities. Mueller finds that polls consistently 'show blacks to be more dovish than whites'[106].) The familiar stereotype of women as more pacifist than men is not entirely convincing if one considers the careers of those few females who have gained entry into inner foreign policy circles. Dulles or Kirkpatrick would hardly fit the stereotype, for example; neither would Frances Willis (1899–1964), the first female to gain class one rank as a career diplomat. On the other hand, one may cite the career of Jeannette Rankin (1880–1973), the first woman elected to the House of Representatives and the only legislator to oppose US entry into both world wars. McGlen and Sarkees conclude: 'where the organizational culture is conducive to liberal or pacifist views, women may exhibit such issue stands. In contrast, where the environment demands conservative or hawkish positions, women may adopt, or already come equipped with, such views.'[107]

During a 1987 informal Congressional hearing organised by the Women's Foreign Policy Council, Vivian Derryck of the Democratic Institute for International Affairs, addressed the assumption that 'women in decisionmaking roles will necessarily be more interested in equality, economic advancement, and social justice'. According to Derryck, this is not always the case: 'Because by the time a woman gathers the expertise to be effective in these kinds of jobs ... she has come through a male system. She has learned concepts and learned language that are gender-neutral or that connote maleness.' Former Representative Bella Abzug commented: 'My experience ... is that large numbers of [women], even those with conservative views, tend to be more willing to question policies that they have not been associated with ... They didn't create the atom bomb ... I think women can make a difference.'[108]

Notes

1 W. Lippmann, *Public Opinion* (New York, Free Press, (1922) 1965), p. 35; W. Lippman, *The Public Philosophy* (London, Hamish Hamilton, 1955).
2 G. F. Kennan, *American Diplomacy: 1900–1950* (Chicago, University of Chicago Press, 1957), p. 59.
3 See F. L. Klingsberg, *Cyclical Trends in American Foreign Policy Moods: The Unfolding of America's World Role* (Lanham, University Press of America, 1983); J. E. Holmes, *The Mood/Interest Theory of American Foreign Policy* (Lexington, University Press of Kentucky, 1985). The examples are taken from S. Welch, 'American public opinion: consensus, cleavage and constraint', in D. P. Forsythe, ed., *American Foreign Policy in an Uncertain World* (Lincoln, University of Nebraska Press, 1984), pp. 22–3; and C. W. Kegley and E. R. Wittkopf, *American Foreign Policy: Pattern and Process* (New York, St. Martin's, 1996), p. 265. See also R. B. Levering, 'Public opinion, foreign policy, and American politics since the 1960s', *Diplomatic History*, 13 (1989), pp. 383–93.
4 T. G. Paterson, *Meeting the Communist Threat* (New York, Oxford University Press, 1988), p. 80.
5 See R. J. Rosentone, 'Economic adversity and voter turnout', *American Journal of Political Science*, 26 (1982), pp. 212–32.
6 J. E. Rielly, ed., *American Public Opinion and US Foreign Policy*, 1991 (Chicago, Chicago Council on Foreign Relations, 1991), p. 9.
7 W. R. Schneider, 'Rambo and reality: having it both ways', in K. A. Oye, D. Rothchild and R. J. Lieber, eds, *Eagle Resurgent* (Boston, Little, Brown, 1983).
8 See, e.g., T. W. Smith, 'American attitudes toward the Soviet Union and com-

munism', *Public Opinion Quarterly*, 47 (1983), pp. 277–92; T. W. Smith, 'Nuclear anxiety', *Public Opinion Quarterly*, 52 (1988), pp. 557–75; W. R. Schneider, 'Public opinion', in J. S. Nye, ed., *The Making of America's Soviet Policy* (New Haven, Yale University Press, 1984).

9 See, e.g., the table reproduced in W. LaFeber, *The American Age* (New York, Norton, 1989), p. 636.

10 See R. B. Levering, *The Public and American Foreign Policy, 1918–1978* (New York, Morrow, 1978), p. 103.

11 See W. R. Schneider, 'Conservatism, not interventionism: trends in foreign policy opinion, 1974–82', in K. A. Oye, D. Rothchild and R. J. Lieber, eds, *Eagle Defiant* (Boston, Little, Brown, 1983); R. Sobel, 'Public opinion about United States intervention in El Salvador and Nicaragua', *Public Opinion Quarterly*, 53 (1989), pp. 114–28.

12 See J. E. Mueller, *War, Presidents and Public Opinion* (New York, Wiley, 1973).

13 See B. Russett, 'The revolt of the masses: public opinion on military expenditures', in B. Russett, ed., *Peace, War and Numbers* (Beverly Hills, Sage, 1972); L. Kriesberg and R. Klein, 'Changes in public support for US military spending', *Journal of Political and Military Sociology*, 10 (1980), pp. 275–97; Schneider, 'Rambo and reality'.

14 See R. H. Johnson, *Improbable Dangers* (New York, St. Martin's, 1994).

15 See B. Russett, *Controlling the Sword* (Cambridge, Mass., Harvard University Press, 1990), p. 46; Kegley and Wittkopf, *American Foreign Policy*, p. 271; Rielly, ed., *American Public Opinion and US Foreign Policy, 1991*, p. 32; B. W. Jentleson, 'The pretty prudent public: post post-Vietnam American opinion on the use of military force', *International Studies Quarterly*, 36 (1992), pp. 49–74.

16 J. A. Nathan and J. K. Oliver, *Foreign Policy Making and the American Political System* (Baltimore, Johns Hopkins University Press, 1994), p. 156.

17 See Holmes, *The Mood/Interest Theory of American Foreign Policy*; M. Ruskin, 'From Pearl Harbor to Vietnam: shifting generational paradigms', *Political Science Quarterly*, 89 (1974), pp. 563–88; O. R. Holsti and J. N. Rosenau, 'Does where you stand depend on when you were born?', *Public Opinion Quarterly*, 44 (1980), pp. 1–22. See generally M. Nincic, *Democracy and Foreign Policy* (New York, Columbia University Press, 1992), ch. 2.

18 See T. W. Graham, 'Public opinion and US foreign policy decision making', in D. A. Deese, ed., *The New Politics of American Foreign Policy* (New York, St. Martin's, 1994) p. 192.

19 O. R. Holsti and J. N. Rosenau, *American Leadership in World Affairs: Vietnam and the Breakdown of Consensus* (Boston, Allen and Unwin, 1984).

20 M. Mandelbaum and W. R. Schneider, 'The new internationlisms', in K. A. Oye, D. Rothchild and R. J. Lieber, eds, *Eagle Entangled* (Boston, Little, Brown, 1979).

21 O. R. Holsti and J. N. Rosenau, 'The structure of foreign policy attitudes: American leaders, 1976–1984', *Journal of Politics*, 52 (1990), pp. 94–125; O. R. Holsti, 'Public opinion and foreign policy: challenges to the Almond–Lippmann consensus', *International Studies Quarterly*, 36 (1992), pp. 439–66; E. R. Wittkopf, *Faces of Internationalism: Public Opinion and American Foreign Policy* (Durham, NC, Duke University Press, 1990).

22 Graham, 'Public opinion and US foreign policy decision making', p. 193.

23 A. Campbell, P. E. Converse, W. E. Miller and D. E. Stokes, *The American Voter* (New York, Wiley, 1960); V. O. Key, *The Responsible Electorate* (New York, Vintage, 1966).

24 R. Y. Shapiro and B. I. Page, 'Foreign policy and the rational public', *Journal of Conflict Resolution*, 32 (1988), pp. 211–47: 224; B. I. Page and R. Y. Shapiro, *The Rational Public: Fifty Years of Trends in Americans' Policy Preferences* (Chicago, University of Chicago Press, 1992).

25 R. Y. Shapiro and B. I. Page, 'Foreign policy and public opinion', in Deese, ed., *The New Politics of American Foreign Policy*, p. 218.

26 Shapiro and Page, 'Foreign policy and the rational public', p. 239.

27 See M. K. Jennings and R. G. Niemi, *Generations and Politics* (Princeton, Princeton University Press, 1981), pp. 386–91; D. Yankelovich and S. Harman, *Starting with the People* (Boston, Houghton Mifflin, 1988).

28 O. R. Holsti, 'Public opinion and foreign policy: attitude structures of opinion leaders after the Cold War', in E. R. Wittkopf, ed., *The Domestic Sources of American Foreign Policy* (New York, St. Martin's, 1994), p. 55; O. R. Holsti, 'American reactions to the USSR: public opinion', in R. Jervis and S. Bialer, eds, *Soviet–American Reactions After the Cold War* (Durham, NC, Duke University Press, 1991); T. Risse-Knappen, 'Masses and leaders: public opinion, domestic structures, and foreign policy', in Deese, ed., *The New Politics of American Foreign Policy*, p. 246; M. Peffley and J. Hurwitz, 'International events and foreign policy beliefs: public response to changing Soviet–US relations', *American Journal of Political Science*, 36 (1992), pp. 431–61.

29 Kegley and Wittkopf, *American Foreign Policy*, p. 275; also, B. Russett, T. Hartley and S. Murray, 'The end of the Cold War, attitude change, and the politics of defense spending', *PS: Political Science and Politics*, 27 (1994), pp. 17–21.

30 Jentleson, 'The pretty prudent public', pp. 49, 73.

31 C. M. Kelleher, 'Security in the new order: Presidents, polls and the use of force', in D. Yankelovich and I. M. Destler, eds, *Beyond the Beltway* (New York, Norton, 1994), p. 236.

32 J. Mueller, *Policy and Opinion in the Gulf War* (Chicago, University of Chicago Press, 1994), pp. 125, 238.

33 See *ibid.*, p. 124; B. Inman, 'Lessons from the Gulf War', *Washington Quarterly*, 15 (1992), pp. 57–74.

34 See E. A. Nordlinger, *Isolationism Reconfigured* (Princeton, Princeton University Press, 1995), pp. 19–20; R. H. Hinckley, *People, Polls and Policymakers: American Public Opinion and National Security* (New York, Lexington Books, 1992), pp. 18–19; A. Richman, 'What the polls say', *US Foreign Policy Agenda* (USIA electronic journals), Oct. 1996, p. 20.

35 Jentleson, 'The pretty prudent public', p. 49.

36 A. J. Bacevich, 'The impact of the new populism', *Orbis*, 40 (1996), pp. 31–43: 38.

37 W. Kristol and R. Kagan, 'Toward a neo-Reaganite foreign policy', *Foreign Affairs*, 75 (1996), pp. 18–32: 24.

38 J. E. Rielly, ed., *American Public Opinion and US Foreign Policy, 1995* (Chicago, Chicago Council on Foreign Relations, 1995), pp. 34–7; J. D. Rosner, 'The know-othings know something', *Foreign Policy*, 101 (1995–96),

pp. 116–29: 124.

39 S. Kull, 'What the public knows that Washington doesn't', *Foreign Policy*, 101 (1995–96), pp. 102–15:102.

40 See B. Crossette, 'Poll finds American support for peacekeeping', *New York Times*, 30 April 1995; Richman, 'What the polls say', p. 17.

41 See Kull, 'What the public knows', pp. 103, 107, 110, 113; P. W. Rodman, 'The paradox of Presidential campaigns', *Orbis*, 40 (1996), pp. 53–61: 54.

42 See Rielly, ed., *American Public Opinion and US Foreign Policy, 1991*, pp. 55–7; Wittkopf, *Faces of Internationalism*, p. 237.

43 See T. G. Paterson, 'Presidential foreign policy, public opinion and Congress: the Truman years', *Diplomatic History*, 3 (1979), pp. 1–18.

44 See A. Spark, 'The myth of the Green Berets in the popular culture of the Vietnam era', *Journal of American Studies*, 18 (1984), pp. 21–42.

45 D. R. Gergen, 'The unfettered Presidency', in J. S. Nye and R. K. Smith, eds, *After the Storm: Lessons from the Gulf War* (Lanham, Madison Books, 1992), p. 183.

46 N. A. Graebner, 'Public opinion and foreign policy: a pragmatic view', in D. C. Piper and R. J. Terchek, eds, *Interaction: Foreign Policy and Public Policy* (Washington DC, American Enterprise Institute, 1983), p. 16.

47 See J. R. Lee, 'Rallying around the flag', *Presidential Studies Quarterly*, 7 (1977), pp. 252–6.

48 Graham, 'Public opinion and US foreign policy decision making', p. 201.

49 See B. Sussmann, *What Americans Really Think* (New York, Pantheon, 1988), p. 5.

50 See B. C. Cohen, *The Public's Impact on Foreign Policy* (Boston, Little, Brown, 1973).

51 See Hinckley, *People, Polls and Policymakers*; also, L. A. Kusnitz, *Public Opinion and Foreign Policy: America's China Policy, 1949–1979* (Westport, Greenwood, 1984).

52 Shapiro and Page, 'Foreign policy and public opinion', p. 233.

53 B. I. Page and R. Y. Shapiro, 'Effects of public opinion on policy', *American Political Science Review*, 77 (1983), pp. 175–90.

54 C. Wlezien, 'Dynamics of representation: the case of US spending on defence', *British Journal of Political Science*, 26 (1996), pp. 81–103. See also T. Hartley and B. Russett, 'Public opinion and the common defense: who governs military spending in the US?', *American Political Science Review*, 86 (1992), pp. 905–15.

55 P. J. Powlick, 'The sources of public opinion for American foreign policy officials', *International Studies Quarterly*, 39 (1995), pp. 427–51.

56 T. J. Noer, 'International credibility and political survival: the Ford Administration's Intervention in Angola', *Presidential Studies Quarterly*, 23 (1993), pp. 771–85.

57 See Powlick, 'The sources of public opinion', p. 448. On attempts to redefine public roles after the Cold War, see Yankelovich and Destler, eds, *Beyond the Beltway*.

58 W. S. Ross, 'The role of foreign policy advisers', *US Foreign Policy Agenda*, Oct. 1996, p. 23 (Rubin). See also, E. M. Uslaner, 'All politics are global: interest groups and the making of foreign policy', in A. J. Cigler and B. A. Loomis, eds,

Interest Group Politics (Washington DC, Congressional Quarterly Press, 1995); also, E. Uslaner, 'A Tower of Babel on foreign policy?', in A. J. Cigler and B. A. Loomis, eds, *Interest Group Politics* (Washington DC, Congressional Quarterly Press, 1991).

59 See A. Garfinkle, *Telltale Hearts: The Origins and Impact of the Vietnam Antiwar Movement* (Basingstoke, Macmillan, 1995).

60 See M. Small, *Johnson, Nixon and the Doves* (New Brunswick, Rutgers University Press, 1988); C. DeBenedetti, with C. Chatfield, *An American Ordeal: The Antiwar Movement of the Vietnam Era* (Syracuse, Syracuse University Press, 1990); T. Wells, *The War Within: America's Battle over Vietnam* (Berkeley, University of California Press, 1993).

61 See D. C. Waller, *Congress and the Nuclear Freeze* (Amherst, University of Massachusetts Press, 1987).

62 See C. J. Arnson and P. Brenner, 'The limits of lobbying: interest groups, Congress and aid to the *contras*', in R. Sobel, ed., *Public Opinion in US Foreign Policy* (Lanham, Rowman and Littlefield, 1993); also, D. Skidmore, 'Foreign policy interest groups and Presidential power: Jimmy Carter and the ratification of the Panama Canal treaties', *Presidential Studies Quarterly*, 23 (1993), pp. 477–98.

63 See D. D. Newsom, *The Public Dimension of Foreign Policy* (Bloomington, Indiana University Press, 1996), ch. 9. Also, D. Forsythe, *Human Rights and World Politics* (Lincoln, University of Nebraska Press, 1989).

64 M. G. Bard, 'The influence of ethnic groups on American Middle East policy', in Wittkopf, ed., *The Domestic Sources of American Foreign Policy*, p. 85.

65 See, e.g., M. E. Ahrari, ed., *Ethnic Groups and US Foreign Policy* (New York, Greenwood, 1987); D. H. Goldberg, *Foreign Policy and Ethnic Interest Groups* (Westport, Greenwood, 1990).

66 See P. Watanabe, *Ethnic Groups, Congress and American Foreign Policy* (Westport, Greenwood, 1984), pp. 167–8.

67 See A. DeConde, *Ethnicity, Race and American Foreign Policy* (Boston, Northeastern University Press, 1992), p. 190; L. L. Gerson, *The Hyphenate in Recent American Politics and Diplomacy* (Lawrence, University of Kansas Press, 1964), pp. xxvi, 235.

68 L. M. Lees, 'National security and ethnicity', *Diplomatic History*, 11 (1987), pp. 113–26: 113.

69 Deconde, *Ethnicity, Race and American Foreign Policy*, p. 1.

70 G. A. Almond, *The American People and Foreign Policy* (New York, Praeger, 1960); N. Glazer and D. P. Moynihan, *Beyond the Melting Pot: The Negroes, Puerto Ricans, Jews, Italians and Irish of New York City* (Cambridge, Mass., Harvard University Press, 1963).

71 DeConde, *Ethnicity, Race and American Foreign Policy*, ch. 8.

72 J. T. Tierney, 'Interest group involvement in Congressional foreign and defence policy', in R. B. Ripley and J. M. Lindsay, eds, *Congress Resurgent* (Ann Arbor, University of Michigan Press, 1993), pp. 94–5.

73 G. F. Kennan, *Memoirs: Volume Two: 1950–1963* (Boston, Little, Brown, 1967), p. 286.

74 D. Kirschten, 'Ethnics resurging', *National Journal*, 25 Feb. 1995, p. 484.

75 DeConde, *Ethnicity, Race and American Foreign Policy*, p. 125.

76 *Ibid.*, p. 195.
77 J. E. Miller, 'Taking off the gloves: the United States and the Italian elections of 1948', *Diplomatic History*, 7 (1983), pp. 35–56.
78 See S. A. Garrett, 'Eastern European ethnic groups and American foreign policy', *Political Science Quarterly*, 93 (1978), pp. 301–23.
79 See D. R. Culverson, 'The politics of the anti-apartheid movement in the United States, 1969–1986', *Political Science Quarterly*, 111 (1996), pp. 127–49; M. Sithole, 'Black Americans and United States policy towards Africa', *African Affairs*, 85 (1986), pp. 325–50; K. A. Hill, 'The domestic sources of foreign policy: Congressional voting and American mass attitudes towards South Africa', *International Studies Quarterly*, 37 (1993), pp. 195–214.
80 See Newsom, *The Public Dimension of Foreign Policy*, p. 185.
81 Kirschten, 'Ethnics resurging'.
82 J. T. Tierney, 'Congressional activism in foreign policy', in Deese, ed., *The New Politics of American Foreign Policy*, p. 117. See also I. L. Kenen, *Israel's Defense Line* (New York, Prometheus, 1981).
83 See Bard, 'The influence of ethnic interest groups on American Middle East policy', p. 82; also, M. Bard, *The Water's Edge and Beyond* (New Brunswick, Transaction Books, 1991).
84 See P. Findley, *They Dare to Speak Out* (Westport, Greenwood, 1985).
85 M. C. Feuerweger, *Congress and Israel* (Westport, Greenwood, 1979), p. 81.
86 E. Tivnan, *The Lobby: Jewish Political Power and American Foreign Policy* (New York, Simon and Schuster, 1987), p. 214.
87 See G. and D. Ball, *The Passionate Attachment: America's Involvement with Israel, 1947 to the Present* (New York, Norton, 1992); S. M. Hersh, *The Samson Option: Israel's Nuclear Arsenal and American Foreign Policy* (New York, Random House, 1991); C. A. Rubenberg, *Israel and the American National Interest* (Urbana, University of Illinois Press, 1986).
88 See W. B. Quandt, *Peace Process* (Washington DC, Brookings, 1993); D. Schoenbaum, *The United States and the State of Israel* (New York, Oxford University Press, 1993).
89 Tivnan, *The Lobby*, p. 256.
90 See P. Stern, *Water's Edge: Domestic Politics and the Making of American Foreign Policy* (Westport, Greenwood, 1979).
91 See I. A. Lewis, 'American Jews and Israel', *Public Opinion*, 11 (1988), pp. 53–5; Uslaner, 'All politics are global', pp. 378–80.
92 See Newsom, *The Public Dimension of Foreign Policy*, p. 190.
93 Kenen, *Israel's Defense Line*, pp. 27–9.
94 A. A. Mazrui, 'Between the crescent and the star spangled banner: American Muslims and US foreign policy', *International Affairs*, 72 (1996), pp. 493–506: 498.
95 M. Thatcher, *The Downing Street Years* (London, Harper Collins, 1993), p. 58.
96 J. Prior, *A Balance of Power* (London, Hamish Hamilton, 1986), p. 219.
97 BBC radio, *Today* programme interview, 22 Sept. 1994.
98 W. Brown, *Manhood and Politics* (Totowa New Jersey, Rowman and Littlefield, 1991), p. 4.
99 See, e.g., M. Conway, D. W. Ahern and G. Steuernagel, *Women and Public Policy* (Washington DC, CQ Press, 1995).

100 J. Hoff-Wilson, 'Of mice and men', in E. P. Crapol, ed., *Women and American Foreign Policy* (Westport, Greenwood, 1987), p. 170.

101 See House Committee on Foreign Affairs, *Women's Perspectives on US Foreign Policy*, Women's Foreign Policy Council informal Congressional hearing, 19 Nov. 1987 (Washington DC, US Government Printing Office, 1988), p. 4 (statement of Congresswoman P. Schroeder). Also, R. Jeffreys-Jones, 'America's missing sisters', *Society for Historians of American Foreign Relations Newsletter*, 26 (1995), pp. 16–28: 25.

102 N. E. McGlen and M. R. Sarkees, *Women in Foreign Policy: The Insiders* (New York, Routledge, 1993), p. 182.

103 R. Jeffreys-Jones, *Women and the Shaping of American Foreign Policy, 1917–1994* (New Brunswick, Rutgers University Press, 1996), p. 10. J. A. Tickner comments: 'While certain radical feminists have supported the claim of women's special affinity with peace, many feminists claim … that this essentialized view of women devalues both women and peace and reinforces barriers between what are typically perceived as women's activities and the tough "manly" world of realpolitik' ('Harbingers of peace?', *Diplomatic History*, 21 (1997), pp. 157–62: 160).

104 See R. Gatlin, *American Women since 1945* (Basingstoke, Macmillan, 1987), p. 242; P. Norris, 'The 1988 American elections', *The Political Quarterly*, 60 (1989), pp. 204–21: 210; E. Klein, *Gender Politics* (Cambridge, Mass., Harvard University Press, 1984), p. 160.

105 Mueller, *Policy and Opinion in the Gulf War*, p. 43.

106 *Ibid*.

107 McGlen and Sarkees, *Women in Foreign Policy*, p. 215.

108 *Women's Perspectives*, pp. 13, 17.

7

Global, local and private power

1 Globalisation

By the mid-1990s, it had become commonplace to describe the post-Cold War world as playing host to forces of both integration and disintegration. Globalised markets faced local nationalisms; global civil society rubbed against ethnic fragmentation; global thoughts complemented local actions; McWorld peered across to jihad. On the integrative side, 'globalisation' became the organising concept for academic projects in fields as various as sociology, international relations, cultural studies and political economy. New technologies of communication and information analysis seemed to undergird the new order. Sociologist Roland Robertson pointed to 'the compression of the world and the intensification of consciousness of the world as a whole'.[1] Anthony Giddens in 1990 thus described the globalising process of social 'disembedding': 'the "lifting out" of social relations from local contexts of interaction and their restructuring across time and space'.[2] Free capital flows and transferable systems of expert, technical knowledge are generally held to be central components of these globalising social processes. The growth of tourism, 'universal culture', the apparent post-Cold War ascendancy of liberal economic forms, and the proliferation of international organisations, are other key features of the globalisation thesis.[3]

Our primary concern here is with economic globalisation and the putative limits which it places upon national governments. Discussion must begin by acknowledging the potency of transnational economic forces. The internationalisation of financial markets actually impelled one commentator in 1992 to invoke the 'end of geography',[4] with computerised dealing superseding and ignoring national, earth-bound constraints. World capital flows do operate in ways which are beyond the control of traditional nation-states and their governments. Globalisation has made it more difficult for national governments to undertake domestic reform and to conduct autonomous macroeconomic policy. In his study of the early Clinton White House, Bob

Woodward recorded the President's intense shock upon discovering that his plans for public investment were subject to the mercy of the global bond market.[5] Susan Strange wrote in 1995:

> The evidence is there for all to see. No longer can any state today afford to opt out of the global market economy … Competing for world market shares, whether oil or semiconductors or air travel, means accepting the established structures and customs of those markets. Competing for foreign capital means accepting the terms and conditions set by the major financial centres and the major international banks, insurance firms, law firms and accountants.[6]

Despite all this, it is important to avoid running away with the notion that US foreign policy is an inert product of globalised capitalism. For one thing, much of the literature on international political economy tends to exaggerate the extent to which a global economy can be said to have arrived. Localised production continues, as does traditional inter-state trade. The international economy was almost as integrated before 1914 as in the 1990s.[7] The recent growth in free financial flows is associated – as Paul Hirst and Grahame Thompson noted in 1992 – with particular events and conditions: floating exchange rates; oil price rises and developing country indebtedness; the rise of the petrodollar; 1970s recession; widespread structural balance of payments imbalances; and the decision by important national governments to liberalise markets. At least some events and conditions 'may be temporary' and are 'not irreversible'. National governments may be constrained by global markets, but 'they remain political communities with extensive powers to influence and sustain economic actors within their territories'.[8] In recent years, national governments have tended to pursue regionalist strategies, thus resisting the absolutist imperatives of globalisation.[9] Moreover, if states do still retain power, the most powerful state of all – the USA – retains the greatest power. Eric Helleiner, for example, in his account of 'the declining policy autonomy of states', makes an important exception in the case of the United States. During the 1970s and 1980s, the USA 'actively cultivated the globalisation phenomenon':

> Globalization benefited the US because of its hegemonic position in the new open global financial system, a position derived primarily from the unique attractiveness of US and Eurodollar financial markets to foreign investors. This power was then used in what Gilpin calls a 'predatory' fashion by the US to finance its growing current account and fiscal deficits.[10]

Helleiner's point, of course, flies in the face of those nationalist economists (notably Pat Choate) who inveigh against foreign investors and foreign lobbyists. Inward investment into the United States and foreign lobbying, are important features of globalisation. (These issues were raised in 1996 not only by the Ross Perot–Choate Presidential campaign, but by allegations that the Clinton White House had been the target of improper influence-buying by Indonesian lobbyists.) By the late 1980s, the United States had become the world's largest host for inward foreign investment, which increased six-fold between 1980 and 1991. In such an environment, foreign governments themselves become powerful lobbyists within the United States. In their study of the 'Japan lobby', Hrebenar and Thomas conclude that 'Japan's lobbying efforts appear to be commensurate to the stakes it holds in its relations with the United States'. There is evidence that the lobby has 'shifted its emphasis away from the use of expensive lobbyists toward the utilization of American organizations and Japanese subsidiaries to get its message to American political leaders'. The annual expenditure of the Japan lobby has been estimated at $400 million. Other countries also spend significant amounts.[11] Regulation of foreign lobbying presents intrinsic difficulties and is a matter of legitimate concern. However, America's experience with foreign direct investment essentially replicates the experience of other major industrial countries. The evidence does not suggest that such investment is either uncontrollable or that it has primarily negative effects on the host economy.[12]

A good snapshot of the global economy emerges from tables showing the world's largest economic entities. In 1992, it was estimated that, of the largest one hundred economic units (countries and corporations), forty-one were multinational corporations (MNCs). General Motors had an annual product significantly larger than that of Indonesia, South Africa or Turkey. By the early 1990s, over 40 per cent of the world's leading corporations were American (compared to nearly 70 per cent in 1965).[13]

The implications of globalised production and marketing are far-reaching. Before he joined the Clinton Administration as Labour Secretary, Robert Reich argued that 'American' MNCs 'are rapidly becoming global entities with no special relationship' to the 'home' economy.[14] Richard Barnet and John Cavanagh note that 'by the miracle of globalization "Japanese" cars are transformed into "American" cars as Honda ships its Accords to Taiwan, Korea, and Israel from its Ohio plant':[15]

> It is now a fact of global life that multinationals, whatever flag they fly, can use overseas subsidiaries, joint ventures, licensing agreements, and strategic alliances to assume foreign identities when its suits their purposes – either to help them slip under tariff walls or to take advantage of some law of another country.[16]

How far, in fact, should US-based MNCs be regarded as an integrated part of 'American power'? Conversely, how far have MNCs developed into authentically transnational corporations – 'genuine footloose capital, without specific national identification'?[17] It should, firstly, be remembered that MNCs themselves vary considerably. Blake and Walters suggest a threefold classification: the 'parent-dominant, subsidiary-subservient' type; the quasi-'international holding company in which the various subsidiaries operate with a high degree of autonomy'; and 'the integrated international enterprise' with parent and subsidiary company operations being 'incorporated into an overall managerial effort'.[18] The third type appears to be increasingly important. Ford Motor's global integration in the early 1990s seemed to exemplify the new internationalism. There are signs also of American MNCs dropping their traditional caution regarding the sharing of ownership of subsidiaries with local, host interests.[19]

Such trends indicate some of the problems of attempting too close an identification between 'American' MNCs and 'American' power. A limited case can be made for MNC 'anationalism'. Washington is not always successful in securing MNC cooperation in the pursuance of US foreign policy objectives. Too little attention has been paid to the quasi-independent role of corporations as transnational bargainers with states and with other corporations (such activity is now far from being confined to large Western MNCs).[20] Upholders of the 'anationalism' of 'American' MNCs would argue that their true character was camouflaged in the post-1945 era by the apparent identity between US security and American business interests. As Bergsten, Horst and Moran put it, in the post-1945 period, 'restoration of an open, multilateral economic system ranked alongside "no more Munichs" as a cornerstone of foreign policy'.[21] The economic institutions of the Cold War – the regime of 'embedded liberalism'[22] – provided the environment for US corporations to expand and prosper. The rise of interdependency, and the putative decline in American economic hegemony, made it possible to argue that American MNCs were now beginning a new career as more autonomous bodies, 'putting the use of their oligopoly power increasingly at the service of diverse national claimants'.[23] The ending of the Cold War may, on one reading, be interpreted as tending further to release MNCs from the reins of US security. (On the other hand, the rise of the 'economic security' agenda, as a major priority for the Clinton Administration's foreign policy, would seem to point in the opposite direction.)

Against 'anational' interpretations of MNC power are ranged realist (including 'neo-mercantilist') theories of state power, as well as Marxian theories of economic imperialism. Taking the latter first, it should be remembered that Marxian theory is concerned primarily with the structure and power of capital itself, rather than with the power of particular nation-states. Marxist interpretations of the contemporary global political economy tend to focus on the 'spatial decentralisation of the power of transnational capital'. However, within the recent Marxian tradition, core capitalist interests are generally identified with the USA, albeit a 'late-imperial' USA.[24] Rejecting pluralist accounts of foreign policy-making, Marxian theory tends to see US foreign policy as the product of the desire and/or need to secure overseas markets, to protect business interests and to maintain access to raw materials. 'Neo-mercantilists' also tend to discount conventional ideas of pluralism in foreign policymaking. If retained at all, the notion of a plural policymaking process tends to serve as an explanation for policies which distort the furtherance of the authentic national interest. 'Neo-mercantilists' reverse the Marxian insistence on interpreting US foreign policy as a mechanism for supporting US business interests. Rather, their emphasis is on the 'promotion of international economic power and domestic prosperity' as 'aspects of the larger objective of preserving national strength in relation to other states'.[25] (Formulated in these terms, realist-inclined 'neo-mercantilism' conforms rather closely to the stated 'economic security' aims of the Clinton Administration[26].)

Where does all this leave our inquiry into the relation between corporate MNC and American national power? Certainly, MNCs are susceptible to political and economic analysis without constant reference to parent, or indeed host, states. However, any notion of complete MNC autonomy or transcendent 'anationalism' is overdrawn. Several studies published in the early 1990s tended to argue that the extent of genuinely *trans*national direct investment capital was not as great as often presumed. MNCs may have the ability to abandon particular national markets, but very often choose not to do so.[27] Entrenchment in local and regional markets tends to militate against genuinely 'footloose' investment. As Mitchell Bernard argues, regionalism has also been driven by 'the desire of corporate and state elites in North America and Europe to respond to Japanese innovation by enlarging the "economic space" that can be considered part of a home market'.[28]

Resistance to the idea of unqualified MNC 'anationalism' should not be confused with a failure to recognise the degree to which the world's economy has moved towards a kind of *regionalised* globalisation. State policy-making structures should not be considered as autonomous units, unaffected by the wider regional or international political economy. There is substance to the case argued by Petras and Morley that US state sponsorship of 'American' MNCs tends to divert resources to international circuits of capital: 'given the present-day structure of US capitalism, more state subsidies to large outward-oriented corporations will only extend the gap between global empire and domestic decay'.[29] However, the main point now being made is that the state – even the 'weak' American state[30] – should not be considered a mere epiphenomenon. Marxian ideas of 'relative autonomy' point away from epiphenomenal treatments of the state.[31] So does a large body of state-centred, 'domestic structures' writing which seeks to carve out an 'independent' role for the state, even in a world of globalised and complex interdependence.[32]

Business and governmental elites in the United States overlap and interpenetrate. They share the same liberal values and commitments to mutually reinforcing capitalism and democracy. However, the state, 'relatively autonomous' and influenced by its own traditions and bureaucratic histories, does impinge upon business autonomy. It sets trade and anti-trust policies. It may prohibit trade with 'enemy' nations. It will grant most-favoured-nation trading status to all but a few. As one recent critic of unreflective theories of globalisation has put it: 'No other institution has emerged to supplant the state in its traditional functions ... the state is still needed as infrastructure-operator, rule-setter, and peace-maker.'[33] Empirical investigation into the relationship between the American state and American corporations reveals a tale of complex linkages, overlapping but not identical interests, potential and actual disputes.

2   Corporations and US foreign policy

Studies of business influence on US foreign policy tend to concentrate on foreign economic and trade policy. As noted above, however, any neat division (whether in Cold War or post-Cold War conditions) between 'economic' and 'security' categories is misleading.[34] Many authorities see trade policy as having both 'strategic' and 'manipulative' dimensions. The former is designed to promote a liberal world order, rooted in (increasingly regionalised) free trade. The latter involves devices like sanctions and most-favoured-nation trade relationships.

Despite the difficulties of separating economics from security, it is clear that business is not interested equally intensely in all foreign policy questions; nor do all foreign policy issues offer equal opportunities for the expression of (aggregated or disaggregated) corporate interests. Conventionally delineated issue areas are regulative, distributive, redistributive and security. Of these categories, security issues are generally regarded as the least domestically divisive, and are more usually settled at an elite, state level. Distributive politics involve the dispersal of tangible benefits where 'everyone who counts politically'[35] gains something. Distributive politics are the stuff of the Congressional pork-barrel and the subject of relatively disaggregated business lobbying. Regulative politics – seen in the cases of NAFTA and GATT – involve clear winners and losers, and are the subject of highly complex governmental and societal interactions. Intense conflicts in the redistributive area may involve fundamental issues and even mass public mobilisation (Zimmerman cites the domestic conflict over the Vietnam War as an example[36].)

Realist accounts tend either to assume or to argue for the primacy of security issues. Stephen Krasner's landmark study, *Defending the National Interest* (1978), demonstrated the possibility of (real and perceived) divergence between state and business interests, and the ability of the state to achieve its 'security' ends. In concentrating on American MNCs involved in the extraction of raw materials, Krasner assaulted those cruder Marxian accounts which postulate clear, determined correlations between such activity and state policy. In fact, it is not especially difficult to find examples of business and state interests diverging, with the state emerging victorious. Congressional cancellation, in the mid-1970s post-Vietnam War environment, of the

Overseas Private Investment Corporation is one such example.[37] Restrictions on free trade resulting from Cold War rivalries also harmed the immediate interests of American MNCs, and offered opportunities to rivals. Proponents of close, determined correlation between MNC interest and state policy also have to address questions of policy inconsistency. H. B. Malmgren declared in 1972 that he only wished that foreign economic policy was as coherent as radical critics claimed.[38]

If the American state does not always pursue policies which are to the immediate and obvious advantage of giant corporations, then the reverse is also true. MNC currency speculation in the early 1970s and cooperation in the Arab embargo on oil supplies to the United States in 1973–74 are cases in point.[39] Some radical interpretations of post-Cold War globalisation see the US state as having been co-opted by the new model of transnational capital.[40] In fact, empirical investigation tends to reveal complex governmental–MNC relationships, based on a strong sense of shared interest, but with significant disruptions and malfunctions. One important study, published in 1995, commented on these issues in the context of the efforts of the US government to enforce Administration-led sanctions against Nicaragua and Libya, and Congressional sanctions against South Africa during the 1980s. Kenneth Rodman concluded that Washington had not always been able or willing to determine the behaviour of foreign affiliates of American-owned corporations. However:

> In Nicaragua and South Africa, the hostility of the US government (Congress in the latter case) increased the external risks faced by firms regarding any venture that anticipated a long-term payoff (as opposed to arm's length trade). In Libya and South Africa, firms had to weigh the internal risks of losing access to governmental services or contracts … Even in the absence of conscious public decisions to manipulate private behavior, these risks dissuaded MNCs from pursuing certain global economic interests but were at variance with intensely held state preferences.[41]

MNCs have been used to enforce US foreign policy: for example, by denying the technology needed to develop a French nuclear force in the 1960s. They have been used for intelligence-gathering and have been involved in grey areas of foreign policy, deliberately kept at one remove from the public domain and subject to the doctrine of 'plausible deniability'. The role of International Telephone and Telegraph in mobilising opposition to the Allende regime in Chile in the early 1970s is now widely acknowledged. David Rockefeller, chairman of Chase Manhattan Bank, was an influential actor in USA–Iranian relations prior to the 1979 Iranian revolution. The 1980s saw repeated reports of corporations channelling money to the Contra rebels in Nicaragua. In the mid-1980s, White House irregular Colonel Oliver North openly solicited money from private sources to fund Contra operations. According to the Tower Commission report on the

Iran–Contra issue, such abuses gave 'private and foreign sources potentially powerful leverage in the form of demands for return favours or even blackmail'.[42]

As noted above, the Clinton Administration quickly moved to position itself as a stout defender of American business abroad. Clinton himself asserted that the United States was 'like a big corporation competing in the global marketplace'.[43] US Trade Representative Mickey Kantor argued that the government had for too long been too coy about exercising pressure on behalf of American business: 'For years we have allowed our workers to be hurt and our companies left out because we wouldn't pick up the phone.'[44] Kantor was careful to insist that pressure should be 'proper' and not include bribery. In 1996 he threatened retaliatory action against countries that were less punctilious.[45] Yet during the 1996 Presidential election campaign, various press allegations centred on putative links between corporate donations to the Democrats and the smoothing (especially by the Commerce Department under the late Ron Brown) of access to foreign markets. The admixture of the Clinton Administration's 'neo-mercantilism' with the apparent logic of 'anational' globalised capital gave an insight into the paradoxes of the post-Cold War order. Rodman also points out that the early Clinton years saw indications that foreign affiliates of US multinationals were not always willing to obey American law. Such affiliates – at least before 1995 – took the apparent insouciance of the Administration over the issue of trade with Cuba as a cue to disobey the 1992 Cuban Democracy Act, which extended the embargo.[46]

In discussing the 'independent' power of corporations, it is important to avoid conspiracy theory. MNCs for the most part exert their influence in fairly obvious ways. At one level, their influence is an inherent and inescapable part of the world capitalist economy. At another, corporate power may be observed in lobbying and political funding activities. The philosophy of corporate influence-buying (with a view to domestic and foreign policy) was illustrated during the 1986 Congressional elections, when General Electric's PAC gave funds to thirty-four House candidates who did not even face an opponent. Such activity is tantamount to a distortion of the democratic process. With their massive lobbying resources, huge corporations are able to embed themselves securely within the 'iron triangles' or 'subgovernments' of policymaking. Through smart footwork and influence in Congress, 130 large corporations managed, in one or more years during the period 1982–85, to avoid paying any taxes on profits whatsoever. This prompted Illinois Democratic Senator Paul Simon to point out that 'the janitor at General Electric pays more taxes than GE'.[47] Economic globalisation has also made it difficult for US taxing authorities to collect revenue from foreign-owned corporations operating in the United States. In 1987, over half of such corporations reported that they had made no profit in the USA and therefore should pay zero tax. Subsequent efforts by state legislatures to close tax loopholes were met by massively expensive lobbying efforts by for-eign-based MNCs.[48]

Again, it should be emphasised that business is not a monolith. Most stud-ies of interest group pressure conclude that 'all groups, regardless of their alleged clout, lose some of the time and win some of the time'.[49] Failure may be due, for example, to unexpected changes of Congressional opinion or personnel, or to the presence of countervailing interests. MNC preferences may also shift and vary. It tends to be assumed, for example, that multina-tionals will always favour low tariffs, with business preference for protection being confined to smaller, national firms in competition with imports. By the later 1980s, however, many US-based MNCs were attempting to steer a new path between protectionism and free trade, towards 'strategic trade policy'. The American semiconductor industry, for example, began to lobby for a closure of domestic markets to Japanese corporations which did not pur-chase US microchips.[50]

Such shifts in corporate strategy led to some surprising alliances with organised labour, which became converted in the 1970s to a 'fair trade' (quasi-protectionist) strategy. Pluralist theory would suggest that organised labour operates as a countervailing force to the power of the corporations. Such an assertion has never been especially convincing, and became partic-ularly unpersuasive in the face of the decline of union power and influence in the 1970s and 1980s. During this period, labour suffered from shifts in American economic activity towards Southwestern areas of traditional union weakness. Organised labour failed to adapt to a service- and informa-tion-based economy, and suffered because of the ability of American MNCs to use profits from foreign operations to undermine the bargaining position of domestic trade unions.[51] Labour's 1993 defeat in the NAFTA ratification battle exemplified this weakness, despite subsequent efforts by the Clinton Administration to mend fences. (The possibility of a reinvigorated labour–Administration relationship was widely discussed in 1995, in the context of leadership changes at the American Federation of Labour–Con-gress of Industrial Organizations. Labour Secretary Robert Reich began to cultivate closer relations, while progress was made in the arenas of union rights and the minimum wage[52].)

Defence contracting firms constitute a special case of corporate power. The Cold War created the kind of unaccountable, vested interests – the 'mil-itary industrial complex' – about which President Eisenhower warned in his 1961 Farewell Address. The Reagan Administration's military spending in the early 1980s produced massive defence contractor profits. In 1984, the ten largest defence contractors achieved an average 25 per cent return on equity. This should be contrasted with the average corporate figure of 12.8 per cent. Lockheed reported a 42 per cent profit as percentage of equity, General Dynamic 30 per cent. The explanation for such profits did not lie in greater efficiency relative to non-defence corporations, but rather in the privileges accruing to leading actors in the Cold War 'military–industrial complex'. Under its contracting system, the Pentagon regularly compensated contractors who tendered unsuccessful, even unsolicited, bids. Defence firms were able to defer paying taxes on profits, often for many years. The whole system was lubricated by frequent personnel interchange between the Pentagon, defence contractors and various research agencies, which acted as 'transmission belts' between the contractors and its governmental client. A familiar Cold War joke was that the Pentagon ran, after the Kremlin, the world's second largest planned economy.[53]

In a sense, the very fact that the Cold War did come to an end indicates that the 'military–industrial complex' is not all powerful. As Gordon Adams wrote in 1994: 'The power of the military–industrial complex, if it was real, ought to have been sufficient to prevent severe budget decline, hardware cancellation, and base closing, the very events taking place in the 1990s'. He argued that 'defence decisions and budgetary allocations have always been influenced by international forces and events, fiscal and economic requirements, bureaucratic behavior, and domestic politics'.[54] The ending of the Cold War had immediate effects on Pentagon procurement levels, which experienced a fall of 20 per cent between 1987 and 1992. Defence authority spending totals in the mid-1990s reflected inter-branch rivalries just as much as an entrenched defence contractor interest. (In 1993, for example, the Democratic Congress sliced $2.6 billion from the Clinton Administration's defence authority requests. In 1995, the Republican Congress *added* $7.1 billion.)

Appreciation of the wider environment of defence budgeting is not, however, tantamount to denial of the lobbying power of defence contractors. The survival of the V-22 Osprey (a vertical take-off transporter, initially opposed by the Bush Administration) illustrates the resilience of military–industrial power centres.[55] The C-17 cargo jet procurement became mired in complex interactions between the Pentagon and McDonnell Douglas. Defence Secretary Les Aspin remarked in 1993: 'The story of the C-17 program reflects on the unwillingness on the part of some high-ranking acquisition professionals to acknowledge program difficulties and to take decisive action.'[56] The post-Cold War defence shakeout saw a major restructuring of the US arms industry. (In 1992, for example, Lockheed purchased General Dynamics' fighter jet division, while Martin Marietta acquired General Electric's aerospace unit.) Industry lobbyists also turned, with considerable success, to the Clinton Administration for assistance with foreign arms sales. Martin Marietta's foreign sales moved from 8 per cent in 1991 to over one-fifth by 1994. Government loan guarantees and some federal governmental reorganisation eased this transition. In 1993, the Pentagon and the State Department helped US contractors achieve $36 billion worth of arms agreements. This version of Clinton's neo-mercantilism soon attracted intense criticism (as when, in 1995, Turkey used US arms against Kurds in

Iraq). Efforts were mounted in Congress (notably by Republican Senator Mark Hatfield and Democratic Congresswoman Cynthia McKinney) to subject the new 'arms bazaar' to a code of conduct.[57]

3   The news media

It is common currency that the media have both a tendency to distort the news, and considerable political power in their own right. James Reston referred in 1967 to the 'tyranny of technique', encouraging 'a startling, even a breathless, presentation of the news, featuring the flaming lead and the big headline'.[58] Broadcasters and journalists are regularly accused of trivialisation, the lack of any institutional memory, 'pack journalism' and intellectual laziness. James Fallows addressed the White House press corps in 1996:

> Why not *read a book* – about welfare reform, about Russia or China, about race relations, about anything? Why not imagine, just for a moment, that your journalistic duty might involve something more varied and constructive than doing standups from the White House lawn and sounding skeptical about whatever announcement the President's spokesman put out that day?[59]

Bored and uninformed scepticism is often seen by government officials and politicians as alternating with 'feeding frenzy' and with 'lynch mob' censoriousness. (In his memoirs, Robert Gates, former deputy to William Casey at the CIA, described his experience at the 1986 Senate Iran–Contra hearings: 'What I was unprepared for … was the media frenzy … I felt as if I was being taken to the dock for trial.'[60])

The view of the media as (at least potentially) a threat to, rather than an integral part of, democratic government has gained added credence with the growth of new technologies. Live, non-stop television coverage of international news arguably forces leaders into precipitate and ill-considered responses. Leadership and accountability may be compromised. Former Secretary of State George Shultz has remarked that Cable News Network (CNN) 'puts everybody on real time, because everyone is seeing the same thing'.[61] Eric Alterman has argued that President Bush was pressured into an excessive reaction to Saddam Hussein's 1990 invasion of Kuwait by an irresponsible 'punditocracy'.[62] Once he had gone to war, Bush was able to operate with little concern for Congress, but could not afford to ignore the media. It is also frequently argued that the uncertain agenda of post-Cold War foreign policy encourages media irresponsibility. News organisations may 'parachute' correspondents into the latest hotspot in a random way. James Schlesinger wrote in 1993: 'In the absence of established guideposts our policies will be determined by impulse and image … National policy is determined by the plight of the Kurds, or starvation in Somalia, as it appears on the screen.'[63]

Several qualifications need to be made to this portrayal of media irresponsibility. For one thing, the independent power of the media is often exaggerated. The post-Vietnam War notion that public opinion had swung away from the war because of crusading journalism and vivid photography is little more than romantic myth. Most newspapers and TV journalists tended to present a patriotic and pro-war coverage; their attitudes shifted significantly only when sharp elite divisions had already become apparent. President Johnson's own communication failures – his inability to invoke an effective 'rhetoric of limited war' – were more damaging to the war cause than activities of crusading cameramen and 'punk kid reporters'.[64]

Foreign policy journalists represent a kind of semi-disengaged feature of elite opinion. Ted Galen Carpenter, writing under the auspices of the anti-interventionist Cato Institute, argues:

> [C]orrespondents, editors, pundits, and publishers who work for major media outlets tend to see themselves as members of an opinion-making elite. They consider themselves on an intellectual and social par with high-level policy-makers, an attitude that increases the prospect of their being co-opted by ambitious and determined policymakers.[65]

Carpenter and others maintain that the Gulf crisis saw a blatant co-option of elite journalists. President Bush may still have had to worry about the press when he went to war. However, the Pentagon's 'pool' system proved effective in orchestrating the coverage. Jonathan Alter recorded the 'sad fact' that 'we "covered" the war, but we didn't report the war'.[66] David Gergen wrote later: 'In the Persian Gulf, the military snookered the press.'[67]

Critical coverage of foreign policy tends to emerge where (as in the case of the Vietnam War) there are intense elite divisions. At one level, conflict between the main players (in Congress, State, the Pentagon and the White House) will almost always generate potentially damaging coverage. Where sustained elite division – over the Vietnam War, over Reagan's policies in Central America, over the thrust of post-Cold War internationalism – exists, media reportage is more likely to penetrate and shape public views.[68] In general terms, however, it is misleading to imagine that such influence is either consistent or direct. The public tends to interpret news coverage in ways consistent with preconceived ideas and belief systems.[69] In the face of public 'defensive avoidance' and selective attentiveness, media shaping may tend to impact most strongly on people with unusually unformed views. (In the case of foreign policy, of course, this description can apply to a large section of the population.) Major televised *coups de théâtre* – like President Nixon's 1972 visit to China – will command mass attention. Generally, however – as discussed in Chapter 6 – foreign policy is not high on any list of public priorities. It should also be remembered that the press, at least during times of peace, is dominated by domestic stories. In the mid-1980s, Doris Graber estimated that only 11 per cent of newspaper stories related to foreign affairs. The ending of the Cold War has also further inclined American news-

papers to locate international news on the back pages.[70] Foreign coverage in
the US media is of a high quality, but it is largely confined to self-consciously
'elite' or 'prestige' segments of broadcasting.

The media's agenda-setting function has long been recognised. Bernard
Cohen wrote in 1963: 'The press may not be successful much of the time in
telling people what to think, but it is stunningly successful in telling it what
to think *about*.'[71] Unquestionably, as James Schlesinger noted in 1993, new
media technologies have increased the likelihood of policy managers being
embarrassed and surprised by the raising of 'news' issues. Yet the media's
agenda-setting often occurs in concert with governing elites. The foreign
policy press, at least to some degree, operates within limits set by elite direction. It serves – especially if one includes specialist journals like *Foreign
Affairs* and *Foreign Policy* – as an instrument of intra- and inter-elite communication. It is (as will become clear in the following section) hazardous to
generalise about foreign policy elite behaviour. However, in the post-1945
era, foreign policy elites in the United States have tended to favour 'liberal'
interventionist and internationalist strategies, and to equate the promotion
of democracy with the promotion of free trade. The foreign policy press has
generally reinforced these views and, in the process, has upset both conservative and leftist opinion. For Ted Galen Carpenter, the media are unthink-
ingly interventionist and committed to 'foreign policy as social work'. For
the left, the media represent a reflection of the interests of corporate America. Marxist media theory, deriving from the work of Antonio Gramsci, suggests that the press exists to disseminate and reinforce dominant hegemonic
ideology. It seeks to 'correct' the degree to which personal experience, rea-
soning and intuition tends to contradict dominant views.[72] Certainly, there is
evidence for the view that the media 'frame' stories in ways which mirror
elite evaluations and cut off options. Press coverage of the 1990 Gulf crisis
arguably inclined to shut off the option of proceeding with sanctions against
Iraq 'long before', as Lance Bennett writes, 'there was any empirical basis for
so doing'.[73] In the absence of clear external censorship, the US press may also
be seen as practising a variety of self-censorship. This might operate at the
level of ownership. It also, however, involves the degree to which the media
are structured so as to keep information and comment within 'acceptable'
bounds. D. C. Hallin points out that early Vietnam War protesters gained
quasi-sympathetic coverage only if they could be presented as stout individ-
ualists, acting – however misguidedly – out of eccentric conscience. A 1967
CBS report on an Indiana schoolteacher, fired for anti-war activity, ended
with the line: 'In a small town, it's difficult to be different.'[74] Media self-censorship seems especially acute after an apparent re-forming of elite consensus. In the early Reagan years, for example, only Jack Anderson, among
'prestige' journalists, appeared willing seriously to challenge the new Administration's foreign policy.[75]

Sections of the media appear to be oriented as much to service foreign policy governing elites as to serve the general public. In his 1995 memoir, *The Politics of Diplomacy*, former Secretary of State James Baker recalled his news management efforts during the January 1992 Coordinating Conference in Washington on post-Soviet reform:

> I also wanted to add a touch of drama that would break through the typical media coverage of such a diplomatic event. I wanted to create a story line that might be transmitted by CNN and other international media to help instill hope in those in need in the former Soviet Union, while also galvanizing a public consensus (and private efforts) in the United States.[76]

The result was 'Operation Provide Hope' – an airlift of food and medicine to the new, post-Soviet republics. The State Department regularly uses press briefings not only to communicate on a world scale, but to send messages to Congress and to other executive agencies. As Adrienne Jamieson writes: 'News is a reflection of the messages policy-makers send, the ways in which the press receive and transmit them and the myriad cultural forces in the Washington community which shape the conversation in policy networks.'[77] The press–politician relationship is symbiotic. Policymakers complain about press negativism and sensationalism, yet also acknowledge that the media are vital to the development and elaboration of successful policy.[78] 'Leaks' and trial balloons are effective devices of elite communication. Foreign policy journalists and foreign policy managers tend to drink at the same informational fountain and to define problems in similar terms.

The full implications for the conduct of foreign policy of the new communications technology are immense and unknowable. During the Gulf crisis, CNN reporter Peter Arnett felt quite literally that he 'was being watched by the whole world' – Saddam, the White House, Wall Street, Arab and allied opinion: all seemed to be dancing to the tunes set in the continuous, live CNN coverage.[79] New technology may, with new opportunities for 'narrow-casting', effectively presage the demise of the 'mass' media. It may enhance democratisation. (According to Harry Grunwald, the communications revolution 'that was instrumental in bringing down the Berlin Wall is likely to bring down many walls in our own society'[80].) Of course, elites (as they have in the past) may find new ways of dominating and influencing the new media.[81] Globalised media pervasiveness also brings its own risks and absurdities. News and entertainment values may – perhaps already have – become dangerously intermingled, especially in view of increasing transmedia mergers.[82] Thomas Jefferson did not have globalised infotainment in mind when he observed in 1786: 'Our liberty depends on the freedom of the press, and that cannot be limited without being lost.'[83] Yet, on balance, instant global communication does help the cause of popular information. It also puts the onus on elites to explain themselves.

4   Foreign policy elites

The post-1945 period witnessed the coming to power of, despite many internal divisions, a well-defined, internationalist foreign policy elite. Michael Clough wrote in 1994 (as a Senior Fellow at the Council on Foreign Relations) that US foreign policy in the Cold War era had been run by a 'small cohesive club of academics, diplomats, financiers, lawyers and politicians'. The 'club' believed that politics should stop at the water's edge, and that bipartisan internationalist consensus should rule the day. In contradistinction to earlier eras, 'the Northeast played a dominant role in shaping foreign policy'. (According to Clough, for 'most of the nation's history the influence of the more industrial and Anglophile Northeast was counterbalanced by other regions'.)[84] The discrediting of pre-1941 isolationism, with its roots in the West and Midwest, laid a foundation for Northeastern ascendancy. Even before 1945, however, top foreign policy positions tended to be dominated by white men from legal and/or business backgrounds, with ready access to the 'revolving door' which separates public and private sectors. In *The Wise Men* (1986), Isaacson and Thomas traced the interlocking backgrounds and careers of six central figures in the foreign policy elite of the 'American Century': Dean Acheson, Charles Bohlen, Averell Harriman, George Kennan, R. A. Lovett and J. J. McCloy. Figures such as these tended to dismiss the notion of any socially exclusive foreign policy 'establishment': 'Skull and Bones, Groton, that sort of thing.'[85] McCloy, sometime chairman of Chase Manhattan Bank, director of the Council on Foreign Relations and president of the World Bank, was born in relatively humble circumstances in Philadelphia in 1895. Certainly, the foreign policy elite was open, in the words of Isaacson and Thomas, to talented outsiders 'who are eager to accept its cultivating process'. McCloy came to embody elite attitudes of public service, Wall Street–governmental partnership and the primacy of continuity over political partisanship. 'Damn it, I always forget', exclaimed President Franklin Roosevelt upon being reminded that McCloy was not a Democrat.[86]

The interpenetration of American social, governmental, legal and business elites has been well documented, and continued into the post-Cold War era. President Bill Clinton's 1993 Cabinet appointees did, in some important respects, 'look like America'; they were certainly more diverse in terms of gender and ethnicity than any such appointments in history. Yet of the fifteen original appointees, nine (including Secretary of State Warren Christopher) came from legal backgrounds. The Clinton appointees tended to possess advanced educational qualifications, but were also highly 'networked'. 'Friendships formed at elite colleges and law schools have been sustained through an archipelago of think tanks, foundations, councils, and associations.'[87] The Aspen Institute, an internationalist group geared to the development of arms control, actually furnished almost the entire early Clinton foreign policy team.

The 'foreign policy elite' comprises really quite a small number of senior foreign policy managers – around forty State Department officials, for example, hold posts of Assistant Secretary or above – as well as senior academics, journalists, think-tankers, and what Thomas McCormick calls 'ins-and-outers'. According to McCormick, around one-third of the Cold War foreign policy elite came from the career civil, military or diplomatic service. (Examples would include George Kennan, Charles Bohlen – Soviet experts on the State Department Policy Planning Staff – and Reagan's first Secretary of State Alexander Haig, from a career military background.) The remaining two-thirds were 'ins-and-outers', switching between private and public employment. Around 40 per cent of these came from corporate management – including Defence Secretaries Charles Wilson (1953–57), Robert McNamara (1961–67) and Caspar Weinberger (1981–87). Another 40 per cent came from law firms, with most of the remaining 20 per cent from academia. According to McCormick:

> What set the foreign policy elite apart from all other groups was its coherent and cosmopolitan world view ... The ins-and-outers especially, because of the multiple functions they performed and the double-tracked perspectives they gained from public and private spheres, were stimulated to see the world as a system ... It was this *long-term globalism* that set them apart from Congress, the middle bureaucracy, and much of the business community, each of which has a more acute concern for special interests, organizational imperatives, or short-term profits.[88]

In this reading of the Cold War era, the foreign policy elite was able to supply a kind of internationalist corporate continuity to US foreign policy. Elitist and ademocratic, it operated in an environment relatively free of meaningful public accountability and even of debilitating 'bureaucratic politics'.

The Cold War did see significant challenges to the world of the 'ins-and-outers'. Various assertions of Congressional authority, public anxieties about nuclear weapons and American over-extension, above all the defeat in Vietnam: all these threatened elite domination, but did not entirely cancel it. Following the Vietnam War, the elite tended to be less socially exclusive and more professionalised. Nelson Polsby in the early 1990s described:

> [an] establishment [which tended] to be from the top of the class in an academic rather than a social sense, who got their basic cognitive grounding in how nations behave from reading Quincy Wright and Hans Morgenthau in graduate school rather than from listening to the exhortations of Endicott Peabody [long-time headmaster at Groton] and reading the book of Common Prayer.[89]

Yet what tends to surprise Europeans is the extent to which the internationalist 'in-and-out' elite appeared to dominate, after as well as before the Vietnam War, both Democrat and Republican Administrations. President Jimmy Carter's Cabinet contained three people who had been on the board of

International Business Machines. The Council on Foreign Relations (CFR), the best known of all foreign policy elite organisations, tends to be associated with policies advocated by the Democratic party. Its offshoot, the Rockefeller-funded Trilateral Commission, provided ideas and personnel to the Carter Administration. It might be assumed that the CFR lost influence in the early 1980s to organisations like the strongly anti-Soviet Committee on the Present Danger and the institutions of the New Right. Yet Reagan's second Secretary of State, George Shultz, was a former CFR Director. (A seasoned 'in-and-outer', Shultz had served previously as Nixon's Labour Secretary, Budget Director and Treasury Secretary.) Vice-President George Bush, Secretary of Defence Weinberger, CIA director William Casey (a former president of the Export-Import Bank) and Shultz's predecessor Alexander Haig, were CFR members as well. (By the late 1970s, the CFR had, in fact, already moved to a more confrontational posture towards the USSR.) Key Bush Administration figures – notably NSA Brent Scowcroft and Defence Secretary Dick Cheney – had strong CFR associations, as did Clinton's NSA Anthony Lake. President Bush himself actually resigned from the CFR in the face of right-wing attacks on its traditions of liberal internationalism.[90]

Elite continuity fuels conspiracy theory, and the CFR has been attacked from the left as an imperialist Rockefeller interest, and from the right as an instrument of Wall Street 'one worldism'.[91] Transnational elite bodies, like the Bilderberg group, have similarly been caught in a right–left pincer movement.[92] Of course, in a country like the United States, with a strong consensual commitment to free enterprise capitalism, the existence of strong links between governmental and (especially) business personnel is scarcely surprising. Influential foreign policy think-tanks, like Kissinger Associates, exist to make a profit. Business elites may show a slight disposition to hawkish foreign policy attitudes, but there is little evidence for the assumption that they are driven in these attitudes by narrow formulations of the business interest. As McCormick argues, a defining feature of the 'ins-and-outers' (even those from relatively narrow business backgrounds) has been the ability to think globally – to combine an ideal of public service with a vision for the advancement of democratic capitalism on a world scale.[93]

Even during the Cold War, the elite was riven by fashions and factions, illustrated in the complex web of foreign policy think-tanks. In *The Idea Brokers* (1991), James Allen Smith listed thirty 'leading think tanks', of which seventeen – all based in Washington DC – dealt in some shape or form with foreign policy.[94] In 1996, David Newsom isolated the ten most prominent: the Carnegie Endowment (founded 1910); the Brookings Institution (founded in its present form in 1927, primarily geared to the development of liberal domestic policy); the American Enterprise Institute (founded in 1943 to provide a rightist, business-oriented counterpart to Brookings); the Centre for Strategic and International Studies (a 1962 foundation, oriented towards anti-Sovietism and modelled on the Institute of Strategic Studies in

London); the Institute for Policy Studies (founded in 1963 by Marcus Raskin and Richard Barnet as a left-leaning contributor to the Democratic party agenda); the Heritage Foundation (dating from 1973 and, by the early 1980s, the most aggressive advocate of rightist foreign policy positions); the anti-interventionist, libertarian Cato Institute; the Joint Centre for Political and Economic Studies (established in 1970 as a think-tank for issues affecting African Americans); the Centre for National Policy (founded in 1982 as a left-of-centre grouping, initially associated with former Senator and ex-Secretary of State Edmund Muskie); and the US Institute of Peace (founded and funded by Congress, originally under the 1985 Defence Authorization Act).[95] Other important Cold War think-tanks included the Rand Corporation (founded in 1948, originally linked to Air Force weapons research) and the Mitre Corporation (dating from 1958, and primarily associated with Pentagon contract research).

The majority of think-tanks depend on a mixture of individual, governmental and corporate funding (either via foundations like Ford and Rockefeller, or directly). Some, including Brookings and the Centre for Strategic and International Studies, have been criticised in recent years for rather uncritical acceptance of Japanese funding.[96] According to Newsom: 'A think tank scholar must walk a tight rope between integrity and the continuation of support.'[97] Richard Higgott and Diane Stone note that think-tanks 'are on the boundaries of philanthropy, government, the media and education'.[98] They mirror and set fashion, continually reflecting shifts in the loci of power. During the Cold War, the quasi-apolitical 'managerialism' characteristic of 'defence intellectuals' in the 1950s and early 1960s was both advanced and challenged in think-tanks. The Centre for Strategic and International Studies represented, in its inception, a reaction against the 'systems analysis managerialism' of Robert McNamara. Think-tanks attempt to set the agenda for incoming Administrations.[99] They provide information and are the sites of elite interaction and rotation.

Since the end of the Vietnam War, think-tanks have – to some degree – changed in ways consonant with Nelson Polsby's analysis of developments within the foreign policy elite itself. They have become more professionalised, more attuned to academe and, certainly, more directly concerned with policy advocacy. They seem to have developed in ways suited to serve the needs of Congress and the media as much as the executive-branch-oriented 'Wise Men' tradition. Their focus has also tended to become more diverse, and globalised.[100] The ending of the Cold War has magnified these tendencies. Some commentators have seen the growing heterogeneity of the think-tanks as a sign of challenge to elite domination. 'Without a clear and present danger', writes Michael Clough 'the public is no longer willing to trust the expert.'[101]

5 Foreign policy at state and local levels

Both globalisation and the ending of the Cold War have encouraged advocates of anti-expert, grassroots foreign policy. Local economic units and 'region states' may be seen as more appropriate focuses of power within a global economy than national governments. Foreign and domestic concerns intermix in surprising ways. According to Kenichi Ohmae, the logic of globalised interdependence is for the federal authorities to allow regions to conduct their own foreign economic relations: 'For the Clinton Administration, the irony is that Washington today finds itself in the same relation to those region states that lie entirely or partially within its borders as was London with the North American colonies centuries ago.'[102] If California were regarded as an independent nation, its gross annual economic product would put it around eighth largest in the world. J. O. Goldsborough concluded in 1993:

> The best hope is for California to pursue aggressively its own foreign policy. The state must rediscover its old relationship with Mexico, which offers the best means for dealing with its economic problems, as well as its immigration problem. In addition, California must also look westward, over the horizon, to the region that has become the most dynamic economic area in the world – the Pacific Rim. California's natural assets remain incomparable, but the state let itself grow too dependent on the Pentagon, too oriented toward the east.[103]

State and local governmental activism, in areas normally thought to lie within the exclusive purview of Washington, has increased considerably since the early 1980s. At one level, this new activism sprang from local opposition to the Republican foreign policy of the Reagan–Bush era. The Local Elected Officials project, the leading information network for the new local liberal activism, grew out of the nuclear freeze movement. (By the early 1990s, nearly one thousand localities had passed resolutions supporting a nuclear arms freeze. Over one hundred localities had refused to cooperate with nuclear war exercises sponsored by the Federal Emergency Management Agency[104].) In 1987, the Local Elected Officials project began publishing its own journal, the *Bulletin of Municipal Foreign Policy*. In the same year, the city of Seattle set up its own Office of International Affairs with a quarter of a million dollar annual budget. Among other tasks, the office was concerned with maintaining relations with Seattle's thirteen sister cities, including Managua. A sample of headlines from 1988 and 1989 issues of the *Bulletin* indicates the range of activities involved in this new activism: 'Detroit Endorses INF Treaty'; 'San Francisco urges Pope to Recognise Israel'; 'Alaska officials battle Plutonium Flights'; 'The Viability of Nuclear-Free Zones'; '39 Mayors Sign Anti-*Contra* Initiative'; 'Missouri and the MX'; 'Jersey Town Fights Rights Abuses in Brazil'.[105]

Gestural position-taking such as this is not new, nor does it automatically run in a liberal direction. (In the 1980s, for example, Alabama teachers were required by local legislators to emphasise 'ways to fight communism'. In 1982, Glen Cove, on New York's Long Island, protested Soviet action in Afghanistan by banning Soviet diplomats from its beaches and golf courses.)[106] Local elected officials have frequently taken high-profile positions on foreign issues, especially when seeking to generate support among local ethnic interests. When San Francisco mayor Willie Brown in 1996 ceremoniously emptied a bottle of Bushmill's Irish whisky into the sea (in protest against sectarian hiring practices at Bushmill's Ulster distillery), he was setting himself in this long tradition. At the state level, protectionist 'buy American' laws have also long operated in certain states as a constitutionally dubious assertion of subnational authority.

The ending of the Cold War lessened the attraction of liberal gesturing. However, it tended to increase enthusiasm for decentralised foreign policy in other areas. Patrick Lloyd Hatcher noted in 1996 that US–Cuban relations had shifted from a national to a regional stage. With the Cold War's end, 'few Americans focus on Cuba, except in South Florida, where a large, dynamic, and politically active Cuban exile community retains its animus against Castro and dreams of liberating Havana'. By the 1990s, it made 'more sense ... to see American relations with Cuba ... as an issue in Florida's foreign policy'.[107]

The main post-Cold War priority for subnational foreign policy was, unsurprisingly, trade and investment promotion. In 1988, Booth Gardner (Governor of the state of Washington and chairman of the National Governors' Association Committee on International Trade and Foreign Relations) declared that states did not need any leads in this area from the Department of Commerce: 'I see Commerce being a facilitator. I see states being the line of action.'[108] The average state budget earmarked for trade and investment promotion rose by 141 per cent between 1984 and 1988. States began to outbid each other in offering incentives to attract foreign investment. Washington State established its own office in Tokyo, promoting the state's trade, investment and agricultural interests. California, through its World Trade Commission, began to present itself as a quasi-independent player in global trade issues. By the late 1980s, state governments had become financial actors on the world stage, contributing to the globalisation of capital. States had amassed substantial investment portfolios and were selling bonds on the world market.[109] The rise of the 'region state' also pointed up the degree to which several border cities and regions of the United States participate in cross-border economies. Examples include the Northern Washington–British Columbia region, and the Paso del Norte – including the city of El Paso (Texas) and Juarez (Mexico).

The legal and constitutional status of state and local foreign policy is complex. Yet the weight of received legal opinion comes down against local and state initiatives. The Constitution's 'supremacy' or 'kingpin' clause (Article 6), as well as the constitutional disbarring of subnational obstruction of foreign commerce, point clearly in this direction. In *Hines* (1941), Justice Black wrote for the Court as follows: 'Our system of government is such that the interest of the cities, counties and states, no less than the interest of the people of the whole nation, imperatively requires that federal power in the field affecting foreign relations be left entirely free from local interference.'[110] In fact, several Supreme Court decisions, notably *Zschernig* v. *Miller* (1968),[111] suggest that federalism stops at the water's edge. In 1990, a federal court found against the Californian city of Oakland's establishment of a 'nuclear free zone'. The Supreme Court also quashed efforts by a number of states to prevent their National Guard contingents from training in Honduras. (These states were seeking to withdraw their forces from any possibility of fighting alongside the Nicaraguan Contras.)

Not all the legal and constitutional arguments pull in this centralising direction.[112] Especially in the area of trade and economic foreign policy, local and state initiatives appear extremely difficult for Washington to resist. The Bush Administration's legal assault against state and local foreign policy was directed mainly at non-economic areas. It is also worth bearing in mind that arguments directed at state and local foreign policy are generally made on grounds of 'efficiency' rather than of constitutionality. As such – although admittedly to a much lesser degree – they share some of the weaknesses of 'efficiency' arguments directed against Congressional foreign policy. The executive branch is not the sole repository of efficiency; and efficiency without accountability is rarely efficiency at all. Obviously, unchecked local and state foreign policy would lead in absurd and anarchic directions. Nevertheless, the claim that US foreign policy must always speak with one voice may always be countered by Michael Shuman's comment: 'America has never spoken in one voice in foreign policy – and never will.'[113]

Notes

1 R. Robertson, *Globalisation* (London, Sage, 1992), p. 8.
2 A. Giddens, *The Consequences of Modernity* (Cambridge, Polity Press, 1990), p. 21.
3 See also S. Lash and J. Urry, *Economics of Signs and Space* (London, Sage, 1994); C. Bretherton and G. Ponton, eds, *Global Politics: An Introduction* (Oxford, Blackwell, 1996).
4 R. O'Brien, *Global Financial Integration: The End of Geography* (London, Routledge/RIIA, 1992).
5 B. Woodward, *The Agenda* (New York, Pocket Books, 1995), p. 84.
6 S. Strange, 'Political economy and international relations', in K. Booth and S. Smith, eds, *International Relations Theory Today* (Cambridge, Polity Press, 1995), pp. 60–1. Also, R. O. Keohane and H. V. Milner, eds, *Internationalization and Domestic Politics* (Cambridge, Cambridge University Press, 1996).
7 See J. Tomlinson, *Can Governments Manage the Economy?* (London, Fabian Society, 1988); P. Hirst and G. Thompson, 'The problem of "globalization":

international economic relations, national economic management and the formation of trading blocs', *Economy and Society*, 21 (1992), pp. 357–96, 366.

8   Hirst and Thompson, 'The problem of "globalization"', pp. 367, 371. See also P. Hirst and G. Thompson, *Globalization in Question* (Oxford, Polity, 1996).

9   See A. Gamble and A. Payne, eds, *Regionalism and World Order* (Basingstoke, Macmillan, 1996).

10 E. Helleiner, 'From Bretton Woods to global finance', in R. Stubbs and G. R. D. Underhill, eds, *Political Economy and the Changing Global Order* (Basingstoke, Macmillan, 1994), p. 173; R. Gilpin, *Political Economy of International Relations* (Princeton, Princeton University Press, 1987), p. 90.

11 R. J. Hrebenar and C. S. Thomas, 'The Japanese lobby in Washington: how different is it?', in A. J. Cigler and B. A. Loomis, eds, *Interest Group Politics* (Washington DC, Congressional Quarterly Press, 1995), pp. 365, 361. See also P. Choate, *Agents of Influence* (New York, Knopf, 1990); N. J. Glickman and D. P. Woodward, *The New Competitors* (New York, Basic Books, 1989).

12 See R. J. Kudrle, 'Good for the gander?', *International Organization*, 45 (1991), pp. 418–24.

13 See B. Hocking and M. Smith, *World Politics* (London, Prentice Hall, 1995), p. 100; D. H. Blake and R. S. Walters, *The Politics of Global Economic Relations* (Englewood Cliffs, Prentice-Hall, 1987), pp. 90–4.

14 R. R. Reich, *The Work of Nations* (New York, Knopf, 1991), p. 5.

15 R. J. Barnet and J. Cavanagh, *Global Dreams: Imperial Corporations in the New World Order* (New York, Simon and Schuster, 1994), p. 281.

16 *Ibid.*, p. 280.

17 See Hirst and Thompson, 'The problem of "globalization"', p. 362.

18 Blake and Walters, *The Politics of Global Economic Relations*, pp. 98–9; S. Gill and D. Law, *The Global Political Economy* (Hemel Hempstead, Harvester-Wheatsheaf, 1988), p. 194.

19 See Hocking and Smith, *World Politics*, p. 99; Blake and Walters, *The Politics of Global Economic Relations*, p. 99.

20 See S. Strange, 'Rethinking structural change in the international political economy: states, firms, and diplomacy', in Stubbs and Underhill, eds, *Political Economy and the Changing Global Order*.

21 C. F. Bergsten. T. Horst and T. H. Moran, *American Multinationals and American Interests* (Washington DC, Brookings, 1978), pp. 309–10.

22 See J. G. Ruggie, 'International regimes, transactions and change – embedded liberalism in the post-war economic order', *International Organization*, 36 (1982), pp. 379–415.

23 Bergsten *et al.*, *American Multinationals*, p. 328. See also, K. A. Rodman, 'Sovereignty at bay? Hegemonic decline, multinational corporations, and US economic sanctions since the pipeline case', *International Organization*, 49 (1995), pp. 105–37.

24 See M. Davis, 'The political economy of late-imperial America', *New Left Review*, 143 (1984), pp. 6–38; J. Petras and M. Morley, *Empire or Republic? American Global Power and Domestic Decay* (London, Routledge, 1995), pp. 1–25; W. I. Robinson, 'Globalisation: nine theses on our epoch', *Race and Class*, 38 (1996), pp. 15–31: 19.

25 Bergsten *et al.*, *American Multinationals*, p. 324. See also S. Krasner, *Defend-*

ing the National Interest (Princeton, Princeton University Press, 1978); G. J. Ikenberry, D. A. Lake and M. Mastanduno, 'Introduction: approaches to explaining American foreign economic policy', *International Organization*, 42 (1988), pp. 1–14.

26 See J. Dumbrell, *American Foreign Policy: Carter to Clinton* (Basingstoke, Macmillan, 1997), pp. 181–4.

27 See Hirst and Thompson, 'The problem of "globalization"', p. 368; S. Ostry, 'The domestic domain', *Transnational Corporations*, 1 (1992), pp. 7–26.

28 M. Bernard, 'Post-Fordism, transnational production, and the changing global political economy', in Stubbs and Underhill, eds, *Political Economy and the Changing Global Order*, pp. 222–3.

29 Petras and Morley, *Empire or Republic?*, p. 55.

30 See Ikenberry *et al.*, 'Introduction: approaches to explaining American foreign economic policy', p. 3.

31 See P. McGowan and S. G. Walker, 'Radical and conventional models of US foreign and economic policy making', *World Politics*, 33 (1981), pp. 346–82.

32 See, especially, P. B. Evans, D. Rueschemeyer and T. Skocpol, *Bringing the State Back In* (Cambridge, Cambridge University Press, 1985).

33 D. D. Marshall, 'Understanding late twentieth-century capitalism: reassessing the globalization theme', *Government and Opposition*, 31 (1996), pp. 193–215. See also B. Crawford, 'The new security dilemma under international economic interdependence', *Millennium*, 23 (1994), pp. 25–56.

34 See, e.g., T. W. Zeller, *American Trade and Power in the 1960s* (New York, Simon and Schuster, 1992).

35 W. Zimmerman, 'Issue-area and foreign policy process', *American Political Science Review*, 67 (1973), pp. 1204–12: 1206; M. Evangelista, 'Issue-area and foreign policy revisited', *International Organization*, 43 (1989), pp. 147–72; T. J. Lowi, 'American business, public policy, case-studies and political theory', *World Politics*, 16 (1964), pp. 677–715.

36 Zimmerman, 'Issue-area', p. 1209.

37 See R. T. Kudrle and D. B. Bobow, 'US policy toward foreign direct investment', *World Politics*, 34 (1982), pp. 353–79: 370; Krasner, *Defending the National Interest*.

38 H. B. Malmgren, 'Managing foreign economic policy', *Foreign Policy*, 6 (1972), pp. 39–51.

39 See K. L. Teslik, *Congress, the Executive Branch and Special Interests: The American Response to the Arab Boycott* (Westport, Greenwood, 1982).

40 See Petras and Morley, *Empire or Republic?*.

41 Rodman, 'Sovereignty at bay?', p. 106.

42 *The Tower Commission Report* (New York, New York Times Books, 1987), p. 98.

43 Cited in P. Krugman, 'Competitiveness: a dangerous obsession', *Foreign Affairs*, 73 (1994), pp. 28–44: 29.

44 *Newsweek*, 6 March 1995, p. 10.

45 See K. Victor, 'Dirty dealing', *National Journal*, 20 April 1996, pp. 869–73.

46 Rodman, 'Sovereignty at bay?', p. 136.

47 P. M. Stern, *The Best Congress Money Can Buy* (New York, Pantheon Books, 1988), pp. 31, 10. See also W. Greider, *Who Will Tell the People?* (New York,

Simon and Schuster, 1992).

48 See Barnet and Cavanagh, *Global Dreams*, pp. 345–6.

49 R. A. Pastor, *Congress and the Politics of US Foreign Economic Policy 1929–1976* (Berkeley, University of California Press, 1980), p. 7.

50 See H. V. Milner and D. B. Yoffie, 'Between free trade and protectionism', *International Organization*, 43 (1989), pp. 239–71.

51 See R. W. Cox, 'Labor and the multinationals', *Foreign Affairs*, 54 (1976), pp. 344–65; K. Cowling and R. Sugden, *Transnational Monopoly Capital* (Brighton, Harvester, 1987), p. 73.

52 See, e.g., *Congressional Quarterly Weekly Report*, 14 Jan. 1995 (on minimum wage).

53 See J. Goodwin, *Brotherhood of Arms: General Dynamics and the Business of Defending America* (New York, New York Times Books, 1985); W. L. Bennett, *Inside the System* (New York, Harcourt Brace Jovanovich, 1994).

54 G. Adams, 'The politics of the defense budget', in E. R. Wittkopf, ed., *Domestic Sources of American Foreign Policy* (New York, St. Martin's, 1994), pp. 106–7.

55 See Bennett, *Inside the System*, pp. 290–300.

56 1993 *Congressional Quarterly Almanac*, p. 451.

57 See W. D. Hartung, 'Nixon's children', *World Policy Journal*, 12 (1995), pp. 25–35; also, E. Kapstein, 'America's arms monopoly', *Foreign Affairs*, 73 (1994), pp. 14–21.

58 J. Reston, *The Artillery of the Press* (New York, Harper and Row, 1967), p. 15.

59 J. Fallows, 'Why Americans hate the media', *The Atlantic Monthly*, Feb. 1996, pp. 45–64: 55. See also S. Armstrong, 'Iran–Contra: was the press any match for all the President's men?', *Columbia Journalism Review*, May–June 1990, pp. 27–35.

60 R. M. Gates, *From the Shadows* (New York, Simon and Schuster, 1996), p. 415. See also L. Sabato, *Feeding Frenzy* (New York, Free Press, 1991).

61 Cited, J. E. Hoge, 'Media pervasiveness', *Foreign Affairs*, 73 (1994), pp. 136–44: 137. See also S. Sarfaty, ed., *The Media and Foreign Policy* (New York, St. Martin's, 1991).

62 E. Alterman, 'Operation pundit storm', in Wittkopf, ed., *The Domestic Sources of American Foreign Policy*.

63 J. Schlesinger, 'Quest for a post-Cold War foreign policy', *Foreign Affairs*, 72 (1993), pp. 14–20: 18.

64 See D. Halberstam, *The Powers That Be* (New York, Knopf, 1979), pp. 429–30; D. C. Hallin, *The 'Uncensored War': The Media and Vietnam* (Berkeley, University of California Press, 1986), pp. 129–31; K. J. Turner, *Lyndon Johnson's Dual War* (Chicago, University of Chicago Press, 1985), p. 6; S. C. Taylor, 'Reporting history: journalists and the Vietnam war', *Reviews in American History*, 13 (1985), pp. 451–61.

65 T. G. Carpenter, *The Captive Press: Foreign Policy Crises and the First Amendment* (Washington DC, Cato Institute, 1995), p. 15.

66 Cited, D. R. Gergen, 'The unfettered Presidency', in J. S. Nye and R. K. Smith, eds, *After the Storm: Lessons from the Gulf War* (Lanham, Madison Books, 1992), p. 187.

67 *Ibid.*, p. 189.

68 See W. L. Bennett, 'The media and the foreign policy process', in D. A. Deese, ed., *The New Politics of American Foreign Policy* (New York, St. Martin's, 1994).

69 See *ibid.*; W. L. Bennett, *News: The Politics of Illusion* (New York, Longman, 1988).

70 D. A. Graber, *Mass Media and American Politics* (Washington DC, Congressional Quarterly Press, 1985), p. 308; also, interview with Z. Brzezinski, *US Foreign Policy Agenda*, 1 (1996) (USIA electronic journal).

71 B. Cohen, *The Press and Foreign Policy* (Princeton, Princeton University Press, 1963), p. 62.

72 See M. J. Parenti, *Inventing Reality* (New York, St. Martin's, 1986); C. Mouffe, 'Hegemony and ideology in Gramsci', in C. Mouffe, ed., *Gramsci and Marxist Theory* (London, Routledge and Kegan Paul, 1979).

73 Bennett, 'The media and the foreign policy process', p. 182; also, S. Iyengar, *Is Anyone Responsible? How Television Frames Political Issues* (Chicago, University of Chicago Press, 1992).

74 Hallin, *The 'Uncensored' War*, p. 196.

75 See M. Hertsgaard, *On Bended Knee: The Press and the Reagan Presidency* (New York, Farrar, Straus, Giroux, 1988).

76 J. A. Baker, *The Politics of Diplomacy* (New York, Putnam's Sons, 1995), p. 618.

77 A. M. Jamieson, 'The messenger as policy maker', *Democratization*, 3 (1996), pp. 114–32: 128.

78 See M. Linsky, *Impact, How the Press Affects Policymaking* (New York, Norton, 1986).

79 P. Arnett, *Live From the Battlefield* (London, Corgi, 1994), p. 372. See also K. Hindell, 'The influence of the media on foreign policy', *International Relations*, 12 (1995), pp. 73–83.

80 H. A. Grunwald, 'A new world needs a new journalism', *Foreign Affairs*, 72 (1993), pp. 12–16: 16.

81 See J. Neuman, *Lights, Camera, War: Is Media Technology Driving International Politics?* (New York, St. Martin's, 1995).

82 See B. Kovach, 'Do the news media make foreign policy?', *Foreign Policy*, 102 (1996), pp. 169–79: 179; D. D. Newsom, *The Public Dimension of Foreign Policy* (Bloomington, Indiana University Press, 1996), p. 50. See also A. Smith, *The Age of Behemoths: The Globalization of Mass Media Firms* (New York, Priority Press, 1991).

83 Cited in D. N. Mayer, *The Constitutional Thought of Thomas Jefferson* (Charlottesville, University Press of Virginia, 1994), p. 170.

84 M. Clough, 'Say good-bye to the "Wise Men"', *Foreign Affairs*, 73 (1994), pp. 2–7: 3.

85 W. Isaacson and E. Thomas, *The Wise Men* (London, Faber, 1986), p. 27 (remark of J. J. McCloy). 'Skull and Bones' refers to a Yale University club; Groton refers to a Connecticut private school.

86 *Ibid.*, pp. 66, 29; also, K. Bird, *The Chairman: John J. McCloy, the Making of the American Establishment* (New York, Simon and Schuster, 1992).

87 D. Ignatius, 'The best and the brightest, 1990s style', *Washington Post National Weekly Edition*, 14–20 March 1994, p. 24 (cited in C. W. Kegley and E. R. Wittkopf, *American Foreign Policy: Pattern and Process* (5th edn, New York,

St. Martin's, 1996), p. 296); also, T. R. Dye, *Who's Running America?: The Clinton Years* (Englewood Cliffs, Prentice-Hall, 1995); A. J. Bennett, *The American President's Cabinet* (Basingstoke, Macmillan, 1996), p. 205.

88 T. J. McCormick, *America's Half Century* (Baltimore, Johns Hopkins University Press, 1995), pp. 12–16: 15–16.

89 N. W. Polsby, 'The foreign policy establishment: towards professionalism and centrism', in Wittkopf, ed., *The Domestic Sources of American Foreign Policy*, p. 213.

90 See Kegley and Wittkopf, *American Foreign Policy*, p. 297. On the Committee on the Present Danger, see A. Tonelson, 'Nitze's world', *Foreign Policy*, 35 (1979), pp. 74–90; J. W. Sanders, *Peddlers of Crisis* (Boston, South End Press, 1983).

91 For an attack from the left, see L. H. Shoup and W. Minter, *Imperial Brain Trust* (New York, Monthly Review Press, 1977). See also P. Thompson, 'Bilderberg and the West', in H. Sklar, ed., *Trilateralism* (Boston, South End Press, 1980), p. 188 (on right-wing conspiracy theory).

92 See Thompson, 'Bilderberg and the West'.

93 McCormick, *America's Half Century*, p. 16. See also B. M. Russett and E. C. Hanson, *Interest and Ideology* (San Francisco, W. H. Freeman, 1975), pp. 244–50; Isaacson and Thomas, *The Wise Men*, p. 27; R. D. Schulzinger, *The Wise Men of Foreign Affairs* (New York, Columbia University Press, 1984); J. K. Galbraith, 'Staying awake at the Council on Foreign Relations', *Washington Monthly*, Sept. 1984, pp. 40–3; I. Parmar, 'The issue of state power: the Council on Foreign Relations as a case study', *Journal of American Studies*, 29 (1995), pp. 73–96.

94 J. A. Smith, *The Idea Brokers* (New York, Free Press, 1991).

95 Newsom, *The Public Dimension of Foreign Policy*, ch. 8.

96 See J. B. Judis, 'The Japanese megaphone', in Wittkopf, ed., *The Domestic Sources of American Foreign Policy*.

97 Newsom, *The Public Dimension of Foreign Policy*, p. 161.

98 R. Higgott and D. Stone, 'Foreign policy think tanks in Britain and the USA', *Review of International Studies*, 20 (1994), pp. 15–34: 33.

99 See, e.g., C. D. Heatherly, ed., *Mandate for Leadership* (Washington DC, Heritage Foundation, 1981); A. Anderson and D. L. Bark, eds, *Thinking about America* (Stanford, Hoover Institution, 1988).

100 Polsby, 'The foreign policy establishment'; Higgott and Stone, 'Foreign policy think tanks', pp. 22–3; D. E. Abelson, *American Think Tanks and their Role in US Foreign Policy* (New York, St. Martin's, 1996), p. 121. See also D. M. Ricci, *Transformation of American Politics: The New Washington and the Rise of the Think Tanks* (New Haven, Yale University Press, 1993).

101 Clough, 'Say good-bye to the "Wise Men"', p.4.

102 See K. Ohmae, 'The rise of the region state', *Foreign Affairs*, 72 (1993), pp. 78–87: 87.

103 J. O. Goldsborough, 'California's foreign policy', *Foreign Affairs*, 72 (1993), pp. 88–96: 96. See also S. P. Mumme, 'State influence in foreign policymaking', *Western Political Quarterly*, 38 (1985), pp. 620–40; B. Hocking, *Localizing Foreign Policy: Non-Central Governments and Multilayered Diplomacy* (London, Macmillan, 1993); G. L. Warren, 'From San Diego', *Foreign Policy*, 88 (1992), pp. 53–6.

104 See M. H. Shuman, 'Dateline Main Street: courts v. local foreign policies', *Foreign Policy*, 86 (1992), pp. 158–77: 158.

105 *Bulletin of Municipal Foreign Policy*, 2 (1988); 3 (1989).

106 See M. H. Shuman, 'Dateline Main Street: local foreign policies', *Foreign Policy*, 65 (1986–87), pp. 154–74: 160; J. Dull, *The Politics of American Foreign Policy* (Englewood Cliffs, Prentice-Hall, 1985), p. 114.

107 P. L. Hatcher, 'How local issues drive foreign policy', *Orbis*, 40 (1996), pp. 45–52: 46.

108 *Business America*, 15 Feb. 1988, p. 14.

109 See P. J. Spiro, 'Who should conduct foreign policy? (taking foreign policy away from the feds)', *Bulletin of Municipal Foreign Policy*, 2 (1988), pp. 6–21: 17; J. Leigland, 'States sell bonds worldwide', *Journal of State Government*, 61 (1989), pp. 137–41; B. Hocking, 'Globalization and the foreign-domestic policy nexus', in A. McGrew, ed., *Empire* (London, Hodder and Stoughton, 1994), p. 154.

110 *Hines* v. *Davidowitz* (1941), 313 US 52.

111 387, US 429. See also *US* v. *Pink* (1942), 315 US 203.

112 See Shuman, 'Dateline Main Street' (1992).

113 Shuman, 'Dateline Main Street' (1986–87), p. 9.

Two case-studies and conclusion

This final chapter begins with two case-studies in post-Cold War foreign policy: the Bush Administration's 1992 decision to send troops to Somalia, and the Clinton Administration's policy towards Northern Ireland. The case-studies are intended to illuminate various issues in post-Cold War American internationalism.

1 1992: humanitarian intervention in Somalia

(a) *Background* Prior to 1992, it was far from evident that the Bush Administration had any clear policy for post-Cold War Africa, beyond hopes for economic and political liberalisation. In his 1995 memoirs, Secretary of State James Baker recalled the view that there were 'new opportunities to clear away some of the regional underbrush of the US–Soviet relationship'.[1] Yet Africa appeared increasingly remote both from US post-Cold War priorities and even from the kind of US-led multilateralism outlined in Bush's New World Order speech of September 1990. Academic opinion tended to conclude that US activism in the developing world would be concentrated on issues of access to oil, nuclear proliferation and areas (like drugs and immigration) with acute domestic impact.[2] By these criteria, Africa seemed unlikely to top the agenda. In July 1991, the Administration announced, unilaterally and controversially, the lifting of sanctions on South Africa in the light of the pace of reform there. In relation to the rest of the continent, however, the White House seemed to prefer a combination of benign neglect and willingness to defer to Congress.

With Soviet/Russian influence no longer of primary concern, the growing disorder in Somalia scarcely attracted Administration interest until the summer of 1992. The occasion of crisis was the ouster of (sometime US-backed) dictator Syad Barre in early 1991. A combination of drought, civil war and the availability of modern weaponry rapidly brought the already fractured country to a state of chaos. Information about impending humanitarian disaster was delivered, firstly by the relief agencies, and subsequently by Congress and the media. As early as 30 January 1992, Andrew Natsios, of the US Agency for International Development (AID) testified to the House Select Committee on Hunger on relief agency reports on Somalia. He anticipated 'the greatest humanitarian emergency in the world'.[3] In the early months of 1992, United Nations relief work was fractionated and ineffectual. In July 1992, Senator Nancy Kassebaum (Kansas Republican) urged President Bush to lobby the UN to establish a force 'to ensure that food gets to those in need'.[4] (Holly Burkhalter, director of Human Rights Watch, later accredited Kassebaum, alongside Democratic Senator from Illinois Paul Simon and Congressman John Lewis (Georgia Democrat), with bringing the Somalia issue to national attention.[5]) The Administration's view was that no UN force should enter in the absence of an effective cease-fire. Assistant Secretary of State John Bolton informed Congressional critics that the United States had made available over $60 million in emergency assistance since January 1991. Leading Representatives from the Select Committee on Hunger opposed the White House's caution. Bolton warned of UN personnel being 'killed for the boots and berets'.[6] In early August, both House and Senate passed resolutions requiring Bush to seek UN action.

On 14 August 1992, White House press secretary Marlin Fitzwater announced a 'leading role' for the United States in ensuring 'that food reaches those who so desperately need it'.[7] Between August and December 1992, the United States participated in an international effort to airlift 17,000 tons of food and other supplies. By September, the Somalian famine had become the focus of intense media attention, recalling memories of the 1985 Ethiopian crisis. As Colin Powell (JCS chairman) later recalled: 'The world had a dozen other running sores that fall, but television hovered over Somalia and wrenched our hearts, night after night, with images of people starving to death before our eyes.' (Powell 'was not eager to get us involved in a Somalian civil war, but we were apparently the only nation that could end the suffering'[8].)

(b) *The decision to commit troops*   Against a background of heightened Congressional and media interest, the Bush Administration began to consider initiating a UN effort in Somalia. Some early indications were that the White House might back a five-hundred-strong UN peacekeeping force. By early November, Assistant Secretary of State Robert Gallucci and Acting Secretary of State Lawrence Eagleburger had become committed to more forceful US action under UN authorisation. (Eagleburger succeeded to James Baker's post in August 1992, when the latter departed for election campaign duties.) On 19 November, Leslie Gelb reported in the *New York Times* a White House meeting the following day, when 'key aides' would tell the President 'that he should not duck the mass slaughter and starvation of Somalia's civil war and then drop the problem on Bill Clinton'. Gelb described a division between advocates of action. Senator Kassebaum was pressing for US participation in a UN operation, while key relief experts (notably Frank Cuny) were despairing of the UN, and wanted a unilateral American effort.[9] Under-Secretary of Defence Paul Wolfowitz seemed to back Cuny's position, while Admiral David Jeremiah (vice-chairman of the JCS) promised that US forces could 'do the job'. In various White House meetings between 20 and 26 November, Pentagon doubts began to surface. Defence Secretary Richard Cheney and JCS chairman Powell were briefed by US commanders involved in the airlift operation to the effect that any US troop commitment could turn out to be dangerously open-ended. Nevertheless, Powell presented Bush with plans for Operation RESTORE HOPE, a 'mercy mission' led by US forces. NSA Brent Scowcroft commented: 'Sure, we can get in. But how do we get out?'.[10] On 25 November, Bush delivered to the NSC his firm decision that 'we want to do something about Somalia'.[11] He outlined three options: increased backing for the airlift; an American-led multinational effort not involving US ground troops; and a major international commitment, led by US ground forces. Powell essentially supported the third option, but expressed doubts about the feasibility of a quick and smooth operation. Advocacy of the third option was, however, particularly associated with the State Department. (John Bolton later located such advocacy specifically with 'State Department careerists'[12].) Bush appeared enthusiastic too, while Scowcroft's doubts lessened. Yet still the President demanded a tight timetable, preferably with troops being withdrawn by the date of Clinton's inauguration (19 January 1993). Bush insisted to his advisers: 'I don't want to stick Clinton with an ongoing military operation[13].) Despite Defence Secretary Cheney's view that such a timetable was unrealistic, President Bush decided to prepare the way for the third option.

Bush immediately, and with no public announcement, contacted UN Secretary-General Boutros Boutros-Ghali with the offer of US forces. The authorising resolution, passed by the UN Security Council on 3 December, reflected conflicting sentiments within the UN. Several African states lobbied to avoid another abdication of UN authority to the United States. (Such nations felt that the latter had enjoyed too free a hand during the 1991 Gulf War.) The authorising resolution gave the Secretary-General some control over the force's command structure and provided for the Security Council to be consulted regarding the duration of the operation. It also set up a fund whereby poorer nations could be compensated for joining the force. Despite all this, the authorisation effectively recognised that the force would be commanded by the United States.

On 4 December, Bush addressed the nation on television and announced the deployment of up to 28,000 troops as America's contribution to the multinational force. The President announced: 'Every American has seen the shocking images from Somalia.' He emphasised that 'the United States alone cannot right the world's wrongs'. Nevertheless: 'we also know that some crises in the world cannot be resolved without American involvement, that American action is often necessary as a catalyst for broader involvement of the community of nations'. Bush promised that objectives were limited. With the creation of a 'secure environment', US troops would be pulled out and the mission handed 'back to a regular UN peacekeeping force'.[14]

(c) *Divisions, disagreements and Congressional reactions*   The most obvious cleavage within Administration views on the troop commitment concerned the likely duration of the operation. On 31 December, the White House was still briefing journalists to the effect that troops could be out by the time of Clinton's inauguration. Powell, however, was reported as talking in terms of a commitment lasting 'a few months'.[15] Behind these concerns lay the 'Vietnam syndrome' and worries about US forces being sucked into what television journalists were already calling a 'quagmire'.[16] Vietnam parallels were repeatedly raised in the press. (On 1 December, for example, Raymond Bonner, a prominent chronicler of the Central American conflicts during the Reagan years, wrote: 'Somalia is not another Vietnam. America is not likely to get bogged down in a military quagmire.' He felt the Somalia 'gangsters' could 'be quickly vanquished'[17].) Administration spokespersons were anxious to depict Somalia as 'not too significant a military operation'.[18] On 11 October, Bush had promised: 'I am not going to commit US forces until I know what the mission is, until the military tell me that it can be completed, until I know how they can come out.'[19] Though prepared to back the Somalian intervention, Powell later recorded his uneasiness over the President's third condition: 'How were we going to get out of Somalia without turning the country back to the same warlords whose rivalries had produced the famine in the first place?'[20]

Powell remained opposed to US intervention in the former Yugoslavia. The Somalia decision inevitably raised the issue of why the United States was so reluctant to tackle the humanitarian crisis in Bosnia. *New York Times* columnist Anthony Lewis posed this question directly, while some public figures (notably former National Security head W. E. Odom and former Balkans specialist at State, G. D. Kenney) urged direct US intervention in Bosnia.[21] Cheney took pains to explain to the press that Somalia's level desert offered easier military problems than Bosnia's mountain forests. Eagleburger argued that Somalia warlords hardly compared to the military commands in Bosnia: 'In the case of what was Yugoslavia, it ought to be clear to everyone that the use of force as a means of bringing that war to an end would require far more in the way of troops and far more in the way of commitment.'[22]

Undergirding the disputes connected with Bush's decision to intervene in Somalia was the question of how the New World Order was to be operationalised after the Gulf victory. On 4 December, the *New York Times* editorialised:

Backstage comment in Washington has centred on the need to assure that US forces will be solely under US command in Somalia, as if that mattered most. At least as important, surely, is insuring wide participation of other nations, European and African, rich and poor, especially if UN blue helmets are to pick up the pieces after Americans pull out.[23]

Within a few days of Bush's decision, it was obvious that a serious rift existed between the United States and the UN Secretariat. The latter, in John Bolton's words, really favoured 'something very like a traditional, small-scale UN peacekeeping operation'.[24] On 4 December, it was reported that Morocco, Algeria, Kuwait and Egypt would be sending troops; but it was manifest that this was essentially an American operation.

A further area of dispute centred on the role of President-elect Clinton and on the propriety of Bush embarking on a potentially major military commitment in his 'lame-duck' period. Congressman R. E. Andrews (Democrat from New Jersey) put the point bluntly: 'if Bush had won the election, there would have been a lot more thought given to the long-term consequences' of the operation.[25] Clinton himself supported the decision, commending Bush 'for taking the lead in this important humanitarian effort'.[26] The UN Secretariat repeatedly expressed worries about how the policy would develop under Clinton. Samuel Berger, who headed Clinton's foreign policy transition team, was briefed on a daily basis by Brent Scowcroft. Yet, as the *New York Times* editorialised on 5 December: 'Mr Bush has executed a dramatic takeoff. Bill Clinton, who backs the mission but seems not to have been consulted, may well be stuck with a messy crash landing.'[27]

All these various disputes and disagreements were reflected in the reactions of Members of Congress. The intervention announcement (like Bush's key Gulf crisis escalation decisions of November 1990) was made while Congress was in recess. Congressional leaders were formally briefed on 4 December. House Speaker Thomas Foley (Washington Democrat) immediately announced: 'The president has acted wisely, and in a circumstance where he had very little choice without grave humanitarian consequences resulting.'[28] On 10 December, Bush issued a letter to Congressional leaders, making clear his position in regard to war powers legislation. There was no intention for US forces to 'become involved in hostilities'. The letter was 'consistent with the War Powers Resolution', but neither conceded any executive obligations under the legislation, nor accepted that the Somalian intervention fell under its purview.[29] Leading Democrats on Capitol Hill were happy to let the legislation remain in abeyance. According to Senate Majority Leader George Mitchell (Democrat of Maine) it was 'unclear' whether the War Powers Act applied. The mission was 'to assist in the distribution of supplies' and should not 'involve Americans in a shooting war'.[30] By early February 1993, both House and Senate had passed resolutions in support of the intervention. The Senate resolution urged the earliest possible transfer of the mission to a UN-led force. It also stated that the operation, and the authorising resolution, was 'consistent' with legislative war powers.[31]

Congressional acquiescence chimed in with positive public acceptance of Bush's decision. A CNN–*USA Today* poll in mid-December 1992, found three-quarters of respondents approving the effort.[32] Individual Members of Congress, however, did offer important lines of criticism. Senator Sam Nunn, chairman of Armed Services, asked: 'Is this a precedent for going into Liberia? How do we rationalize this with what's going on in Bosnia?' Congressman James Murtha (Pennsylvania Democrat and chair of the Defence Appropriating Subcommittee) declared himself unable to 'see the national interest'. People were 'starving in a lot of different places, and we can only afford so much'. Lee Hamilton, incoming chairman of House Foreign Affairs, also noted that 'not all the suffering takes place in Somalia'. Congressional liberals generally supported the intervention, reflecting the new ideological divisions of post-Cold War foreign policy. The Congressional Black Caucus applauded the concern for humanitarian values in Africa. (The Reverend Jesse Jackson noted that 'for the first time we've been willing to risk the lives of American soldiers to save an African people'.) To Representative Toby Roth (Wisconsin Republican), however, the operation really came 'under the heading of wishful thinking, and that's gotten us into some big problems'. Senator Larry Pressler (Republican of South Dakota) said that here was another example of the American taxpayer playing 'the Santa role' for the New World Order. (In one of his final acts as President, Bush offered a list of defence cuts – primarily research grants – to offset the expense of the operation[33].)

(d) *Somalia, 1992–1995*   On 8 December, the first US forces (Navy SEAL commandos) landed in Somalia. They were met by a collection of television lights and cameras. The commandos were the advance guard for a 25,400-strong force. After some initial apparent success, the intervention indeed developed into a messy crash landing for Clinton. The United Task Force, led by the United States, provided at least a degree of safety for the relief work between December 1992 and April 1993. During this early phase, US public support for the intervention remained reasonably high. Events swung out of control following the April–May 1993 transition to UN control. The Security Council, encouraged by US Ambassador Madeleine Albright, adopted a 'nation-building' resolution. Clinton himself spoke of the need for 'patience in nation-building'.[34] In June 1993, twenty-three Pakistani peacekeepers were killed. The ambush was blamed upon Mohamed Farah Aideed, and US forces were set the difficult task of arresting him. By August 1993, eight US soldiers had been killed. On 3 October 1993, US forces (under US command) lost eighteen members in a Mogadishu firefight. The 'nation-building' phase of UN involvement effectively ended in October, 1993. Under intense Congressional pressure, Clinton announced that all US troops would be withdrawn by April 1994. Congress raised the prospect of a funding cut-off thereafter, although limited US deployments were allowed until March 1995.

2 The Clinton Administration and Northern Ireland

(a) *Background*   The post-1992 Northern Irish 'peace process' – its inception and stuttering progress – bore the clear imprint of Washington's influence. Throughout the 1992 Presidential election campaign, and subsequently, President Clinton insisted that the United States, as a 'nation of diversity' must 'help in any way that we can'.[35] Senator Patrick Leahy (Democrat from Vermont) commented in February 1995 on the 1993 Downing Street Declaration, the 1994 paramilitary cease-fires and the subsequent Framework Document: without Clinton's 'personal involvement we would not have seen this day'.[36]

Before 1992, US involvement in the Northern Irish conflict occurred primarily at the level of Irish-American interest groups and their allies in Congress. At various times, militant Irish republicanism gained succour from the Catholic Irish diaspora in the United States. Involvement in Northern Irish affairs at the executive level was severely limited, especially before 1977, by inhibitions about 'interfering' in the internal affairs of the United Kingdom, a close and strategically important Cold War ally. This tradition of executive caution was breached by President Carter, who issued a statement in 1977, promising US investment in the event of a settlement. It was widely felt in Washington that such a 'settlement' would emerge along the lines of formalised 'power-sharing' between the opposing factions. Significant, if still limited, executive branch activism continued into the Reagan years (especially in connection with the 1985 Anglo-Irish Agreement). The Bush Administration, however, returned to a policy of caution, in line with the traditional preference of the State Department.[37]

Bill Clinton's 1992 stance on Northern Ireland represented a clear attempt – in a Presidential campaign otherwise distinguished by a high level of foreign policy consensus – to establish distance from the Bush approach. Clinton later averred a long-standing interest in the province, deriving from his arrival to study at Oxford just as the modern Troubles were starting: 'I could see it coming, that religious differences were likely to lead to the same kinds of problems that racial differences had in my childhood.'[38] Ten days before polling day in 1992, candidate Clinton issued a statement on Northern Ireland. Drafted by Nancy Soderberg, former aide to Senator Edward Kennedy, the statement took the form of a letter to a group called 'Irish Americans for Clinton and Gore'. The group had been founded by ex-Democratic Congressman (and former Clinton law school classmate) Bruce Morrison. The statement criticised the 'wanton use of lethal force by British security services'; it upheld the MacBride principles ('fair employment' requirements for US-owned firms operating in the province) and proposed a peace envoy for the province, as part of a future Clinton Administration commitment to 'peace and justice'.[39]

(b) *The policy*   Clinton's letter was widely interpreted as a slightly desperate attempt by a Southern Protestant governor – Carter's 1992 equivalent – to garner Northern Catholic votes. It was also widely noticed that the letter had been issued in a situation in which the British government, under John Major, was actively helping the Bush cause in the election. Events soon proved, however, that the new Administration's interest in Northern Ireland was far more profound than such comments tended to suggest.

The 'peace envoy' idea, though not implemented, was kept alive. Clinton linked the proposals to his concerns over human rights in Washington talks with John Major in February 1993. The British Prime Minister's statement on returning from Washington attempted to supply an optimistic gloss to a difficult situation: 'An envoy may still be sent, but as a fact-finder rather than as a mediator.'[40] Clinton was under considerable pressure in Congress, led by Congressman Joseph Kennedy, actually to appoint a mediator-envoy. Yet the proposal represented primarily a warning to London that the United States was expecting some progress.

London was acutely concerned lest Clinton reverse the practice of five former Presidents by granting a visa to Sinn Fein leader Gerry Adams. Despite election campaign indications to the contrary, Adams was twice refused a visa in 1993. Clinton declared that the decision should go against Adams, since he 'is no longer a Member of Parliament'.[41] However, following the 1993 Downing Street Declaration – hailed by Clinton as a breakthrough to peace – Adams was granted a two-day visa, against the advice of Raymond Seitz, US Ambassador to London. Seitz blamed the visa decision on White House 'munchkins'.[42] The CIA also joined with the State Department in opposing any move which could be seen as extending approval to Sinn Fein and the Provisional Irish Republican Army (IRA). The visa was opposed by House Speaker Tom Foley, though endorsed strongly by most leading Irish-Americans on Capitol Hill. The main visa sponsors were NSA Anthony Lake and European specialists (notably Soderberg) on the NSC staff. Gerry Adams's February 1994 visit to the United States rapidly became interpreted as a turning-point on the road to the subsequent IRA cease-fire. The trip gave prominence to the idea, long trailed by Northern Irish Social Democratic and Labour Party (SDLP) leader John Hume, of a 'peace dividend', deriving from private and public sources in the United States. Bruce Morrison (whose group invited Adams, along with unionist politicians) later depicted the February visit as Sinn Fein's 'opportunity to come in from the cold'.[43] Adams was being rewarded for participating in the dialogue with John Hume which had produced the 1993 Downing Street Declaration, and which would eventually lead to the IRA cease-fire. Soderberg declared that the Adams visa enabled Irish America to 'underscore the benefits of peace'.[44]

During 1994, the key elements of the Administration's strategy fell clearly into place. The 1993 Hume–Adams agreement, and the Downing Street Declaration, had a clear American dimension, supplied by Hume's extensive transatlantic links, by prospects of US investment, and by close diplomatic ties between Washington and the Dublin government of Albert Reynolds. Through Bruce Morrison and his associates, the Administration was able to operate a species of plausible deniability. Failures need not be acknowledged directly (or, as Godfrey Hodgson later wrote, laid at the door 'of the ancient intransigence of the British').[45] The Morrison group's August 1994 visit to Belfast, where leading Irish-American businessmen joined Irish-American labour leaders, was at once recognised as instrumental in delivering the IRA cease-fire.

The Clinton strategy involved the application of pressure on both London and Sinn Fein. At one stage, London faced the prospect of, in effect, being excluded from the developing Dublin–Washington–Sinn Fein–SDLP nexus. By the spring of 1994, John Major was being advised by Sir Robin Renwick (British ambassador to Washington) to swallow his pride and accept a mediation role for the United States.[46] Anthony Lake opened a correspondence with Gerry Adams, demanding, in effect, some movement on a cease-fire in return for the visa and American recognition. Clinton's strategy also involved the wooing of moderate unionists. By April 1994, Jean Kennedy-Smith (US Ambassador to Dublin and sister of Senator Edward Kennedy) had developed and led a new strategy.[47] Official Unionist leader James Molyneaux was persuaded to participate in a dialogue with Vice-President Al Gore. Molyneaux was assured of America's good faith towards both Irish traditions. (The Administration thus ensured that there would not be a repetition of united unionist opposition to the 1985 Anglo-Irish Agreement.) Both the moderate unionists and Sinn Fein were told – as Clinton had declared in 1993 – that the Northern Irish conflict could not 'be resolved by the language of victory or defeats'.[48] The August 1994 IRA cease-fire was followed by the granting of a second visa to Gerry Adams.

In December 1994, the White House finally named an envoy for the province – a 'special adviser for economic initiatives in Ireland'. Retiring Senate majority leader George Mitchell was charged with coordinating US efforts to promote Northern Irish economic regeneration. Announcing the appointment, Clinton declared: 'There must be a peace dividend in Ireland for the peace to succeed. Peace and prosperity depend upon one another.'[49] A major investment conference took place in Washington in May, 1995, with Commerce Secretary Ron Brown actively promoting the province to US private investors. By this time, in fact, it had become apparent that any 'peace dividend' was more likely to come from the private rather than from the public purse.[50] The Administration's requested increase in International Fund for Ireland contributions amounted to only $10 million. (The Republican leadership, which took control of Congress in January 1995, proved predictably unwilling to make substantial increases in Irish aid, though it was one of the few areas to be protected from actual cuts.) In January 1995, US Ambassador to London William Crowe offered to remove restrictions on Sinn Fein fundraising in the United States as a way of tying the IRA into the peace process, and possibly breaking the impasse over arms decommissioning. By 1996, Sinn Fein was operating a $200,000-a-year office in downtown Washington.[51]

Clinton's November 1995 visit to Belfast – the moment when 'hope and history rhymed' – represented a uniquely high-profile attempt to use America's influence to promote a Northern Irish settlement. Nancy Soderberg expressed misgivings over the press 'focusing on the president pulling a rabbit out of the hat'.[52] The visit put only temporary life into the peace process. It promoted the 'twin-track' approach (beginning talks, while treating decommissioning separately) with only very limited success. In December 1995, George Mitchell took over as chairman of the international commission charged with the task (defined differently in Dublin and London) of advising on arms decommissioning. Following the breakdown of the IRA cease-fire, events veered beyond any agenda envisaged by the White House. The assembly elections, promoted by David Trimble (Molyneaux's successor as Official Unionist leader) constituted an effective setback for the line set by Clinton during his Belfast visit. Trans-party talks, under Mitchell's chairmanship, continued into 1997.

(c) *Explaining Clinton's activism*   The Clinton Administration saw a qualitative change in US executive branch attitudes towards intervention in the Northern Irish troubles. Many commentators, especially London journalists, condemned Clinton as – in Hugo Young's words – 'only the latest example of an American politician shoring up his domestic position at the expense of Ireland'.[53] Simon Jenkins reacted to the granting of the visa to Adams by suggesting that London 'give Americans a taste of their own crassness' by inviting 'Haiti's General Cedras to a taco party on the British embassy lawn in Washington'.[54] In August 1996, former British Northern Ireland minister Michael Mates wrote of 'Clinton's cynical playing to the green Irish vote … Close to the President, there is his small group of advisers whose vote-winning agenda is not so much peace, as giving Irish Republicans what they want at almost any price.'[55]

Clearly, Clinton was concerned to win the support of Irish-American voters if at all possible. Irish-Americans did contribute, probably disproportionately, to the ranks of 'Reagan Democrats' in the 1980s. Yet Mates's point about cynical hunting of green votes was simplistic. Irish-America is demographically complex, suburbanised and concerned with a wide range of issues. In 1992, Clinton defeated Bush fairly easily in states with high numbers of Irish-American voters. There was no reason for Clinton in his first term to imagine that he needed to make special efforts to court such states.[56] In fact, by 1996, Clinton found himself at odds with organised sections of Irish-American opinion. The Irish National Caucus (the important lobbying organisation led by Father Sean McManus) broke with Clinton over his failure to provide consistent support for the MacBride principles. (McManus announced in 1996 that Bob Dole, Clinton's electoral challenger, had actually positioned himself to the 'green' side of Clinton by supporting MacBride.) In June 1996, the Ancient Order of Hibernians – the largest Irish-American group – criticised Clinton for supporting late term abortions, and withdrew an invitation to address its national convention.[57]

Explanations of Clinton's activism need to go deeper than mere vote-chasing. The context for the alliance between the Clinton Administration and the kind of Irish-American business elites represented in the Morrison group was set by changing US strategic interests. At one level, this linked into the erosion of the 'special relationship' between London and Washington: the coolness between the two capitals following the Major government's clumsy interventions in the 1992 election; the fact that only 20 per cent of Americans now claim British origin;[58] the signs of a Pacificised American foreign policy. In 1996, James Baker claimed that 'the result has been the worst relationship with our closest ally, Britain, since the Boston Tea Party'.[59] Those commentators who see Clinton as following the nationalist agenda take the argument a stage farther. According to Robert Fisk, for example, US interventions in Ireland are always 'carefully calculated to produce a winner, a side with whom Washington feels comfortable, an ally upon whom it can rely in the future'.[60] (Such arguments recall the argument, long made by J. Enoch Powell, regarding the strategic attraction to the United States of a united Ireland within NATO[61].)

Again, Clinton's Irish interventions belie such simple explanations. The role of mediator, 'honest broker' and conciliator of moderate unionism has been more than mere nationalism in subtle disguise. At the heart of Clinton's activism lay the opportunities offered by Northern Ireland in the context of post-Cold War foreign policy. In his first term, Clinton sought an amalgam of selective engagement, democratic 'enlargement', peace-promotion and pursuit of US economic interests. As Adrian Guelke has argued, the Irish policy 'fits in with the role (the Administration) has sought to play in the resolution of other conflicts, as it has attempted to establish the basis for an outward-looking foreign policy after the end of the Cold War'.[62] On the economic front, George Mitchell has argued before American business audiences that investment in a peaceful Northern Ireland can constitute a valuable bridgehead into the European Union market. Average labour costs in Northern Ireland are approximately one-third less than in the United States, 60 per cent less than in Germany.[63] Above and beyond all this, the ending of the Cold War made it easier for Washington to ignore London's sensibilities (and the sensibilities of those in the State Department who counselled against the new activism). As Niall O'Dowd (Irish-born publisher and prominent member of the Morrison group) related: 'We were taking on forty-five years of Anglo-American relations.'[64] London's post-1994 adoption of a slightly more positive attitude towards American involvement seemed to embody an acceptance of the new, post-Cold War power relations.

3   Reflections on the case-studies

The two case-studies illustrate the sheer uncertainty associated with military or diplomatic intervention in complex international processes. Bush's Somalian intervention was uncharacteristic of the cautious, reactive American conservatism which had previously characterised his management of foreign relations. It was as if, spurned by the electorate in November 1992, the outgoing President felt a new freedom to take gambles on behalf of the New World Order. Criticised for equating the New World Order with access to Middle Eastern oil during the Gulf conflict, Bush took the chance to demonstrate that the United States was prepared to intervene – as head of a multilateral operation – in pursuit of less tangible goods. The Somalian deployments would also demonstrate that, in Bush's own phrase, following the Gulf victory, the United States had 'kicked the Vietnam syndrome once and for all'.[65] Future Presidents, seeking to guarantee the New World Order, would not have continually to contemplate the lessons of Vietnam. By 1995, it was common to find the view expressed that the Clinton Administration, not its predecessor, was responsible for the Somalian débâcle of 1993–94. According to this view, Bush's well-defined, humanitarian operation had succeeded. It was the open-ended, 'nation-building' phase of May to October 1993 which saw the intervention spinning beyond Washington's control, threatening post-Cold War internationalism.[66] Such a view has its merits. However, even Bush's intervention had its political, 'nation-building' dimension. It was always prone to 'mission shift' and likely to impel the incoming President beyond narrow, 'humanitarian' limits. As William Schneider wrote in December 1992:

> The Administration insists that America will not try to disarm the warring clans or bring about a political settlement. Then why is special envoy Robert B. Oakley arranging talks between Somali warlords? The Administration says he is not engaging in politics. He is doing what is necessary to protect the relief supplies.[67]

Like Bush's decision to intervene in Somalia, Clinton's Northern Irish activism involved a conscious attempt to stake out an agenda for post-Cold War internationalism. Associated risks were far less than in the case of Somalia. No Americans were likely to die as a result of the new policy. At the outset at least, failures could be finessed through the agency of the Morrison group. As indicated above, the Administration could simply blame British intransigence or the ancient intractability of the Irish question. The White House would almost certainly gain some credit as a mediator. Yet risks did exist. Was it worth investing time and energy in a complex and difficult area which did not directly or obviously affect immediate US interests? The Clinton strategy – pressuring London and Sinn Fein, attempting to include moderate loyalists, working with Dublin – was carefully and intelligently developed. However, it did not really offer anything new, being essentially an operational form of the strategy inherent in Carter's 1977 statement. Especially when it became evident that Ireland could not expect any huge injection of US public funds, there was a danger of Clinton being seen as a bungling amateur and raiser of false hopes. The new activism would certainly upset London, and possibly expose divisions within the Administration. It was also bound to stimulate at least some domestic criticism. (In April 1995, Carter's former Energy Secretary James Schlesinger argued: 'Northern Ireland is, after all, a province of the United Kingdom … For us to butt in (no other expression seems suitable!) for domestic political reasons appears both ignorant and bumptious'[68].) Beyond mere vote-grubbing, Clinton could be seen as following the agenda of 'foreign policy as social work'.[69] In the last analysis, a failed and discredited Irish activism would hardly further the cause of selective engagement as a feature of post-Cold War internationalism.

Despite the ending of the IRA cease-fire, the internationalist thrust of Clinton's foreign policy was augmented by at least the attempt to encourage a peace process. In contrast, Bush's Somalian intervention resulted in a setback for post-Cold War internationalism. The two case-studies nevertheless offer interesting parallels. Ethnic lobbies were important in both instances, albeit in not altogether predictable ways. In December 1992, liberal African-Americans in Congress and outside tended to support a Republican Presidential decision which conservatives inclined to question. Clinton's Irish policy was supported by Catholic Irish-American groups. But expectations were raised to the point where groups like the Irish National Caucus began to doubt his real commitment. Both cases illustrated the difficulty of developing adequate criteria for post-Cold War activism. When should Washington work with or through the UN? If Somalia was appropriate for intervention, why not elsewhere? Would diplomatic intervention in Northern Ireland be followed by open engagement in the internal affairs of other allies? If so, which ones, and why? Each of the case-studies also points up the role of the media: most obviously in bringing the Somalian famine to public attention. It was Ronald Reagan who remarked in 1985 that 'a hungry child has no politics'.[70] Pictures of starving children shook the ground underneath those who favoured caution in Somalia. In the Irish case, it can be argued that media coverage tended to encourage the expectation that a new Democratic Administration would reverse the caution of the Bush years.[71]

How do the case-studies relate to wider patterns of foreign policy decision-making? Each certainly exhibited a strong 'bureaucratic politics' com-
ponent. In December 1992, State Department personnel were strongly in
favour of an internationalism which went beyond the narrow identification
of American 'interest'. They tended to view the Pentagon's caution as an
unnecessary concession to the forces of neo-isolationism. At the Defence
Department, memories of Vietnam were more insistent and the New World
Order more an object of circumspection. The November–December 1992
Somalian debate also clearly revealed the vital role of the President in adju-
dicating 'bureaucratic politics', at least when the phenomenon surfaces in
top-level discussion. The Irish example saw 'bureaucratic politics' operating
in a slightly more exposed and less elite manner. Essentially, the State
Department and the London embassy stood for caution (particularly over
the Adams visa, but over US involvement generally); the NSA and relevant
staff promoted what became Clinton's strategy. For most of 1993, State's
line on the Adams visa held. However, by the end of 1993 – with the Morrison group apparently making headway, and some kind of breakthrough in
prospect – Clinton was prepared to lend his weight to Lake and Soderberg.
Again, one is struck by the President's ability to adjudicate and prioritise
issues. Neither case-study offers much in the way of encouragement to those
who would accord Congress a leading role on the post-Cold War foreign
policy stage. The legislature took a lead in bringing Somalia's plight to White
House attention. However, Congress was not involved in any direct way in
the key decisions, and was – certainly in the short term – prepared to abdi-
cate its war powers. The legislative role in relation to Northern Ireland was
more complex. Before 1993, Congress – or at least interested parties within
Congress – had generally been the main force applying US pressure to the
affairs of the province. Clinton continued to respond to Congressional calls
for peace activism. However, it was manifestly the executive which took
over the reins of policy in 1993. It is impossible to imagine Congress following the kind of concerted strategy adopted by Lake, Soderberg,
Kennedy-Smith and Clinton. Individual Members (notably Senator
Kennedy) remained central to the new initiatives, but Congress *as an institution* figured only when it came to voting foreign aid.

Finally, what was the role of public opinion? The 1992 Somalian intervention – a limited exercise designed to achieve defined humanitarian ends
– was shaped, at one level, to respond to public demands to do something
about the starving children. However, as a 'lame-duck' President, Bush was
not especially concerned to court public approval. His desire to further, and
to popularise, the New World Order agenda was paramount. Clinton's Irish
interventions were generally popular, but were hardly the product of excited
and widespread public demand. Again, the desire to educate the American
public in the ways of post-Cold War internationalism appears a likely factor
of importance. In both the Somalian and the Irish cases, key decisions were

made in narrow, elite circles: in the Bush NSC (technically the NSC Deputies Committee) meetings, and in interactions between President Clinton and his NSC staff. Nevertheless, both sets of decisions took place in the context of a reasonably open public debate on the issues and options involved. (As we have seen, even Bush's closeted NSC meetings were subject to leaks – both before and after the event – and to extensive and detailed press coverage).

4 Conclusion: democracy and American foreign policy

During his 1976 campaign, Jimmy Carter made the assertion that every 'time we've made a serious mistake in foreign affairs' it was 'because the American people have been excluded from the process'.[72] Such a statement may appear naive, especially perhaps in view of the experience of the Carter Administration. (By 1979, the leadership being exerted by Carter and NSA Zbigniew Brzezinski was not characterised by much desire to share power with Congress or the public.) As was implicit in David Barrett's argument in Chapter 3, post-1945 US foreign policy has been shaped by Presidential leadership and the NSC system. It is not easy to visualise any alternative to this. Even in post-Cold War conditions, the public and foreign policy elites look to the White House to shape the agenda. Congress does not impress as a force either able or willing to assume leadership. The lesson of the 104th Congress (1995–96) was surely that even an exceptionally partisan and disciplined legislative majority had neither the incentive nor the ability to 'lead' foreign policy in any sustained manner. Nonetheless, it is worth noting a few factors that point towards a more positive relationship between democracy and foreign policy, and which point away from Tocqueville's famous conclusion in *Democracy in America*: 'I have no hesitation in saying that in the control of society's foreign affairs democratic governments do appear decidedly inferior to others.'[73]

Examination of recent American history leads to the conclusion that Tocqueville's hypothecated antagonism between democracy and efficiency is misleading. For one thing, successful foreign policy management is inherently difficult for *any* regime – centralised or decentralised, accountable or unaccountable, democratic or undemocratic. As James Reston wrote in 1964: 'This is the devilish thing about foreign affairs: they are foreign and will not always conform to our whim.'[74] In a complex international context, unfettered executive power tends to promote abuses of power, bureaucratism and the persistence of error. In this connection, Kenneth Waltz in 1967 offered an interesting comparison between British and American practice, neatly reversing some familiar assumptions. Of course, the fact that this comparison appeared in a book published in 1967 should put us on our guard against praise for an American system engaged in policy mismanagement in Vietnam. Nevertheless, his general points are worth considering. In Britain, the 'fusion of powers and the concentration of responsibility encourage governments to avoid problems'. By contrast, decentralised processes facilitate 'the quick identification of problems, the pragmatic quest ... for solutions ... the open criticism of policies'.[75] It should also be stressed that Carter's 1976 assertion, about foreign policy mistakes being linked to the exclusion of the American people, had more than an element of truth about it. H. J. Morgenthau once famously pointed out that a popular foreign policy is not necessarily a good one.[76] However, the mistakes of post-1945 US foreign relations are not persuasively to be attributed to excessive democratic control and participation. Hall and Ikenberry offer the following excellent reply to Morgenthau:

> [I]t is entirely proper to remember that the American people were perfectly pre-pared to fight the 'good' war of 1941–5, and that they, rather than the experts, were right to refuse to continue the war in Vietnam ... Democratic control of foreign policy is ultimately ... a positive resource because of its capacity to weed out poor policies.[77]

The record of Presidential domination of foreign policy is one, not of measured efficiency, but of disregard for the law and the use of foreign policy powers to enhance political standing. According to I. M. Destler, Leslie Gelb and Anthony Lake, post-1964 Presidents in particular 'squandered their own authority to construct steady majorities'.[78] By using foreign policy to enhance their personal positions, Presidents stimulated calls for greater openness and accountability. This was as true of Reagan and Bush as it was of Johnson and Nixon. As Melvin Small has concluded: 'Perhaps Tocqueville was not so prescient after all.'[79]

Democratic foreign policy is one where Presidents generally lead, but where they also share power and respect legal and constitutional constraints. One where the CIA, executive branch bureaucrats and the military are subject to control by elected civilian politicians. It is one where Congress controls the purse-strings and exposes the executive to public inspection. It is one in which the US obeys international law, and where open, informed public debate is the norm. Defined in such terms, democratic foreign policy will remain a necessary aspiration rather than a reality. Proponents of open foreign policy processes are wise to concede this, and to admit that – from time to time – the system will have to admit of secretive, elite direction. Larry George, for example, notes that 'governments must from time to time make decisions in secret and limit access to certain types of information in order to prevent leaks that could jeopardize operations, endanger agents or informants, or undermine negotiations'. (George notes that 'this is true in the domestic as well as in the international arena'; and that democratic governments 'should be given the authority to conduct covert operations or to classify information relevant to issues of public concern only under extraordinary circumstances'.)[80] There is here the irreducible problem of defining 'extraordinary circumstances'. Acceptance of this does not amount to a denial of democratic foreign policy. Rather, it involves commitment to the view that, ultimately, accountability under the law is the safeguard. In slightly different terms, Volkman and Baggett present the following worth-while conclusion:

> No one has yet been able to figure out a system where the Legislative and Exec-utive branches can share responsibility for the conduct of foreign policy – and at the same time act with great speed in the event of a sudden crisis. It is one of democracy's central flaws. Still, democracy is a flawed process, and it may well be that this central question will remain a permanent source of tension, so long as there is a constitutional system.[81]

The first edition of this book cited four major enemies of democratic for-eign policy. The first of these was termed the 'logic of executive compe-tence': the view that policy made in secret by relatively unitary structures is superior to that made in public, especially involving strong legislative branch input. The second enemy of democratic foreign policy was held to be public ignorance and elite manipulation of public opinion. The third and fourth forces were militarisation of the US economy (the 'military–industrial com-plex') and the unaccountable power of giant corporations. It is now the intention to review these various forces in the light of international devel-opments since 1990.

Various objections to the 'logic of executive competence' have already been made, and the point does not need to be laboured. What is clear is that presumptions of executive competence, already compromised in the Cold War era, are further undermined in post-Cold War conditions. The 'inter-mestic agenda', debates over immigration, the new prioritisation for trade and economic foreign policy, the opening of global markets: all these factors tend to weaken the argument that national interests will always be best aggregated in a competent executive. Post-Cold War issues, no longer hier-archically organised around 'national security' and the 'Soviet threat', tend to affect domestic groups differentially, and can only be resolved in a rela-tively decentralised process. Foreign policy expertise tends increasingly to be multifarious and not restricted to members of the federal executive branch. The more that domestic and foreign policy arenas intertwine, the more argu-ments for a special executive foreign policy competence lose power. New actors, including the state governments, assert their claims. Of course, decentralisation can be taken too far. Yet, despite warnings and book titles to the contrary, we are a long way from foreign policy domination by an 'imperial Congress' or a thousand Main Streets.

It was argued in Chapter 6 that public opinion is more 'rational' than commonly supposed. The post-Cold War era has seen many expressions of fear about US public opinion turning inward. Secretary of State Warren Christopher argued in his 1993 confirmation hearing: 'Today, foreign policy makers cannot afford to ignore the public or there is a real danger that the public will ignore foreign policy.'[82] High levels of public education and access to information are essential to the proper functioning of democracy. New media technologies can expand access to information, converting 'mass opinion' into 'public judgement'.[83] Foreign policy leaders should not simply defer to imagined 'mass opinion'. As George Elsey, adviser in the Truman Administration, put it: 'You can't sit around and wait for public opinion to tell you what to do ... You must decide what you're going to do and do it, and attempt to educate the public to the reasons for your action.'[84] Too often, however, leaders have confused easily manipulated 'mass opinion' with the 'public judgement' of settled and mature second thoughts. Cold War conditions encouraged rather crude selling of foreign policy, invariably in terms of the struggle against communism. Yankelovich wrote in 1979: 'Some (perhaps all) ... government statements harbor the assumption that the public is simpleminded, capable of holding only one extreme alternative in mind at a time – black *or* white, for *or* against, friend *or* foe.'[85] President Bush's selling of his Gulf policy in 1990–91 further exemplified Yankelovich's point. Successful and prolonged opinion leadership in post-Cold War conditions will require more subtlety and more respect for the variegated structure of public opinion in an era of global interdependence.

As noted in Chapter 7, the first decade of the post-Cold War era did not see a drastic demilitarisation of American power. Indeed, it witnessed a major Middle Eastern conflict in which the United States provided the major military force against Saddam. As the world entered the late 1990s, 100,000 American troops remained in Europe. (It was George Kennan who remarked that one day US troops *would* leave Europe[86].) A major post-Cold War priority for US policymakers is to achieve a new balance between military and diplomatic international leadership. Despite the desire of Congressional Republicans to augment Pentagon spending after 1994, the most likely course for the United States is a slow demilitarisation. William Hudson simply echoed common sense when he wrote in 1995: 'While the United States devotes a huge share of its GNP to building high-tech weapons systems, our economic competitors build high-tech automobiles, VCRs, and other industrial products American consumers buy.'[87] Excessive militarisation is also the enemy of democracy.

However, the power of defence contractors (and the wider 'national security state') is no longer quite the threat to democratic integrity as it was in the early to mid-1980s. The same cannot be said about private, corporate power generally. In the post-Cold War era, the task of making corporate power accountable to democratic processes has become complicated by the reality and myth of globalisation. As argued in Chapter 7, globalisation does raise severe problems both for democracy and for national governments. In so far as globalised processes (whether social, cultural of economic) are becoming increasingly 'decentred', even the government of the United States will find many traditional foreign policy tools outmoded. However, as indicated in Chapter 7, it is far too early to proclaim the death of either national governments or of 'American' foreign policy. Too often in the post-Cold War years, national governments have invoked the apparently irresistible forces of globalisation as a way of ducking difficult policy decisions.

Invocation of a relentless globalisation is but one aspect of the pessimism which took hold in some quarters in the years following the Cold War's end. In actuality, the Cold War was a terrifying period in world history – an era of bloody proxy wars, democratic retreats, Soviet and American imperialism, and the ever-present threat of nuclear annihilation. That a kind of frenzied stability was also involved was far more evident with hindsight than when the Cold War was in train. The end of the Cold War raised opportunities for a new kind of American internationalism, a reconfiguration of the liberal ideology which has traditionally dominated US foreign relations. A successful new internationalist foreign policy of 'principled pragmatism' will be anti-imperialist, cooperative, not excessively moralistic, but committed to democratic procedures and values.[88] It will not so much try (in Dean Acheson's phrase) to 'grab hold of history and make it conform',[89] as recognise that prudent international retrenchment is not the same as isolationist retreat. Above all, a successful post-Cold War internationalism will accept that the United States cannot achieve its goals by acting alone.

Notes

1 J. A. Baker, *The Politics of Diplomacy* (New York, Putnam's Sons, 1995), p. 218.

2 See, e.g., S. R. David, 'Why the Third World still matters', in E. R. Wittkopf, ed., *The Future of American Foreign Policy* (New York, St. Martin's, 1994).

3 J. Clark, 'Débâcle in Somalia', *Foreign Affairs*, 72 (1993), pp. 109–23: 112.

4 *Congressional Almanac*, 1992, p. 535.

5 *Congressional Quarterly Weekly Report*, 5 Dec. 1992, p. 3760.

6 *Congressional Almanac*, 1992, p. 535.

7 *Public Papers of the Presidents of the US: George Bush, 1992–93*, vol. 2 (Washington DC, US Government Printing Office, 1993), p. 1360.

8 C. Powell, *A Soldier's Way* (London, Hutchinson, 1995), p. 564.

9 *New York Times*, 19 Nov. 1992.

10 Powell, *A Soldier's Way*, p. 565.

11 *Washington Post* national weekly edition, 14–20 Dec. 1992 (D. Oberdorfer, 'The road to Somalia').

12 J. R. Bolton, 'Wrong turn in Somalia', *Foreign Affairs*, 73 (1994), pp. 56–66: 58.

13 Powell, *A Soldier's Way*, p. 565.

14 *Public Papers, 1992–93*, vol. 2, pp. 2174–75.

15 *New York Times*, 4 and 5 Dec. 1992.

16 See D. D. Newsom, *The Public Dimension of Foreign Policy* (Bloomington, Indiana University Press, 1996), p. 75.

17 *New York Times*, 1 Dec. 1992.

18   *Ibid.* ('senior Administration official').
19   *Public Papers, 1992–93*, vol. 2, p. 1788 (Presidential election debate).
20   Powell, *A Soldier's Way*, pp. 565–6.
21   See D. C. Morrison, 'US troops in Somalia: where next?', *National Journal*, 12 Dec. 1992.
22   *Ibid.*, also, W. Schneider, 'Vietnam or Gulf: pick your syndrome', *National Journal,* 19 Dec. 1992.
23   *New York Times*, 4 Dec. 1992.
24   Bolton, 'Wrong turn in Somalia', p. 61.
25   *Congressional Quarterly Almanac*, 1992, p. 537.
26   *Ibid.*, p. 536.
27   *New York Times*, 5 Dec. 1992.
28   *Congressional Quarterly Almanac*, 1992, p. 536.
29   *Public Papers, 1992–93*, vol. 2, pp. 2179–80.
30   *New York Times*, 4 Dec. 1992.
31   *Congressional Quarterly Almanac*, 1992, p. 538.
32   *National Journal*, 19 Dec. 1992, p. 2926. See also C. J. Logan, 'US public opinion and the intervention in Somalia', *Fletcher Forum of World Affairs*, 20 (1996), pp. 155–80.
33   *Congressional Quarterly Alamanc*, 1992, pp. 536–8; *Congressional Quarterly Weekly Report*, 5 Dec. 1992, p. 3760.
34   *Public Papers of the Presidents of the US: William J. Clinton, 1993*, vol. 1 (Washington DC, US Government Printing Office, 1994), p. 987 (2 July 1993).
35   *Ibid.*, p. 315.
36   *Congressional Record*, S2917 (27 Feb. 1995).
37   See R. N. Haass, *Conflicts Unending: the United States and Regional Disputes* (New Haven, Yale University Press, 1990), ch. 6; J. Dumbrell, 'The United States and the Northern Irish conflict, 1969–94: from indifference to intervention', *Irish Studies in International Affairs*, 6 (1995), pp. 107–25.
38   *The Times*, 9 Dec. 1995.
39   See M. Holland, 'Irish notebook', *Observer*, 8 Nov. 1992.
40   *Independent*, 26 Feb. 1993.
41   *Public Papers*, 1993, vol. 1, p. 669.
42   *Guardian*, 16 April 1994.
43   *Newsweek*, 12 Sept. 1994, p. 10.
44   BBC interview, *The World this Weekend*, 4 Sept. 1994.
45   G. Hodgson, 'It's foreign policy, stupid', *Prospect*, Jan. 1996, p. 51. See also J. Stevenson, 'Northern Ireland: treating terrorists as statesmen', *Foreign Policy*, 105 (1996–97), pp. 125–40. See also C. O'Clery, *The Greening of the White House* (Dublin, Gill and Macmillan, 1996).
46   M. Walker, *The President We Deserve* (London, Fourth Estate, 1996), p. 279.
47   *Belfast Telegraph*, 18 April 1994 (Gavin Esler). See also R. Wilson, 'Days like this', *New Statesman and Society*, 15/29 Dec. 1995.
48   *Public Papers*, 1993, vol. 1, p. 314. See also J. O'Grady, 'An Irish policy born in the USA', *Foreign Affairs*, 75 (1996), pp. 2–7.
49   *Public Papers of the Presidents of the US: William J. Clinton, 1994*, vol. 2 (Washington DC, US Government Printing Office, 1995), p. 2129.
50   See A. J. Wilson, *Irish America and the Ulster Conflict, 1968–1995* (Belfast,

Blackstaff, 1995), p. 300.

51 See S. Breen, 'Not an ounce?', *Fortnight*, Jan. 1996, p. 7.

52 *Fortnight*, Dec. 1995, p. 23.

53 *Newsweek*, 12 Sept. 1994 ('The Ulster disease').

54 *Spectator*, 15 Oct. 1994, p. 29.

55 *Mail on Sunday*, 25 Aug. 1996.

56 See M. J. Brady, 'Democratic audit', *Fortnight*, Dec. 1995, p. 8.

57 K. Cullen, 'The fraying of the green', *Fortnight*, June 1996, p. 8.

58 See *The Economist*, 18 March 1995 (Lexington, 'When Irish eyes are brimming').

59 *The Times*, 16 Aug. 1996.

60 R. Fisk, 'No use relying on Uncle Bill', *Fortnight*, Jan. 1996, pp. 19–20.

61 For Powell's view, see *Parliamentary Debates*, 6th Series, vol. 87, 27 Nov. 1985, pp. 954–5 (on Anglo-Irish Agreement); J. E. Powell, 'Aligned with the IRA', *The Times*, 10 Aug. 1994. For similar conclusions, arrived at from a completely different political perspective, see S. Cronin *Washington's Irish Policy, 1916–1986* (Dublin, Anvil Books, 1987). See also J. Hume, 'The Irish question: a British problem', *Foreign Affairs*, 58 (1979–80), pp. 300–13.

62 A. Guelke, 'The United States, Irish Americans and the Northern Ireland peace process', *International Affairs*, 72 (1996), pp. 521–36: 536.

63 See M. Spillane, 'Northern exposure', *The Nation*, 19 June 1995; C. C. O'Brien, 'The wearing of the greenbacks', *National Review*, 17 April 1995.

64 *Guardian*, 1 Dec. 1995.

65 Cited in R. W. Tucker and D. C. Hendrickson, *The Imperial Temptation* (New York, Council on Foreign Relations, 1992), p. 152.

66 See C. A. Crocker, 'The lessons of Somalia', *Foreign Affairs*, 74 (1995), pp. 2–8; J. L. Hirsch and R. B. Oakley, *Somalia and Operation Restore Hope* (Washington DC, US Institute of Peace, 1995).

67 *National Journal*, 19 Dec. 1992, p. 2926.

68 *Congressional Record*, S5679 (25 April 1995).

69 See M. Mandelbaum, 'Foreign policy as social work', *Foreign Affairs*, 75 (1996), pp. 16–32.

70 Clark, 'Débâcle in Somalia', p. 113.

71 On US coverage of the Northern Irish conflict, see J. Holland, *The American Connection* (Dublin, Poolbeg, 1989); J. Thomas, 'Bloody Ireland', *Columbia Journalism Review*, 27 (1988), pp. 31–7; J. F. McCarthy, *Dissent from Irish America* (Lanham, University Press of America, 1993); Wilson, *Irish America and the Ulster Conflict*.

72 *The Presidential Campaign 1976: vol. 3, The Debates* (Washington DC, US Government Printing Office, 1979), p. 97.

73 A. de Tocqueville, *Democracy in America* (New York, Anchor, 1959), p. 226.

74 *New York Times*, 16 Dec. 1964.

75 K. N. Waltz, *Foreign Policy and Democratic Politics* (Boston, Little, Brown, 1967), pp. 304, 307.

76 H. J. Morgenthau, *A New Foreign Policy for the United States* (New York, Praeger, 1969), p. 151.

77 J. A. Hall and G. I. Ikenberry, *The State* (Milton Keynes, Open University Press, 1989), p. 100.

78   I. M. Destler, L. Gelb and A. Lake, *Our Own Worst Enemy: The Unmaking of American Foreign Policy* (New York, Simon and Schuster, 1984), p. 21.

79   M. Small, *Democracy and Diplomacy* (Baltimore, Johns Hopkins University Press, 1996), p. 170.

80   L. N. George, 'Democratic theory and the conduct of American foreign policy', in D. G. Adler and L. N. George, eds, *The Constitution and the Conduct of American Foreign Policy* (Lawrence, University Press of Kansas, 1996), p. 70.

81   E. Volkman and B. Baggett, *Secret Intelligence* (London, Allen, 1989), p. 228.

82   Quoted in D. A. Sharp, 'Preamble', in D. Yankelovich and I. M. Destler, eds, *Beyond the Beltway* (New York, Norton, 1994), p. 16.

83   See D. Yankelovich and S. Harman, *Starting with the People* (Boston, Houghton Mifflin, 1988), pp. 9–10.

84   Quoted in C. W. Kegley and E. R. Wittkopf, *American Foreign Policy: Pattern and Process* (5th edn, New York, St. Martin's, 1996), p. 289.

85   D. Yankelovich, 'Farewell to "President knows best"', *Foreign Affairs*, 57 (1979), pp. 671–92: 687.

86   Cited in C. Layne, 'Superpower disengagement', *Foreign Policy*, 77 (1989–90), pp. 17–40: 40.

87   W. E. Hudson, *American Democracy in Peril* (Chatham, Chatham House, 1995), p. 193.

88   On 'principled pragmatism', see M. Nincic, *Democracy and Foreign Policy* (New York, Columbia University Press, 1992), ch. 6. See also S. Talbott, 'Democracy and the national interest', *Foreign Affairs*, 75 (1996), pp. 47–63.

89   Quoted in B. Schwarz, 'Why America thinks it has to run the world', *The Atlantic Monthly*, June 1996, p. 101.

Index